GLORY IN
GOTHENBURG

GLORY IN
GOTHENBURG

THE NIGHT ABERDEEN FC
TURNED THE FOOTBALLING
WORLD ON ITS HEAD

RICHARD GORDON

BLACK & WHITE PUBLISHING

First published 2012
by Black & White Publishing Ltd
29 Ocean Drive, Edinburgh EH6 6JL

1 3 5 7 9 10 8 6 4 2   12 13 14 15

ISBN: 978 1 84502 470 3

Typeset by Iolaire Typesetting, Newtonmore
Printed and bound by ScandBook AB, Sweden

CONTENTS

I would like to dedicate this book to my late dad, George Gordon, who introduced me to the game, and more importantly, the team I came to love. And to my son, Kiefer, who as firstborn has assumed the at times onerous responsibility of lifelong devotion to Aberdeen FC.

Also to every player who has ever pulled on that red shirt – thank you all for the joy, the heartbreak and the memories you have given me.

And to Phil Goodbrand, a friend who never grew old.

AUTHOR'S INTRODUCTION

My name is Richard Gordon and I am, for better or worse, an Aberdeen fan.

There are times when it has brought me the greatest of joy, others when it has left me on the verge of desolation, but that hardly singles me out. Virtually every single football supporter knows that range of emotions. It is what defines us, what makes us keep going back for more.

My devotion began at Muirton Park, Perth, in 1970 where the Dons were contesting the Scottish Cup semi-final with Kilmarnock – it was to be some years before I discovered Killie didn't actually play in Perth, the notion of neutral venues being foreign to me at the age of nine. My three main memories of that day are of being pinned against the perimeter railings with my oversized rosette attached firmly to my anorak; that the Kilmarnock goalkeeper Sandy McLaughlan was wearing what looked like hand-knitted white gloves; and that Derek – thereafter nicknamed 'Cup-tie' – McKay scored the only goal of the game. Aberdeen were off to Hampden (wherever that was)!

The Dons indeed won that Scottish Cup Final, an improbably decisive 3-1 win over Jock Stein's Celtic, and by the next season I was a regular at Pittodrie, not just at first-team games, but at reserve matches as well. Initially I went with my dad and sat where all little boys sat back then, on the wall around the pitch, legs dangling over.

Occasionally, if he had been whipped off shopping or was otherwise occupied, a few of us would wander down George Street, cut through Froghall, over the hill and down Merkland Road, and enter for free when the gates were opened shortly after half-time.

By the end of that first campaign Aberdeen were serious title challengers and a win in the penultimate fixture, at home to all-conquering Celtic, could have wrapped it up. I was sitting in the Main Stand with my old man (a rare treat – he must have been given complimentary tickets) when Harry Hood put the visitors ahead early on and I duly burst into tears. Alex Willoughby equalised, and in the second half Arthur Graham – 'Bumper' to his devoted army of fans – rounded Celtic keeper Evan Williams but got held up momentarily. By the time he had spun and rolled the ball goal-wards, Billy McNeill was there to clear it off the line. And that, ladies and gentlemen, was that. The next Saturday Dad and I got the train down to Falkirk where Davie Robb conceded a penalty and the late George Miller stroked home the only goal of the game to give the home side the points.

Over the next couple of seasons that side began to break up. Joe Harper and Martin Buchan – two genuine Dons legends – left for England and the manager Eddie Turnbull returned to his first love, Hibernian. I am somewhat ashamed to admit that I was to follow him to Easter Road not long after. Aberdeen were toiling under Jimmy Bonthrone and Joe Harper had not settled at Everton. The word was that he was coming back to the Dons, but the directors were haggling over a few thousand pounds, and Hibs nipped in. I was distraught and switched allegiance, and suddenly my dear old dad, God rest his soul, was taking me around the country to watch a Hibernian side that boasted not only 'King Joey', but talented players like Pat Stanton, John Brownlie and John Blackley among others.

Throughout that time I would still go along to Pittodrie, and bit by bit I knew I was being drawn back in. In season '74-75 the Dons finished fifth to ensure they would be part of the new look Scottish

Premier Division, but the following campaign was a tortuous one and a first ever relegation in the club's history was a genuine possibility. How could I desert them in their time of need? I went to every home match that season and travelled to a number of away games too. The irrepressible Ally MacLeod had replaced Bonthrone and then in what seemed to me a sign from above, in spring 1976 Joe Harper re-signed for the club. The only problem was that he couldn't play for the first team until after the summer. He could play for the reserves though, and I was among a crowd in excess of 5,000 at Pittodrie as Joey made his comeback against St Johnstone on the same night half that number watched the Dons first team lose 2-0 at already relegated Saints. (The Aberdeen second XI won 6-0, with Harper, naturally, among the scorers.)

One game left to save the season and it was at home to . . . Hibs! Official records show that the crowd that afternoon was just 10,985 – I would have sworn it was nearer 100,000, such was the intense atmosphere inside the stadium.

By now I was going to matches with a group of friends from Aberdeen Grammar School. As with most kids of that age, few of us were known by our given names (in fact to this day I am not sure that I knew all their real names); we were Hand, Bov, Deano, Dom Sullivan (not the real one), Phil, The Bish, Bat Fry and me, Gongy (don't ask!), and whatever the attendance, we were certainly packed into The Paddock where the nervous tension was almost palpable.

Aberdeen won 3-0 with goals from Drew Jarvie, Joe Smith and Davie Robb, and I knew that afternoon that I was where I belonged. Despite all the successes, all the silverware that followed, I am not sure I ever had quite the same wave of emotion as that which I experienced that cloudy afternoon at the end of April 1976.

From there it became just the most incredible rollercoaster. As a group we went to every game home and away; there was even a spell when I was chartering buses and selling tickets around the school, a practice ended by the headmaster Mr Gibb when it was finally brought to his attention!

MacLeod won us the 1976 League Cup Final then departed to take over as Scotland boss in what became the most ill-fated World Cup campaign ever inflicted upon any nation. Billy McNeill was next up and in his single season gave us real hope, but was always likely to be lured back to Celtic. His successor in the Pittodrie hot-seat was Alex Ferguson – just sacked by St Mirren – and we buckled our seat-belts for blast-off!

On leaving school I had begun work for the Clydesdale Bank at the Bridge of Don where Dom Sullivan (the real one!) was among our customers but, such was the pedestal upon which I placed my heroes, I found it incredibly difficult to engage him in conversation. That was a situation I had to remedy pretty quickly a few years later when I was employed by Ken McRobb as Northsound Radio's part-time Aberdeen reporter, and then within four months on a full-time basis as a trainee journalist with particular responsibility for sport.

I was commentating and reporting on Dons games and inter-viewing the players and manager; sadly, by then it was Ian Porterfield in charge and not Alex Ferguson, and life as a Dons supporter very quickly reverted to its more normal course.

In my first decade as an Aberdeen fan the club had won two trophies. From 1986-87 until now there has been a Cup double under Alex Smith and Jocky Scott, and the 1995 Coca-Cola Cup win under Roy Aitken. In the eight years that 'Fergie' ruled the Pittodrie roost he brought home ten major pieces of silverware: three Scottish League titles, four Scottish Cups, one League Cup and, unbelieva-bly, in 1983 the European Cup Winners Cup and European Super Cup. It was quite simply the most astonishing period in Aberdeen's history, one that will never be repeated and one which I feel incredibly privileged to have lived through.

Privileged too that during the course of my working life – I joined the BBC in 1991 after a brief stint at Radio Clyde – I have got to know most of the players who brought that haul of trophies to the north-east. Some I have had more dealings with than others; some have become friends, but all have some wonderful stories to tell of those halcyon days, and that was the starting point for this book.

Gothenburg has featured large in a number of previous publications as part of the overall story of the club, but not as the sole focus, and the 30th anniversary of that triumph seemed a suitable point to rectify that. I wanted not only to relive that glorious event but to fill in the blanks of what has happened to the main characters in the years since. Everyone knows where Sir Alex Ferguson's career has taken him and a number of his team have remained similarly high-profile, but not all of them, and it has been a genuinely rewarding experience catching up with them and discovering what cards fate has dealt them.

In the early part of my preparation for writing this book, all the research and setting up interviews, I one day scrolled through the recent calls on my mobile phone. The list read, one after the other: Willie Miller, Neale Cooper, Jim Leighton, Neil Simpson and John Hewitt, and that just blew me away! They were among the easier ones to pin down. One or two of the others required a bit more persistence but in the end I spoke to all the players from that marvellous side, and a number of the squad men, drawing together their tales and memories to paint the overall picture as each of them warmly reminisced on the 'Glory In Gothenburg'.

INTRODUCTION

As the rain continued to tumble from the dark Gothenburg sky five young Scotsmen in red shirts jostled into position, directed into line by their anxious goalkeeper who barked instructions. As they formed a defensive wall one of them, mercurial winger Peter Weir, looked to the heavens and offered up a prayer, "Please God don't let them score, they don't deserve it". His team, Aberdeen, was on the verge of recording its most sensational victory, of creating a historic moment its supporters would never forget. Two-one up, agonisingly close to the end of extra-time against the legendary Real Madrid in the European Cup Winners Cup Final, the Dons had conceded a free-kick just outside their own penalty area and the next few seconds would determine the outcome.

Weir's thoughts were interrupted by the Spanish striker Juanito who, hoping to catch his opponents unawares, took the free-kick quickly. The ball bobbled harmlessly beyond the wall of Aberdeen players straight into the welcoming arms of Jim Leighton, but their joy was short-lived. The Italian official had not signalled that play should resume. It was to be retaken.

Again the Aberdeen players lined up. Again Leighton bawled instructions. Far away on the touchline the team's manager stood impassively, his hands stuffed into the pockets of his rain jacket. At that moment all Alex Ferguson could do was watch on helplessly, hoping the gods would smile on him and his players.

There were fourteen thousand Aberdeen fans in the Ullevi Stadium that night and I was one of them. We too stood helplessly. For two hours we had sung our hearts out, cheered the two goals scored by Eric Black and John Hewitt, groaned as chance after chance to seal the game went begging. It had been an incredible performance by our team, one that deserved to end in triumph, not in the seemingly traditional Scottish way of glorious failure.

My red and white waterproof suit, bought hurriedly and at considerable expense in a Gothenburg department store – who knew it rained in Sweden! – was plastered to my clothes. We had got soaked earlier and had not dried out. It had been an interminably long, uncomfortable day waiting for the moment to arrive. We had hauled ourselves out to the stadium hours in advance of kick-off and joined in as fellow Aberdeen supporters, already drenched, cavorted in a fountain near the stadium. I had even been interviewed by Swedish radio and confidently predicted a Dons win.

By the time we tumbled into the ground and staked our places inside that huge bowl our nerves were frayed. The ninety minutes of regulation play followed by half an hour's extra-time had hardly helped our state of mind. It had been intense, dramatic and at times almost unbearable.

Now, victory was agonisingly close, but it could yet be snatched away.

This time the full-back Jose Salguero placed the ball meticulously on the sodden turf and paced a few steps backwards, his eyes focused on the spot just beyond our defensive wall and inside Leighton's left post. The keeper crouched on his goal line, satisfied that his team-mates were exactly where he wanted them. He peered into the near distance and waited. Cooper, Weir, Strachan and Simpson locked arms to hold their position; Mark McGhee stood a couple of paces to their left, all determined to throw their bodies in front of the ball. The whistle blew again, the Spaniard charged forward and struck, his right foot a swishing blur. The ball flashed

2

beyond the line of Aberdeen players. They all turned their heads as one and Leighton flung himself desperately to his left. High up on the terracing almost at the other end of the stadium I clenched my red and white scarf against my face. The fans, so raucous throughout, had fallen silent. For a split second it appeared the ball had found its target but then came the joyous realisation that it had in fact sped inches wide of the upright and was now careering off on to the running track which surrounded the pitch. The silence was pierced by a deafening roar all around.

Down on the pitch Peter Weir offered up a silent thank you and Jim Leighton took as long as he humanly could recovering the ball from behind his goalmouth.

Within seconds the final whistle would blow and Ferguson's team would have pulled off the most unlikely of triumphs, stamping an indelible mark on the history of Scottish football. They would emulate the European triumphs of the game's giants, Celtic and Rangers.

Such a scenario would have been impossible to imagine just a few years earlier. Indeed, at no time in the club's eighty years in existence had there been even a hint that such success lay in store. There had been League Cup and Scottish Cup wins following the end of World War II and Aberdeen had been crowned Scottish champions in 1954-55. There was that surprise Scottish Cup victory under Eddie Turnbull in 1970 and another League Cup triumph under the irrepressible Ally MacLeod six years later.

But that was about that.

When Alex Ferguson was appointed to replace Billy McNeill as Dons boss in the summer of 1978 the club's roll of honour listed a mere half dozen major trophy wins in three quarters of a century. The man from Govan was about to rip up the history books and totally transform Scottish football.

He inherited a decent squad of players from McNeill who had been denied silverware only by Jock Wallace's treble-winning Rangers, but there was little evidence during his first season in

3

charge that the new man was going to make much of an impact. 1979-80 began with a 1-0 defeat away to Partick Thistle, and losses to Morton and Celtic soon followed, but the Dons found their feet and the nucleus of the team that would go on to create history was formed. Miller, McLeish, Kennedy, McMaster, Strachan and McGhee all played major roles as Fergie's Aberdeen secured just a second national title for the club, clinching the championship with a breathtaking 5-0 demolition of Hibernian at Easter Road. As we packed on to the huge terracing that bright and sunny afternoon all eyes were on the pitch, all ears glued to radios for word on how our rivals, Celtic, were faring against St Mirren. The veteran Dons goalkeeper Bobby Clark spent much of the second half turning anxiously to the crowd, desperate for updates. Our game had finished, Celtic's had not, but then came conformation of a 0-0 draw and the title race was over. Suddenly Aberdeen players were cavorting across the surface, the supporters a heaving mass of jubilation and Fergie was racing down the pitch and throwing himself into Clark's arms.

It was the breakthrough Ferguson had craved and in doing so he had set down a marker, not only for his team but for the rest of Scottish football. The Dons had put together a fifteen match un-beaten run as they marched to that title, including two of the most significant wins in the club's history. Twice during April Fergie had taken his side to Celtic Park, twice they had headed back up the road with victories. He had instilled in his players the self-belief required to succeed, he had convinced them they could take on and beat their closest rivals in their own back yard in front of their passionate and vociferous home support. He had made them winners.

Ferguson continued to re-shape the side. The following season saw Jim Leighton establish himself as Bobby Clark's successor between the posts. Alex McLeish dropped back from midfield into central defence alongside Willie Miller, a pairing that would become the bedrock for everything that followed. And we Dons fans got our first glimpses of three kids who would become club legends: John Hewitt, Neale Cooper and Neil Simpson. There were to be no domestic trophies in 1980-81 and our European adventure was short-lived as a rampant Liverpool handed out a 5-0 aggregate thrashing, but Ferguson was learning all the time and so were his players.

By now all Alex Ferguson had to do was tinker with his squad. Popular left-winger Ian Scanlon departed for St Mirren in part exchange for Peter Weir and eighteen-year-old Eric Black was introduced. Aberdeen finished runners-up in the Premier Division for a second successive season, but we were given a taste of things to come in Europe. Drawn against the UEFA Cup holders Ipswich Town, the Dons drew 1-1 at Portman Road and then ripped them apart in the return leg at Pittodrie. Gordon Strachan and John Wark exchanged first-half penalties before Peter Weir took centre stage. On a night when he destroyed England's international right-back Mick Mills, the man from Johnstone became an Aberdeen hero scoring twice to clinch a stunning 3-1 success. For the first time the national media had to sit up and take notice of the revolution underway in the north-east corner of Scotland; for the first time we all had a real inkling that something special might just be about to happen to our club. Our UEFA Cup run ended in December at the hands of SV Hamburg, Franz Beckenbauer and all, but the following month we embarked on another Cup run, one that was to lead all the way to that never to be forgotten night in Gothenburg.

It began one dull, grey afternoon in Lanarkshire; Saturday, January 23rd, 1982, the third round of the Scottish Cup.

Aberdeen had been drawn against a Motherwell side flying high in the First Division, one that would ultimately secure promotion back to the top flight of the Scottish game by a clear ten points, rattling in 92 goals along the way. It was therefore a less than straightforward tie, one that could quite easily provide an upset. There were almost 13,000 fans inside Fir Park, including myself and my friend from the Clydesdale Bank, Ken Johnston. As we stood in

5

the enclosure below the main stand, huddled against the chill, the fear persisted that an early Cup exit could be on the cards. And then the game started. The Dons kicked-off, the ball was fed out to right-back Stuart Kennedy and he hoisted a long angled cross to the edge of the Motherwell penalty area where home defender Iain MacLeod miscontrolled. John Hewitt was on the ball in a flash and lashed an angled left-footed shot high past the despairing Hugh Sproat. 9.6 seconds had elapsed; it was the fastest goal ever scored in a competition which had begun in 1873. Game over!

The following month Hewitt was again the hero, netting the only goal against Celtic at Pittodrie. Another home tie followed in the quarter-finals, Kilmarnock disposed of despite having the nerve to take a first minute lead, and then after two hard-fought encounters St Mirren were beaten in the semis, Peter Weir driving in the decider on a rain-soaked Dens Park pitch to snatch the replay 3-2.

When Aberdeen had last reached the Scottish Cup Final they had been well beaten by Rangers in what had been Billy McNeill's farewell match as manager. Four years on, the Ibrox side again lay in wait, but this time the outcome was to be very different. Alex Ferguson was determined to secure another trophy and his team did him proud, blowing away the Glasgow giants in extra-time to record a stunning 4-1 success.

Winning the Scottish Cup for just the third time in the club's history secured a place in the following season's European Cup Winners Cup and that was where the fun really was about to start . . .

CHAPTER ONE

JIM LEIGHTON

ABERDEEN 7-0 SION
Wednesday August 18th, 1982

It is a measure of how Scottish football's fortunes in European competition have declined that our teams are now well accustomed to kicking off their campaigns in advance of their domestic seasons. Back in 1982 Scotland's representatives could expect to have as many as ten league and cup fixtures under their belts before contemplating continental opposition, but that was not the case for Aberdeen as they embarked upon their Cup Winners Cup adventure.

The season had begun with back-to-back draws in League Cup sectional ties, 2-2 away to Morton and then a remarkable 3-3 with Dundee, a game we had dominated but had to settle for a point from when Eric Black completed his first hat-trick for the club just five minutes from the end.

As we trooped out of Pittodrie that warm August afternoon the fans' thoughts were already turning to the following midweek's tie against the unknown Swiss side Sion, against whom we had been unlucky enough to be drawn in a preliminary round. I do recall being a little fearful. The previous season's exploits against Ipswich and Hamburg had given us a real taste for European action and the thought of being knocked out before the Premier Division had even begun was an unpalatable one.

Those fears were however dismissed on a sunny Wednesday night in front of some 13,000 supporters as an imperious Aberdeen performance saw us stroll to a 7-0 victory.

Black settled any nerves with an early goal that night, Gordon Strachan and John Hewitt scored within a minute of each other, and Neil Simpson had us four ahead and coasting with little more than half an hour played. Simpson in particular was in dominant form that night, capping his performance with a fine individual effort, weaving past opponents before cleverly chipping the ball into the net. As we relaxed in the Beach End thoughts were turning to 'how many?' The Swiss central defender Alain Balet prodded in an unfortunate own goal for the fifth, heading a Hewitt cross beyond his own keeper, Mark McGhee helped himself to the sixth from close range and the rout was completed near the end by the ever-popular Stuart Kennedy who plundered the only European goal of his career to the biggest cheer of the night.

The Sion General Manager Leon Walker, quoted in the following night's *Evening Express*, described the match as 'a catastrophe' but for us it was a glorious night to be a football fan, both in terms of the weather and the joy of luxuriating in a romp which had ensured we could anticipate at the very least one further round in the competition.

It was also one of the quietest nights ever enjoyed by our goal-keeper Jim Leighton. He, like us, spent the evening watching his team-mates run rings round their hapless opposition: "I had nothing to do that night, absolutely nothing, but as long as I had a 'nil' at the end of it I was always quite happy. To be honest the score-line could have been even greater, the boys were absolutely unbelievable and it was a joy to watch."

By then, Jim had firmly established himself as Aberdeen's number one with over one hundred first-team appearances. He had been an ever-present in 1981-82, having missed just two games the season before when he had taken on the mantle of replacing club legend Bobby Clark.

It was all very different from his first job after leaving school, as a clerical officer trying to help the 'no-fixed-aboders' who attended the Unemployment Benefit office at Kinning Park in Glasgow.

"You could write a book about that in itself! They were the nicest folk ever, some of them slept on benches or at the old hostel in Duke Street. One might have been a teacher, another a doctor, but something had happened in their lives and they ended up on the streets. They would come in and give you presents and you'd think, 'that's nice', then you'd see the price tag was still on them! There was one guy who had a wooden leg. He used to come over on the Renfrew Ferry, and he came in one day without the leg; he'd been woken by a wrecking ball crashing through the wall of the building he'd been sleeping rough in and he'd had to leave the leg behind when he escaped!"

Having moved up to Aberdeen, Jim had been farmed out to Highland League side Deveronvale in his first season, but by the following summer Clark was injured and Alex Ferguson had to decide which of his young keepers would step in. The Dons had a Monday night friendly against Middlesbrough and it was then I got my first glimpse of Jim Leighton as he played one half and John Gardiner the other in a 3-2 win.

Five days later at a rain-soaked Tynecastle Fergie had made his decision and it was Leighton who took the field for the opening Premier Division encounter against Hearts. It did not exactly start as planned with Eamonn Bannon opening the scoring for the home side in just four minutes. Jim settled quickly however and impressed with his handling, and the Dons got back into the game, Duncan Davidson equalising before Joe Harper edged us in front before half-time. I am unable to report on the second half as by then a group of us, having been gradually penned in and tortured by disgruntled Hearts fans, had made a run for it and I spent those forty-five minutes listening to the commentary on Radio Scotland while cowering under my seat on the coach which was being liberally pelted by rocks, stones and bottles.

Unaware of my troubles, Leighton apparently cruised through the remainder of the match and retained his place in the starting line-up for the first three months of the campaign.

"It was difficult. I was just a kid and there I was having been thrust into the first team without having played even a reserve match. I had posters of some of these players up on my walls at home and now I was playing against them."

He stayed in the side until the end of October, but by then the Dons had lost three league games in a row and with Clark fit again, the veteran was restored to the side for a narrow victory over Dundee United.

"It really did me a favour, Bobby being fit again. It was just beginning to dawn on me that I was operating in a big man's world and it was for the best that I was left out at that time. It had been an incredible learning curve, I had played at Ibrox, I'd played three European ties, but it was all beginning to get a bit much, and later, when I was ready for it, I was back in the team and was never out of it again."

He still had a bit of learning and maturing to do. In the title-winning campaign of 1979-80 Leighton played just once, in a 2-1 home defeat at the hands of Kilmarnock in which he was culpable for conceding the opening goal. His manager however made sure he felt part of the group.

"Fergie made me go out on the open-decked bus with the trophy and the rest of the guys, and while I didn't really feel that I deserved to be there, it definitely gave me a taste for it and made me want more. Little did I know then just how often I was going to enjoy that experience."

It was to be vindication of Jim's decision to leave Elderslie and head north. He had rejected chances to sign for both Morton and St Mirren (where Alex Ferguson was then manager) on part-time contracts, preferring to take his chances as a full-time pro far from his home comforts.

"It might have been the only chance I got and I wasn't going to pass it up. I always promised my mum and dad that the only way

I would be back down the road was if I wasn't good enough, it wouldn't be because of drink or women or gambling. Thankfully I never had to go back."

Instead Jim Leighton became part of a group of young men being moulded and guided by Alex Ferguson into a side which would eventually dominate the domestic game and take on and beat the best that Europe had to offer at that time. He was a key figure in all the major successes, including the 1982-83 Cup Winners Cup run, during which he was an ever-present. The final itself was not one of Jim's busier nights; he did make a couple of saves at important moments, but his major contribution was in conceding the penalty (albeit given little choice by Alex McLeish's slack pass-back) from which Real Madrid equalised. Thankfully that proved immaterial and by the end of the night big Jim was collecting the most prized winner's medal of his career.

While there was flair and potency in Ferguson's team, he never lost sight of the reality that he needed to have a core to it and a defensive solidity. Neale Cooper and Neil Simpson would provide that in midfield, but it was to be a defensive triumvirate that would be the bedrock, a trio whose names still trip off the tongue as naturally for me today as they did three decades ago: Leighton, Miller and McLeish.

In the four seasons from 1980-81 through to 1983-84, perhaps the peak years for that side, Aberdeen played a total of 227 competitive fixtures at home and abroad. Jim Leighton missed just three of those matches, Willie Miller seven and Alex McLeish twenty-three, largely he would tell you because he was the one putting his body on the line while the other two strolled around looking good! In addition to averaging more than fifty club matches each year, there were also the demands of international football with the three being fixtures in Scotland squads through-out that time.

Of course as fans we just took that all for granted. It is only now on reflection that the enormity of what those guys did hits home.

Their level of consistency was remarkable. In those four seasons their goals-against tally in 36 Premier Division matches was 26, 29, 24 and 21. In that final campaign, in which they were crowned Scottish champions, they conceded a mere nine goals in eighteen away matches.

"It's a shame that everyone talks about me, Willie and Alex, as there were other guys who made up that defence. Stuart Kennedy played a major part, Dougie Rougvie did and John McMaster. We had international full-backs, but I guess it was inevitable we were the ones everyone focused on. Every season we started off with the target of conceding under twenty goals. We never quite managed it, we got close a few times, but that was always our aim, that was the standard we set."

Every Monday morning during the season the trio would conduct an inquest if goals had been conceded, trying to pinpoint any mistakes that had been made.

"Quite often we decided it was one of the other players to blame, but if it was one of us, we took steps to make sure that wouldn't happen again. We didn't just gel overnight; it took hours and hours on the training ground and plenty scowls from Willie before we got the unit working as we wanted."

That unit remained intact, apart from occupational hazards like injuries and suspension, through until the summer of 1988 and it was Jim who split it, following Alex Ferguson to Old Trafford in what seemed a dream move.

"Aberdeen were the only club I had ever played for and I had won everything there was to win. When I came back from the 1986 World Cup in Mexico I really wanted to leave then, but I had two years left on my contract and I wasn't allowed to go, which I had no problem accepting."

Two years later there was nothing to hold him and there was significant interest from clubs at home and abroad. Bundesliga outfit KFC Uerdingen were in the bidding, so were Racing Club Paris, and both were offering considerable sums of money, but as soon as Jim knew Manchester United were interested his mind was made up and a £500,000 fee was agreed.

"Fergie had been at me for a while, that was no great secret, and I was delighted when the deal was finally done."

His time at Old Trafford got off to a flying start, with Leighton recapturing his best form.

"Up until the last few games of the season we had the best defensive record in England. The second season was a tough one for me personally. McClair and Hughes had gone about fifteen games without scoring a goal, and if they didn't score nobody did. We would get beat one-nil and I was carrying the can for it, whether it was my fault or not. It was getting crazy at times, all the media had different names for me – 'Jittery Jim' was a favourite I seem to remember – and it had a snowball effect. The supporters were fine with me until the media campaign began. I was the target for abuse from ex-players in the papers, from pundits, and it did start to get to me."

Difficult to take any positives from that time, but looking back, Jim admits it was character forming.

"It did make me a stronger, wiser person. Everything had gone very easily in my career, I'd gone straight from the Highland League into the Aberdeen first-team, and straight into the Scotland team. I'd never had to deal with all that kind of thing before and I needed help. I didn't have a goalkeeping coach that I could rely and depend upon and talk to because it was Alan Hodgkinson who was there and, incredible as it might seem now, he was employed just one morning a week. It felt like I was just left hung out on my own to dry. Fergie never defended anyone publicly. We all defended him, but he wouldn't defend anyone else because he was getting hung out to dry by the media as well. It was a really tough year, I just didn't enjoy it, I absolutely hated it, and that reflected in my performances as well."

Nevertheless, United reached the FA Cup Final and with Crystal Palace the opposition there was an obvious chance for Jim to add to his medal haul and Alex Ferguson to win his first silverware since moving south of the border.

The game finished 3-3 after extra-time and Leighton was in the firing line once again.

"It was my fault for the first goal, I've not got any complaints about that. Gary O'Reilly's header looped off Gary Pallister and because of that deflection I got caught too far off my line and that just summed up how things were going for me at that time. No matter what I did, the ball ended up in the back of the net."

The replay was scheduled for the following Thursday and it was that afternoon, just a few hours before kick-off, that the bombshell was dropped.

"We trained, and then he pulled me aside before the meal and told me I was out. It wasn't the easiest one to take."

If Jim was devastated about being dropped in the way that he was, he could at least take some small comfort from the fact that it was his good friend Les Sealey who took his place.

"Right after the announcement was made I went up to my room and Les came and asked if I'd do him a favour. I knew instantly what he was going to say and I said, 'No, I'm not taking your medal – you wouldn't do it if roles were reversed, would you?' We were best mates. His wife and kids were in London and he had a place in Wilmslow where I stayed, so he was round at my house for half the week having his tea. We were friends before the Final and friends after, and we kept in touch long after we'd left United."

Sealey lasted longer at Old Trafford than Jim did, playing in the 1991 European Cup Winners Cup Final, and even briefly returned to United a few years later, as part of a nomadic conclusion to his playing career, which ended when he became West Ham United's goalkeeping coach. Tragedy struck though when, at the age of just 43, he died suddenly in August 2001.

"I went in to work the next morning and Dave MacDermid (Aberdeen's press officer at the time) was waiting for me and he told me that Les had died. He'd been driving, taken a massive heart-attack, and he was gone, just like that. That was hard. Obviously I was down for the funeral, in fact I was one of the pall bearers along with the West Ham keepers Shaka Hislop and Ludo Miklosko, Dave Jones, the former Cardiff manager, and Stephen Bywater (who later wore the number 43 on his jersey after joining Derby as a mark of respect to Sealey). We never had a cross word, Les and me. We were complete opposites, he was loud and brash, but we got on great."

Jim played just one more game for Manchester United, a League Cup tie away to lowly Halifax Town the following September. United scored twice late on to secure a 3-1 victory, the home side's goal a long-range free-kick which, typically it seems, deflected off one of his team-mates and over Leighton's despairing hands.

"It was a hard time. I wanted away, but it took me eighteen months before I got out of there. He wouldn't let me leave, he wouldn't let me go out on loan, I wasn't travelling with the first team. On Fridays after training me and Ralph Milne used to go on runs just to keep ourselves fit."

Despite having played more than 300 times for Ferguson at Aberdeen, and having helped the manager and his team amass such an impressive roll of honours, Leighton was dropped like a stone. It was as if he no longer existed as far as the manager was concerned.

"You know what he's like: anyone who stands up to him, that's it. It's always his way or no way. I've got my principles and I stood up for them, I certainly paid for them, but at least I could go to my bed at night knowing I'd done what was right. Everyone thinks it was just the Cup Final, but there were lots of other things leading up to that which I don't really want to go into. We had been together for a lot of years – would he handle it any more sympathetically with me than others? The answer was a definite 'no!' and I was hung out to dry again."

The media was full of speculation about why Jim had 'really' been dropped and about his relationship with Ferguson, and Jim at that time wanted to set the record straight.

"He wouldn't let me do it. He was worried that I was going to criticise him, criticise the club, but you know me, I wasn't interested in doing that kind of story. I was offered a lot of money, very nearly a six-figure sum, on the morning after the game but I turned that down. When I eventually did an article it was because I wanted to and it was because everyone had their own version, their own variation on why I'd been left out. There were so many stories, including one that I'd been caught with someone's missus, you know what it's like, everybody just makes up their own story – I just wanted to nail it once and for all and get the truth out there."

It may have been a weight off Jim's shoulders to clear the air and dismiss the rumours, but his decision did not go down well in the manager's office.

"He phoned me and called me every name under the sun and told me that no-one would be interested in my story. He said he'd spoken to the Chairman and that he wasn't letting me do it, so I called Martin Edwards and he wasn't bothered, he told me to go ahead and do the story and to get as much money out of them as I could! That was just one of a whole number of incidents, there wasn't just the one real bust-up, there were plenty of things before and after. After the decision was made at the Cup Final he knew and I knew without having a conversation that I was finished with United. I would have liked to have got away that summer, but he wouldn't let me go. Aberdeen wanted me when Theo [Snelders] got injured and he wouldn't let me – that would have been great because that would have been about three months playing but in the end Aberdeen brought in Bobby Mimms and Andy Dibble instead."

So, has Jim spoken to Sir Alex Ferguson since their acrimonious split?

"No."

I thought for a moment or two Jim was going to leave it at that, but he then continued, albeit briefly . . .

"I can always accept football decisions . . . I'll say no more."

He was allowed to go on brief loan spells with Arsenal and Sheffield United, where he still did not get a game, and with Mark McGhee at Reading, where he at least managed to play eight times, but it was not until he joined Dundee in March 1992 that Jim was able to put his Old Trafford hell behind him. Sadly, all he had done was swap that for Dens Park hell.

"It's one thing getting dropped at Manchester United, but it's an entirely different thing getting dropped at Dundee! Iain Munro was the manager and John Blackley his assistant when I signed. That was on the Thursday and Simon Stainrod signed the same day. On the Monday, Sloop [Blackley] got the sack and the following week Minnie [Munro] got the sack and Simon got his job. That wasn't a good time either . . . wrong club, wrong time."

Jim's career might have taken a completely different twist had he not felt honour bound having given his word to Munro that he would sign.

"I was at Edinburgh Airport at the carousel waiting for my luggage – no mobiles at the time obviously – and I hear an announcement asking Jerome Anderson to take a phone call. Jerome was my agent and he'd gone up earlier to discuss terms with Iain, so I took the call and it was from the office telling us that Werder Bremen had come in for me. They'd played a European tie the night before and their goalie Oliver Reck had got injured and was going to be out for the rest of the season, so they wanted to sign me. I said no, because I'd already promised Dundee I'd sign for them. As it turned out, everything went wrong for me at Dundee and Bremen went on to win the Cup Winners Cup that season!"

Leighton's time at Dens was just as disappointing as his spell with United, so it came as a huge relief when after three horrendous years, Leighton finally got his career back on track when he signed for Hibernian.

"I felt when I went there it was like last-chance saloon and Alex [Miller] was the only one prepared to take a chance on me. When I'd walked into Dundee the first morning there I knew there was something not quite right, but when I went in that first Monday morning into Easter Road I just had the feeling that something special was going to happen. It's like when you're looking for a new house, you get a feeling the moment you walk through the front door . . . and that four years, that was the best I played in my whole career . . ."

At which point I interrupted him – better than the glory years at Pittodrie?

"Oh aye, the best form of my whole career, helped by the way everybody took to me, I got on well with all the staff, the supporters, the directors, everyone. I had a fabulous time."

It was also while at Easter Road that Jim returned to the international fold. Leighton had been stuck on 58 Scotland caps, the bulk of which had been won with Aberdeen, but he had not featured since the 1-0 defeat to Brazil at Italia 90. It was not until November 17th, 1993 that he was recalled, for a World Cup qualifier in Malta, with Jim keeping a clean sheet in a 2-0 win for Craig Brown's side.

"I hadn't been sure about going back. Craig had asked me, but I really didn't want to go travelling all around Europe without playing. That wasn't me being big-time, I was just trying to concentrate on Hibs then, but for that game there was an injury crisis and he called me again. I had to check with my family first, I've got a thick skin but your family take the criticism more personally, and I had to make sure they were ok about it, but actually they knew that I really wanted to go back."

Jim edged his way back in slowly. He and Andy Goram were the stand-out choices for the goalkeeper's jersey, and it was Goram who played the first three qualifiers for Euro 96. But Jim reclaimed the number one position for the defeat in Greece and played in the seven remaining ties as Brown's men booked their place at the Championship Finals in England. That summer, however, there was to be another savage blow for the big keeper, as Goram was chosen to play in all three group matches, the Rangers man's case pressed home by Scotland's goalkeeping coach at the time, Alan

Hodgkinson, who also happened to hold the same post at Ibrox, and had history with Jim from their spell at United.

"It's not up to the goalie coach to make those decisions, it's certainly not the way I work, maybe because of what happened back then. I make a case for all the goalies and the manager decides. If I push one of them too much, then I lose the other ones. That was a sore one. I'd played in all the games leading up to Euro 96, and having fought back from where I had been, playing for Manchester United reserves, for Dundee reserves, to get all the way back to the top and then get dropped, I took that really, really badly. There was never any problem between Andy and me, we were always best of mates and stuck together. I had to handle it, but I decided then that I wouldn't be going back again."

But he did.

Having begun the road to France 98 by taking four points from away games in Austria and Latvia, the Scots faced a vital meeting with Sweden at Ibrox. John McGinlay scored an early goal and Jim then kept the Swedes out for the next 82 minutes to help secure a 1-0 victory.

"That was my 75th cap, so it was a special one. I know lots of people remember that one. I played well, but not as well as people seemed to think; it was all down to the importance of the match and it is certainly one I look back on with a great deal of pleasure."

From there Jim held on to his place throughout the campaign and this time he was given the nod for the Finals, playing in all three group matches against Brazil, Norway and Morocco. That gave him a total of nine appearances in World Cup Finals matches, a record for a Scottish goalkeeper that may never be broken. As usual, we failed to reach the knock-out stages, but Leighton left with the most special memory of his entire career, that opening game against Brazil at the Stade de France.

"I know I've upset some people saying that, given what we achieved with Aberdeen, but coming from where I'd been and then missing out on Euro 96, to be playing against Brazil in the first match of the World Cup, hundreds of millions watching on the telly, my family all watching on. There were many reasons why that game was so important to me."

Jim played just two more games for his country, European Championship qualifiers, a 0-0 draw in Lithuania and a battling 3-2 win over Estonia at Tynecastle. He had won 91 Scotland caps and decided, mainly, he says, because of his worsening relationship with Hodgkinson, that enough was enough.

"That was the biggest reason why I left, I've gone into the details before, everyone knows how I felt, and there's no need to go over them again, but he was the main reason."

He later returned to the international scene as goalkeeping coach to the under-21s, a position he has held for over a decade now.

It was during his time with Hibernian that Jim decided to further his education away from the game. He had got friendly with the headmaster at Auchterarder High School, and rather than take night classes, Leighton was invited to join the pupils in the afternoons once he had finished training.

"I didn't really want to carry on in football after I'd stopped playing . . . the first subject I did was Economics, I got my Higher, then I did Management Information Studies the following year and got my Higher in that. You can imagine the stick I was getting from the lads in the dressing room, but I loved it, and if I'd stayed on, my daughter Claire would have been in the same class as me! The plan was to go and do accountancy at Stirling University, but I had to forget that when I went back to Aberdeen."

The return to his spiritual home came in summer 1997, but the seeds had been sown a few months earlier, just three quarters of an hour before a Scottish Cup replay between the Dons and Hibernian at Pittodrie. As he prepared to go out for his warm-up Leighton had gone into the boot room looking for kit-man Jim Warrander, who always supplied him with a new ball before matches.

"He wasn't there, but the door got closed behind me and Tommy Craig [the Aberdeen assistant manager] stood with his back against it keeping it shut. He said to me, 'Would you come back? We need a goalie in the summer, we need you to come back.' I asked if he was serious – I really wasn't sure if it was him just winding me up before the big game – and when he said yes, I gave him my number. He called me a few days later and we'd agreed everything by the middle of February."

Despite that intervention, Jim went out and kept a clean sheet in a 0-0 draw then saved a penalty from Joe Miller in the shoot-out, allowing Kevin Harper to score the decisive spot-kick in a 5-3 win for the Edinburgh side.

In re-signing for the 1997-98 campaign, Leighton became the only one of the Gothenburg heroes ever to leave the club and return as a player. The old saying 'never go back' could not be applied to Leighton as he turned in a string of fine performances and added another 97 appearances, making a grand total of 535 for the club. He is fifth in the all-time standings in that respect, headed only by Stewart McKimmie, his old mentor Bobby Clark, and the two other members of that great defensive triumvirate, McLeish and Miller.

It was a very different Aberdeen by then. No longer were they challenging for league titles and terrorising the best of continental opposition, but Jim was just delighted to be back home, "This has always been my club", and he did at least reach two more Cup Finals. Sadly, neither was to turn out the way he would have wished for.

Under the haphazard management of eccentric Dane Ebbe Skovdahl the Dons lost the League Cup Final 2-0 to Celtic in March 2000, but there was a chance to make amends in the Scottish Cup Final three months later when Rangers lay in wait.

I remember calling Jim for a chat on the Thursday night before that game and we spoke for a long time about how special it would be for him and the team, how amazing it would be to collect another Scottish Cup winner's medal fourteen years on from his last one. His parting words to me were, "Whatever happens, win or lose, I'm going to take it all in. I'm going to be the last one off the park." On the contrary, he was the first one to leave the pitch that day.

"I had dreamt of a few different finales, but that certainly wasn't one of them."

Rangers broke down the right wing, Reyna fed Kanchelskis, and when he crossed to the near post Leighton and Rod Wallace arrived simultaneously, both desperate to reach the ball. There was just 1 minute and 55 seconds on the clock and the accidental collision left Jim with a shattered jaw. As he was stretchered off, and with no back-up goalkeeper on the bench, it was striker Robbie Winters who had to pull on the gloves. He held off Rangers for half an hour, but eventually the Dons were ground down and were fortunate in the end only to lose 4-0. While all that was happening at the national stadium, Jim was doing a tour of Glasgow hospitals.

"My jaw was fractured in one place, dislocated in another, but they couldn't get me an ambulance, so I'm in the back of a car, still with my strip and boots on, face covered in blood. They took me to one hospital, but they didn't have the proper x-ray machine, so I was taken to another one and by this time I'm getting stuck in all the Rangers traffic and they're all giving me plenty. It was unbelievable! Eventually when I was in the right hospital all the journalists are trying to get to me and the snappers are wanting a photograph, one of them pretended to be my brother, but he was stopped by the nurses who were just great with me. The downside was that it made it difficult for my real family to try to find out how I was!"

As he was being patched up the realisation that his playing career was probably over began to sink in and Jim was left with one huge regret.

"My family has always been great for me, always been there for me, and my one big disappointment is that my kids, Claire and Greg, never saw me win anything. They were at that FA Cup Final with United, they've seen me play against Brazil twice and in a lot of big high-profile games, they saw me in a Cup Final with Hibs and in two Finals that last season with Aberdeen, but they never saw me lift a trophy or collect a winner's medal. I would have liked them to have seen that for everything they had to put up with."

After a lengthy recovery process, it became clear Jim was not going to play again, and in January 2001 it was confirmed he had retired and would take on the role of the club's goalkeeping coach.

"I had no intention of becoming a goalie coach, I'd always thought my future would lie outside football, but it was my big pal Jim Stewart, who'd been my coach at Aberdeen, who got me into it and I'm certainly glad he did."

Leighton began working with Ryan Esson and David Preece at Pittodrie, and has worked with a host of goalkeepers since. He admits he monitors all their careers, and takes great satisfaction from seeing them progress.

"I still watch Ryan at Inverness for instance, but I would never try to take any credit for what any of them have done because it's not me that crosses the white line. Inside though, I do take great pride in seeing them do well."

Jim had been in place for almost a decade when his old team-mate Mark McGhee was appointed Dons manager in summer 2009, and he had no reason to suspect his position was under threat. He could not have been more wrong.

On Saturday, August 22nd Aberdeen had beaten Hamilton 3-0 at New Douglas Park to record their first victory of the season. Forty-eight hours later Leighton was unemployed.

"I never saw it coming. Looking back, there were signs, but then I just never gave it a thought. He pulled me into the office after training and said that was it, I was away. I was dumbstruck, I didn't know what to say or do. I walked out thinking that would be the last time I left the stadium through that door and I shed some amount of tears over the next few days."

I remember being stunned when I heard the news and called Jim, not as a reporter, but as a friend to offer my condolences and to try, probably in vain, to lift his spirits.

"You always know who's going to call in a situation like that, and you're never let down. There might be fifty phone calls in the first five hours and you just say the same things over and over again and you just start breaking down every time. It was a horrible time."

McGhee replaced Jim with Colin Meldrum who he brought from Motherwell. At the time he told the media that Meldrum offered "better value for money" saying he had experience in fitness work, and that "he is young, ambitious and enthusiastic". When I met Mark for this book he admitted it had been hard to sack Leighton, but he stood by his decision.

"I needed somebody who could do more than just keep goal, we couldn't afford to employ a separate fitness guy or someone who could work in the gym with the players. Colin was someone I knew could do both jobs."

Where Mark perhaps made a mistake was in not explaining that decision to the man he had just fired.

"Nobody ever told me why I had been sacked. Willie [Miller] called me three times and I kept asking him for the reason, but he said I'd have to speak to Mark. That was hardly going to happen, was it?"

Jim had thought his relationship with Mark had been solid enough, but did recall to me an incident that had taken place the previous year. The Gothenburg squad was celebrating the 25th anniversary with a series of events, including a game and three high-profile dinners at the Aberdeen Exhibition Centre. Most of the ex-players supported the fund-raising venture, but Mark did not, and that upset Leighton.

"We were playing Motherwell down at Fir Park the weekend of the dinners and that Saturday I had a right go at Mark, asking him why he wasn't doing anything. He said it was all down to how he felt about Fergie and I pointed out that no-one dislikes him more than me! I told him that Archie Knox, Eric Black and Bryan Gunn had all made the effort to fly up and get involved and that it wasn't about Fergie, it was about the players, it was about us and about the fans who must be fed up seeing the same old faces, me, Willie, Johnny Hewitt, Simmy . . . they want to see you and wee Gordon.

He wasn't having it and we were having a right go at each other while the players were doing their warm-up! Anyway, when it came to the payout I was very much against him getting anything and what they did in the end was make a minimal payment across the board and loaded the money on to those who had attended the various events. Whether that had any bearing on what happened later, I don't know . . ."

Whatever the reason, Leighton was now unemployed for the first time in his life and with bills to pay, he had to try to find some work.

"I really had no idea what I was going to do. I went to an employment agency and they told me to bring in my CV, and I had to say my CV wouldn't be of any use to them! I really don't think I ever came to terms with it. My wife wanted me to go and see a doctor because she thought I was getting depressed. I love playing golf, but I'd stopped that. I'd take the dogs for a walk in the morning and by nine o'clock I'd be sitting having my breakfast wondering how I was going to fill the day. I did get one job offer from America and another from the Middle East, but neither was practical. I did start working with Peterhead and Huntly, but Monday to Friday, nine to five, was soul-destroying."

He did join the Sportsound team on Radio Scotland, commentating for us on Dons matches with local reporter Scott Davie, which would have hardly lifted his spirits! Aside from his 'Statler and Waldorf' act with Scott, Jim still had his Scotland under-21 work and set up his own goalkeeping school, which he continues to this day, but there was still a huge void that needed filled.

"Aberdeen have always been my club and I was never going to get another job in football anywhere else. If someone had come in with the offer of a decent job in England I'd have seriously thought about it, but it's a real closed shop down there and goalies coaches are usually appointed through a pal of the manager . . . and I've not got any mates, so there was no chance of me getting a job!"

As Mark's troubled reign entered its final days word reached me that Jim would be back at Pittodrie just as soon as the axe fell. He had to play a waiting game, and although his return seemed inevitable, it was not plain sailing.

"One of the directors, Hugh Little, called me into the office and told me that I was always going to be coming back, but that they needed the new manager to make the appointment. He told me they were meeting Craig Brown the next day and that Craig had said I'd be the first one he'd bring in, then Hugh called me back and told me he wasn't taking the job!"

Chairman Stewart Milne did eventually persuade Brown to quit Motherwell and head north, and within days Leighton was back where he belonged. The day he walked into Pittodrie as an Aberdeen FC employee once again was, he says, one of the happiest of his life.

"I'm an Aberdeen fan, have been since I first came to the city all those years ago, and it was a marvellous feeling returning to the club. Now I want to play my part in trying to bring success back to Pittodrie, that would be just fantastic and would mean so much to all of us, players, coaches and supporters. That's what we're trying to achieve."

Almost every professional footballer's career lurches from highs to lows and back again, it is the nature of the job, but few can have enjoyed, or indeed endured, what Jim experienced during more than two decades in the game. The blows he suffered would have finished a lesser man but Leighton kept coming back for more, spurred on by a self-belief formed during those glory years at Pittodrie, years which saw him crowned Scotland's number one and a major player in Aberdeen FC's most illustrious team, culminating in that never-to-be-forgotten evening in Gothenburg.

"It was an incredible achievement by the lads, really incredible, and to have been part of that is something I will always look back on and treasure. It was an amazing time and I'm so glad I was there to experience it all."

CHAPTER TWO

WILLIE MILLER

SION 1-4 ABERDEEN
Wednesday September 1st, 1982

In the fortnight between the Sion matches Aberdeen got on with ensuring qualification from Section Two of the Scottish League Cup. The competition had been launched in the wake of World War II and had become the traditional curtain-raiser to the Scottish domestic season. As a young fan I loved those group matches which gave me my first glimpse of traditional old teams such as Airdrieonians, Clyde, Queen's Park and Queen of the South. The matches were often high-scoring – in my first year we thumped Airdrie 7-3 at Pittodrie – and allowed the teams to get in some serious competitive match practice ahead of the league campaign getting underway.

It was in such a sectional tie that the man who would become the most influential player in Aberdeen's history made his full first-team debut. Having come on as a substitute for Arthur Graham in the final match of the previous season at Morton, Willie Miller lined-up against Dundee United at Tannadice on Wednesday, August 15th, 1973. Naturally enough, he marshalled his defence securely, keeping a clean sheet in a 0-0 draw.

Almost a decade later Willie was still at the heart of the Dons' rearguard, captaining his side to three successive victories before the trip to Switzerland. Having begun their section with those back-to-back draws Aberdeen demolished Dumbarton, Morton and Dundee, scoring eleven goals in the process, with Gordon Strachan helping himself to half a dozen of those. Being the perfectionist he is, Willie to this day is probably still annoyed by the only one conceded during those games, to Aberdonian Ray Stephen for Dundee in a 5-1 Dons romp at Dens Park. That win ensured the Pittodrie side would make the knockout stages of the tournament, the first objective on the seasonal check-list nicely ticked off.

The following Tuesday morning Willie and his team-mates gathered at Aberdeen Airport for the flight to Geneva, followed by a two-hour coach drive through the scenic Alpine countryside to the small town of Sion. The views were breathtaking, but lost on the club captain, as he did what he always did on these trips, slept! Willie has long been renowned for his ability to nod off anywhere and at the drop of a hat, his relaxed laid-back approach to life off the field a stark contrast to the ferocious competitive edge he brought onto the pitch.

Seventy fans accompanied the seventeen strong playing party and they were treated not only to a picturesque and welcoming stadium, but to another classy performance by the team.

These days a seven-nil home win would have prompted the successful manager to field a virtual reserve side in the second leg, but the thinking was very different in 1982 and the two alterations made by Alex Ferguson were enforced, Neale Cooper replacing the injured Alex McLeish and Peter Weir taking over from Eric Black, who was suffering the after effects of a couple of heavy challenges in the win over Dundee.

The Dons picked up where they had left off in the first leg, finding the net on a number of occasions only, according to the *Evening Express* reporter Alastair Guthrie, to have those efforts ruled out by a 'flag-happy linesmen and an over-fussy Yugoslavian referee'. Incredibly, when John Hewitt did finally plunder a legitimate goal with almost half an hour gone, the Swiss part-timers equalised within seconds, Bregy heading past Jim Leighton, a goal the big keeper was furious about losing.

"Archie Knox was giving Gordon Strachan pelters from the dug-out and wee Gordon was standing there arguing back when the man he should have been marking came through and set up the goal. If we hadn't lost that one we would have had seven European shut-outs in a row, right through to the Bayern Munich game at Pittodrie. I can promise you the wee man got it after that one!"

The second half was again dominated by the Dons and they eventually got the goals their play merited. Willie grabbed his first ever European goal for the club (he eventually amassed a grand total of two in continental competition, the other coming against IFK Gothenburg in the European Cup in March 1986), surging from deep to catch out home keeper Pittier, and a Mark McGhee double secured another comfortable win and an aggregate 11-1 success.

Alex Ferguson later singled out Hewitt and Miller, whom he said he had been urging to venture forward more often, but saved special praise for the club's record buy, Peter Weir, whose tantalising wing play had helped destroy the Swiss.

The affable Leon Walker told the *EE*: "I don't think we have ever seen a better team at our ground", and proved his clairvoyant qualities by offering up this additional quote, "They could finish up in the Final itself."

Willie Miller was not thinking quite that far ahead, he was just basking in the glory of having scored even if he did admit to me, "Everyone scored against Sion!" The good news for us Dons fans however was that Willie was still there and in a position to find the net, as for much of the summer it seemed certain our charismatic captain was on his way out of Pittodrie.

As season 1981-82 had ended, so had Miller's contract with the club. Back in the pre-Bosman days that did not have quite such serious implications, the player's registration was retained and Willie would have commanded a hefty transfer fee, but Alex Ferguson was beginning to view his skipper as irreplaceable and was determined to hold on to him.

Willie, along with club-mates Gordon Strachan, Jim Leighton and Alex McLeish, had headed off to Spain for the World Cup Finals without having put pen to paper, and having featured against both Brazil and Russia, admitted to the local press on his return that 'leading clubs' had been in touch.

One of those clubs was Rangers, whose manager John Greig was desperate to lure Miller to Ibrox, but the finances on offer were no better than at Pittodrie and Willie judged Aberdeen to be a better bet than the Govan side, a wise move as it would turn out.

I well remember the whole 'will he, won't he' saga being played out at the time, and in those days before the internet and rolling TV and radio sports news, the dash for the *Evening Express* each afternoon to find out the latest. It was fascinating almost three decades later to sit wheeling through microfilm at Aberdeen City Library reliving that tantalising episode, and understanding the problems faced by the journalists in filling the back pages with a story which for days on end developed little. On July 21st, 1982 Willie was quoted as refuting suggestions that Manchester United had approached him, but admitted "naturally I would be interested, anyone in the game would be silly not to listen to United." The *Express* headline that day read I'M NOT GOING YET and by Friday, August 6th, more than two weeks later, it was MILLER: STILL 'NO'. In between, Alastair Guthrie and his colleague Iain Campbell had essentially been writing and re-writing the same story. Because he had not re-signed, Willie missed Drew Jarvie's testimonial match against Ipswich Town and Ferguson issued a warning, "We need continuity and we can't wait much longer for Willie to sign."

The impasse continued over the weekend and we were all becoming resigned to him going when, just twenty-four hours before the opening League Cup encounter with Morton, the news we all craved finally arrived. The back-page headline said it all: MILLER SIGNS NEW TWO-YEAR CONTRACT WITH THE DONS. Willie had gone in for the latest in a series of meetings that lunchtime, a few 'minor' points had been agreed, and the captain finally signed on the dotted line. A relieved Alex Ferguson told the paper, with a degree of understatement, "I'm delighted." The weeks-long saga was at last over and Willie had pledged his immediate future to the club. The wrangling had been over the princely sum of £10 a week!

Miller skippered the team in the 2-2 draw at Cappielow. He did however handle the ball in the box with just five minutes to go, allowing Aberdeen's nemesis Andy Ritchie to equalise from the penalty spot!

There were to be other occasional such blips during his remarkable playing career with the Dons; that would be inevitable given his longevity, but there were countless high-points. In seventeen years Willie started 796 competitive matches for the club in addition to that one solitary substitute's appearance against Morton on April 28th, 1973. He scored 32 goals along the way, but it is by the goals he prevented that Willie's worth to Aberdeen has to be truly measured, and his level of consistency was quite staggering. In the decade and a half between the start of the 1973-74 season and the end of 87-88 Aberdeen played 556 league matches. Willie Miller played in 523 of them. Given the position in which he played and the potential for serious injury and, even more likely, suspension, that is a truly astonishing statistic.

As with most young boys Willie's love for the game began early, and having worked his way through the various school and boys club sides he was snapped up at the age of thirteen by the amateur team Eastercraigs. Back then he was a prolific striker and it was as such that he signed for Aberdeen in 1971, turning his back on an offer from Celtic to do so. He was farmed out to Highland League Peterhead and the goals flowed, his tally of 23 making him the club's top scorer, before returning to Pittodrie to continue his apprenticeship in the reserves.

It was in December of 1972 that Willie's career took an unexpected twist, one for which he would be eternally grateful. An injury crisis meant reserve team coach Teddy Scott had limited options from which to select his second XI and he moved the seventeen-year-old Miller into the back four. He cruised through a 2-0 win over Rangers and from that day on Willie was a central defender.

He had to bide his time, waiting more than eighteen months before he was considered a first team regular, but once he got into the team he was there for keeps.

Willie lived through the Jimmy Bonthrone era, seeing off more experienced competition, and really came into his own when first Ally MacLeod and then Billy McNeill set about rejuvenating the club. By the time Alex Ferguson arrived he was captain, had two hundred appearances under his belt, and was displaying the self-assured control which became the hallmark of his play.

As fans we very quickly began to hear suggestions that the pair's relationship was anything but smooth in the early days.

"There were plenty teething troubles between myself and Alex. He came in and he wasn't the smooth, sophisticated chap you see these days. He was young in managerial terms, pretty determined, and there was a bit of conflict."

What irked the Dons skipper more than anything was his manager's continual references to Jackie Copland, a player Ferguson had left behind at St Mirren, but who he clearly rated very highly. During training Miller was regularly being compared, not always favourably, to Copland, and it got to him.

"In the early days when he was setting things up he used to say things like, 'Jackie would do it this way, or that way'. I wasn't a kid at the time, I had my own way of doing things and it got on my nerves a wee bit. Eventually I asked him to stop doing it, he did, and we were fine."

That was not what the rumour mill around the city was suggesting at the time and I was by no means alone in hearing stories of dressing room bust-ups between manager and captain. Three decades on Willie plays down any such suggestions, although he was once substituted at half-time by Ferguson after the pair disagreed over defensive tactics. It was in September 1981 during an apparently routine 2-0 win away to Partick Thistle, but such was the force with which Willie tried to make his point he was 'hooked' and replaced by Neil Simpson.

"We were playing three at the back. I had my opinion on how to play that formation and the manager had his, so we had a disagreement. It was probably just me being stubborn and the manager always wins, so I stayed in the dressing room. There was one other occasion, after we had won a game in the middle of winter, when with us all sitting there freezing he started dissecting the performance. After about ten minutes I said, 'Gaffer, if you want to talk to me I'll be in the bath,' and off I went. There was a bit of a silence and then he just told the rest of the guys to get in. Generally though we were on the same wavelength, we wanted the same things."

The single-minded determination shared by the pair was key to everything the Dons would go on to achieve, with Ferguson the mastermind and Miller pulling the strings out on the pitch. He shared Jim Leighton's utter hatred of conceding goals and soon became one of the most dominant figures in Scottish football, recognised by everyone and rightly feted for his remarkable level of consistency.

Those performances led to the string of successes enjoyed during the Ferguson era and brought to the fore one of the most iconic and enduring images the game has ever known: Willie standing, both arms outstretched, a trophy nestling almost casually in his right hand.

It was a pose he struck with pride in the Ullevi Stadium that rainy night three decades ago. Having watched his side outclass Real Madrid across much of the two hours of play, Miller knew the reward was well-merited and it was with additional relish that he lifted the silver trophy skywards, sending us all into raptures of delight. It was payback for all the hours working hard in training, forging and developing his defensive unit with Leighton and McLeish, and for all the disappointments suffered along the way as Fergie's team took shape.

"At the time I don't think we understood the magnitude of what we were doing. You look at the names on that trophy and we shouldn't be on it, really. I don't think there's another small, provincial club like ours that won it. We didn't have the greatest resources, we didn't have the biggest support, and if you check the other winners virtually all of them are huge clubs compared to us."

To emphasise Willie's point, Barcelona had won the ECWC the season before, Juventus won it the season after, beating the Porto team which had knocked out the Dons in the semi-finals.

The skipper led his side up to collect a trophy on ten separate occasions down the years, beginning with the League Cup win under Ally MacLeod in 1976 and ending with a 2-1 victory over Rangers in the same competition on October 22nd, 1989. Just twenty-four days later his career was all but over.

Willie had won his 64th Scotland cap in a 3-1 defeat away to Yugoslavia in a World Cup qualifier two months earlier, but had been left out for the next match, a 3-0 loss in Paris, as manager Andy Roxburgh turned to a more youthful line-up featuring Alex McLeish and Richard Gough. It had seemed his international career was over, but with the Scots requiring a point from their final game at home to Norway, Roxburgh decided he needed more experience at the back; he needed Willie Miller. It was to prove a fateful decision for the Dons captain.

With little over an hour gone in the match, and Scotland leading 1-0 thanks to an Ally McCoist lob from the edge of the box, Miller tried to turn away from a Norwegian opponent just inside his own half and was caught on his already weak right knee by a late challenge. The joint had previously been severely damaged by Polish midfielder Wlodzimierz Smolarek in a pre-season friendly against Feyenoord in what Willie describes as the worst foul ever perpetrated on him, and now it immediately began to swell and he was forced to leave the pitch. By the time the celebrations were kicking off out on the pitch following a 1-1 draw, Willie was already contemplating his future as he lay on the treatment table in the Hampden dressing room. He was operated on three days later and began his long rehabilitation. My notes from that time suggest the early prognosis was that he would be out of the game 'for at least four weeks', but that was to prove wildly optimistic. He returned through sheer force of will to the Aberdeen side for the last two league matches of the season, but was not deemed ready to play in what would have been a fitting finale, the 1990 Scottish Cup Final against Celtic, won 9-8 in a thrilling penalty shoot-out after a goalless draw.

He worked hard through the summer and led the side out for the first game of the next season, a second-round League Cup tie against Queen's Park at Hampden Park in front of just 2,201 supporters, but he knew the knee had not healed properly, was never going to, and that his time was up.

It is not easy to let go, and Willie delayed the announcement for three months before finally confirming what he, and we, had all feared; he had kicked his last ball for Aberdeen FC. Well, almost. There was one final appearance, in what was his second testimonial match granted by the club, against a World XI chosen and managed, fittingly enough, by Alex Ferguson. It was December 4th, 1990 and after a rousing, emotional and prolonged send-off from the fans, Willie's glorious playing career was over.

He had been that rare breed, a loyal one-club man, and had attained legendary status in the eyes of us Dons fans, not just because of that, but also because of everything he achieved during his time at Pittodrie. He might have left for Rangers that summer of 1982, indeed he might have left earlier as Sunderland had tried to entice him south, but those were the only two occasions there was any serious thought given to leaving Aberdeen.

"I was enjoying my football; I was in the international team, going to World Cups. I was playing for Aberdeen and I was perfectly happy, I didn't have any great ambition to move. Sunderland financially was a fantastic offer, I'd have been making four times my wages and got a big signing-on fee, but I went down and just had that gut feeling that it wasn't for me."

Incredibly there were no more big money moves dangled in front of the skipper and his continued presence became more valuable as one by one his Gothenburg team-mates left for pastures new.

"It was difficult at times, particularly after Sir Alex left and Ian Porterfield came in, because I was the one in the firing line, I was the one getting slaughtered by the press for this and that, and he wasn't there to share it any more, to help relieve the pressure. They wouldn't have done it had he still been around."

By the time Willie hung up his boots, Porterfield had gone to be replaced by Alex Smith and Jocky Scott, the pair being assisted by Dons legend Drew Jarvie. The club realised there was no way Willie could be allowed simply to walk away from Pittodrie, so he was brought into the coaching team working initially with the reserves and then, as part of a reshuffle when Jocky took over as Dunfermline boss, as first-team coach.

He had offers to embark on his own managerial career, but they never seemed the right option at the right time.

"Ayr United asked me, but it was an awful long way to think about going and moving the family, and then Arbroath came in as well, but it was part-time football, and I said no to that one too."

I have often wondered if Willie might have been better served learning the job down the divisions, whether that might have better prepared him for what followed in the Pittodrie hot-seat, but the man himself remains to be convinced.

"I don't think it would have made a big difference. What might have been better is if the club had held on to Alex Smith longer, kept him as manager with me working alongside as coach, that would have helped, that would have been my learning curve."

Indeed that scenario had been agreed and was due to be announced on Monday, February 10th, 1992. Unfortunately, 48 hours earlier the Dons lost 1-0 at home to Hibernian and there was a noisy and angry demonstration by a section of the Aberdeen support immediately afterwards. During the course of that weekend Chairman Ian Donald ripped up the plans and the news conference became an entirely different one. Alex Smith was out and Willie Miller was in, becoming the thirteenth full-time manager in the club's history.

Aberdeen were fifth in the Premier Division table, still well in touch for a European place, but back in the early nineties, with the successes of the previous decade still fresh in the mind, that was not good enough.

"It was unexpected, that's for sure, but what could I do? When you're offered a job like that at a club you love, you've got to take it because you never know when the chance is going to come round again."

Willie's reign began with a 0-0 at Ibrox, one of five draws in the remaining twelve games of the season. Only four were won and Aberdeen slipped down to sixth. Over the summer he set about revitalising the squad and for the next two seasons the Dons came desperately close to reclaiming silverware.

In 1992-93 Willie lost out in both Cup Finals to Rangers and also finished runners-up to Walter Smith's treble-winners in the title race. The following campaign brought defeat to the Ibrox side in the League Cup quarter-finals, a Scottish Cup semi-final exit at the hands of Dundee United in a replay and another second place finish in the Premier Division, the title lost, to Rangers of course, by just three points.

Season 1994-95 was however to be an entirely different story as Willie turned over the squad dramatically in a bid to kick-on.

"I was a young manager at the time, and when I look back now I look at the players I brought in and I can't believe how badly they handled it here, playing for this club. I give wee Doddsy (Billy Dodds) stick, he's a smashing player, but believe me if he'd scored half the chances that he should have scored, then that season wouldn't have been nearly as depressing as it was. I'm not blaming the players in any way because I think when you're the manager you've got to take the responsibility, but I'm still surprised to this day that they just couldn't handle the pressure of playing for Aberdeen."

Willie had been accustomed to playing with players who could cope with that pressure, and admits with hindsight that he should have fought harder to keep his more experienced men at the club a little longer.

"I should have persuaded Jim Bett to stay, could have kept Robert Connor, not let big Alex (McLeish) go to Motherwell, but at the time I thought it was the right thing to do. Second place wasn't good enough for me, I had ambition, I wanted to win things and that was how I thought I could do it."

Three years on from his appointment Willie Miller was sacked as Aberdeen manager. The Dons had just lost 3-1 at Kilmarnock and were languishing in second-bottom place, just two points clear of Partick Thistle. He was devastated, but philosophical, and had no qualms about telling his successor to accept the post.

"Roy Aitken had been offered the job and asked my thoughts and I said, 'Big man, take it, don't think you owe me anything' and that's the way football works. My time had gone, now it was his time."

Less than a fortnight after he had been axed, and just a week after beating Rangers, the Dons lost to Stenhousemuir in a Scottish Cup tie, then the most embarrassing defeat in the club's history. I remember calling Willie at the time and pointing out that at least he had avoided that ignominy; it is typical of the man and his self-belief that his immediate answer was that it wouldn't have happened had he still been in charge!

The end of that season was torture as Aberdeen seemed set for a first relegation in the club's history, but there was to be a late rally. I vividly recall actually shedding a tear or two of relief in the Sportsound studio when Billy Dodds scored a late winner at Tynecastle. They followed that up with victory over relegation rivals Dundee United and a win at Falkirk on the final afternoon doomed United and earned the Dons a two-legged play-off against First Division Dunfermline.

The first match was to be at Pittodrie and Willie was the obvious choice to be part of our commentary team, but he took some persuading. He had not been back at the stadium since being sacked and feared taking the spotlight off the team and its objective, but eventually I talked him into joining us. It was a beautiful sunny afternoon on Sunday, May 21st, 1995 and after the expected early flurry of activity from the press photographers, Willie settled down to discuss the match. Nerves were settled by Stephen Glass's free-kick but Dunfermline equalised through Craig Robertson, ironically one of Willie's closest friends. To the delight of the vast majority of the 21,000 packed into the ground, a Duncan Shearer double earned Aberdeen some breathing space, and survival was ensured with a repeat 3-1 win in the away leg in front of as noisy an away support as I can ever remember on my travels with the Dons. Despite having been kicked out of the club just a few months earlier Willie was as happy and relieved that night as every other Aberdeen fan.

It would be another nine years before Miller was once again an integral part of the club. During that time he became a valued member of the Sportsound team, regularly displaying an astute tactical brain and often surprising both us and the listeners with his wicked sense of humour, an attribute only very rarely seen during his time as Dons manager. While he had to cope with the pressures brought on by his various business ventures, he had been freed from the particularly intense demands of professional football, and I always felt he saw broadcasting as something of a release valve. His timekeeping never improved and we got used to Willie sitting down and pulling on his headphones with just seconds to spare before we went on air. On one occasion, a semi-final at the national stadium, we began the programme by winding him up for another finely judged arrival, but he hit back with the perfect riposte, "I'm not used to going to Hampden without a police escort."

Never one to hold back from expressing his views on how the club he still loved was being run, Willie's comments were not always welcomed within the walls of Pittodrie, but to Stewart Milne's credit the Chairman realised the legend still had something to offer and towards the end of the 2003-04 season I began to hear whispers that plans were being laid for his return. I spoke to Willie privately on a number of occasions as he weighed up the offer and my advice was clear; he had to go for it. I would not for one minute suggest that my comments held any real weight, I know he consulted a number of other friends before taking the plunge, and on Monday, May 22nd he was back where he belonged, joining the Board of Directors as Executive Football Consultant with overall responsibility for all football matters. The title was more than a little cumbersome and in reality irrelevant, the importance lay in the job itself, and it was a huge one.

"Being involved in football was such a huge part of my life and being out of it was difficult and I was very pleased to take on the challenge. It was a big challenge, because the club was in a very poor state at the time. Major surgery was needed."

The Dons had finished second-bottom of the twelve team SPL that season and had been knocked out of both Cup competitions by Livingston. The team had struggled under the at times wayward leadership of Steve Paterson and the big Highlander and his assistant, Dons legend Duncan Shearer, were shown the door on the same day Miller was appointed. By then he had already taken steps towards securing the next manager, Jimmy Calderwood, who was fresh from a fourth place in the league and a Scottish Cup Final appearance with Dunfermline. Willie saw his former schoolmate as a safe pair of hands, someone who would look after the first team while he got on with the task of revamping the youth set-up and scouting network.

And to a large extent it worked. Calderwood brought much-needed stability and a succession of top six finishes, but failed to end the ever-lengthening run without a trophy, enduring along the way a series of Cup embarrassments at the hands of lower league opposition. Miller stood by his man throughout those defeats, but five years down the line the Board had decided another change was required.

"It had been solid in the league and of course we had that great European run, going over to Dnipro, beating Copenhagen, even going to Madrid to take on Atletico and the game here against Bayern, absolutely fantastic, but in the end it was the Cup results that counted against Jimmy. The Queen of the South defeat in the Scottish Cup semi was huge, I knew at the time it was huge, because you're staring at a Cup Final against Rangers knowing you're in with a great chance the way things were going at that time. Not reaching that was . . ." Here Willie took a deep breath and paused for a few seconds, the memory clearly still intensely painful, ". . . hugely disappointing."

I was working at Tannadice where Rangers were going about the business of reclaiming the SPL title when I got a call suggesting that Jimmy would be sacked after Aberdeen's final game of the season, at home to Hibernian. We broke the news on Radio Scotland during the half-time round-up and it was confirmed an hour or so later in the wake of a 2-1 win over the Edinburgh side which clinched a return to European competition. Even that feat was not going to save Calderwood's position and Willie was soon attempting to earmark his successor, with ex-Don Mark McGhee the chosen one.

The years of steadiness were about to come to an end as McGhee toiled on his return to the north-east, beginning with a record European defeat, 5-1 at home to Sigma Olomouc, and all but ending with a club record hammering, 9-0 away to Celtic, although he did linger for a few matches thereafter. It was not a good time to be a director of the football club and Willie admits he found it tough.

"I don't think you can enjoy being a manager or a director, you enjoy playing the game. You know when you join the board that you're not likely to be popular, are there any popular directors? Very few. If things are going well it's nothing to do with you, if things are going badly, 'Sack The Board!' That's the way it is. It is a difficult club to run, it's difficult financially and we've had to try to run the club prudently and that's had an impact on results, particularly in the last couple of years."

Stewart Milne took a more hands-on approach with the appointment of Craig Brown as McGhee's replacement and an internal restructure saw responsibility for contract negotiations and budgets taken over by Chief Executive Duncan Fraser, freeing Willie to spend more time working on the youth set-up, an important area for the club and one he feels passionately about.

"Despite the financial problems, the board has always backed the investment in the development side and I think they will continue to support that, which is vitally important."

On the afternoon I met Willie to interview him for this book we had first watched the Dons under-19s beat Dundee United 4-0 at Balgownie. Within five minutes it was clear to me the club had some highly talented youngsters, kids who, all things being equal, could go on and feature for the first team, perhaps earning large sums of money for the club in future transfers further up the football ladder. It was equally clear that Willie was thoroughly enjoying his newly defined role.

"I'm still a director so I still get the abuse when things go wrong, but I am out of the firing line a bit, and I can concentrate more on what's happening below first team level. We've got teams from under-11s right through to 19s and I'm involved with them all, working with the coaches at each level. We've got some great guys; I brought back Lenny Taylor to take us to Academy status, I've got Peter Weir in Glasgow, Andy Dornan in Edinburgh, there's Neil Simpson and Neil Cooper, and we've got a great philosophy throughout as we try to bring the kids on. We want football played the way it should be and I love standing by the dug-out watching those youngsters do just that."

A few months later that joy was snatched from him as Willie was sacked as part of a boardroom reshuffle. Axed as a director, he also had the development programme taken away from him and seventeen years after being fired as manager Willie once again walked out of Pittodrie Stadium an ex-Aberdeen employee. His reaction was brief and dignified as he declared himself "surprised and disappointed" by the decision.

Having served the club in so many different ways and having achieved so much, Willie Miller will always be a Dons legend. Had he done nothing else other than lead the side to victory in Gothenburg that would still have been the case. All these years later, he had hoped to leave a lasting legacy in the form of a conveyor belt which had already produced the likes of Chris Maguire, Ryan Jack, Peter Pawlett, Clark Robertson and Fraser Fyvie. He was denied the opportunity to see it through, but the work he did in recent years will certainly play a major part in securing the long-term future of the club.

CHAPTER THREE

DOUG ROUGVIE

ABERDEEN 1-0 DINAMO TIRANA
Wednesday September 15th, 1982

The 1982-83 league campaign got underway against Dundee United just three days after the second leg success in Switzerland and there was, as ever, a healthy Dons travelling support in the crowd of 11,683. Aberdeen almost fell behind in the first minute, Jim Leighton touching a Davie Dodds header on to the crossbar, but he was only delaying the inevitable, and by half-time Dodds and Maurice Malpas had both found the net to give United a winning advantage.

It was no disgrace to lose to Jim McLean's team – the Tannadice men were to go on to have the season of their lives – and the following midweek the Dons rounded off the first stage of the League Cup, Bell and Hewitt on target in a 2-1 win over Dumbarton at Boghead.

Our second Premier Division game was at home to Morton, so often a bogey team, and it seemed a bad omen when John McNeil nudged the visitors ahead. The Dons were level soon after when Gordon Strachan netted from the spot, and helped further when Jim Duffy got himself sent off for bringing down Eric Black. Black then snatched a half-time lead and Simpson and Hewitt struck after the interval to see out a comfortable 4-1 victory, earning in the process Aberdeen's first two league points of the campaign. It is interesting to note that reports from the time have the attendance that day down as between 7,500 and 8,000, the size of crowd which when achieved these days brings howls of disappointment and derision.

There was double that number inside Pittodrie the following Wednesday as the Dons continued their Cup Winners Cup campaign with a first-round first-leg tie against an unknown quantity, the Albanian side Dinamo Tirana.

The fans who headed to the stadium were given an inkling as to how Alex Ferguson intended winning the match, the *Evening Express* headline blaring TAKE THE HIGH ROAD! and promising the Dons would launch an 'all-out attack' against opponents 'lacking in inches'.

There was also a little aside in the newspaper revealing that the Dons manager's brother, Martin Ferguson, had parted company with East Stirlingshire, the club at which Alex had begun his managerial career.

The only thing on Fergie's mind however would have been seeing off Dinamo, and it would prove to be a frustrating ninety minutes, something he anticipated in his column in the match programme, The Don, writing, "The tie has that special magic because of its mystery content . . . I don't think the side has played against a team during my time at Pittodrie when we know so little about them . . . there may be something we don't know about that will surprise all of us." The manager's comments were reinforced by the fact the Tirana team-list was left blank in the programme, with the heading 'Squad to be announced over the Tannoy'.

The one goal the Dons did score came on the half-hour mark. Dougie Bell set off on a cross-field run and his attempted pass to Gordon Strachan rebounded off an opponent back to the midfielder. He scuffed his twenty-yard shot, but the Tirana keeper Ilir Luarasi weakly spilled the ball and John Hewitt pounced to tap home from seven yards.

That should have opened the floodgates, and Aberdeen certainly piled on the pressure, carrying out their manager's pre-match instructions, but despite the Albanian keeper flapping on occasion, the Dons could not break through a second time.

Mark McGhee fired over from six yards, Peter Weir saw his effort scrambled off the line and a sequence of shots were blocked or charged down as Dinamo defended in depth. McGhee had us all jumping for joy just two minutes from the end when he blasted the ball into the net, but the goal was ruled out by a linesman's flag, the striker adjudged to have been offside.

By that point frustration had set in, the players becoming over-anxious, and it had long become clear this tie was not going to be killed off in the first leg as the previous one had been. Ferguson later revealed: "During the second half their coaches were staring along in our direction and chanting 'Albania, Albania' – and they weren't shouting that for nothing. They are aware that we could feel ill at ease in their country."

Dinamo were clearly feeling confident and club official Konei Mahmut told the *EE*, "I expected more from Aberdeen and I can only judge that it was a poor performance from them," before warning, "We will be better in Tirana."

While the second leg seemed likely to be a stiff defensive test, the Dons back line had strolled through that first game with Jim Leighton an untested observer. Indeed, Willie Miller and Doug Rougvie – deputising in central defence for the injured Alex McLeish – had spent much of the match operating as auxiliary attackers. Big Doug in particular would have loved that. His rampaging runs forward from full-back had become a trademark of his game, and such was his size and strength that when he got a head of steam up, he was a hard man to stop. By then he had become a firm fans' favourite and the chants of 'Rooogveeeee!! Rooogveeeee!!' often filled the stadium.

As one of the longest-serving players at Pittodrie he was relishing the success being enjoyed, having experienced very different times during his decade with the club.

Doug Rougvie was to prove the hardest of the Gothenburg legends to track down. I had a number for him but it was out of date. I got a different number from within Pittodrie, but it too rang out. I spoke to John Hewitt, who had been his assistant manager at Cove Rangers, but the number John had was not current either.

I knew he had been working in the oil industry, and had spent a few years out in Dubai, but the word was he was back. A few people suggested they had seen him at Dons matches, but no-one could offer a way of contacting him. Eventually I turned to modern technology and posted on Twitter, "For my friends in the north-east – does anyone know whereabouts of Doug Rougvie? My contacts can't find him – he's too big to be lost!" and within half an hour I had the number for his direct line at work thanks to @sand_dancer_94.

It took a few days, but I did finally get to speak to him, and some weeks later we were sitting in his comfortable apartment on the outskirts of Aberdeen filling in the blanks. We began with the start of his Pittodrie career.

"I'd been with Dunfermline in their youth programme, playing for Dunfermline United under-16s and we had a great team, winning the Fife League and Cup and the Scottish Cup without losing or even drawing a single game. Ken Mackie [who later signed for the Pars and famously rejected a transfer to Rangers] and Allan Evans [a European Cup winner with Aston Villa] were both in that side and I thought I'd get called up, but Dunfermline were relegated and began cost-cutting and I got released. Andy Young was chief scout then and he tried to get me to Leeds, but they didn't want me, and because he knew Jimmy Bonthrone [then Dons manager] I ended up in Aberdeen."

That was 1972 and sixteen-year-old Dougie would have to wait more than three years for his competitive debut. He was farmed out to Keith and won his first senior medal when the side lifted the Highland League Cup, and he was given an insight into life as a professional footballer on a somewhat bizarre excursion by the club in the early summer of '74. He pulled on the red jersey for the first time in, of all places, Iran!

"I had been doing well for the reserves so they took me along on their 'world tour' and I made my debut for Aberdeen Football Club against Persepolis in Tehran, coming on as a sub."

This came as a complete surprise to me as I had no recollection of my team undertaking such a venture, but a bit of digging revealed that the Dons had indeed embarked on a somewhat grandly-titled world tour in May and June that year. They lost that match against Persepolis 2-0 before moving on to Australia and New Zealand where they undertook eight more games, a number of them just two days apart, with mixed results. They lost to Queensland in Brisbane and also to Noumea in New Caledonia, and although there were a few convincing victories along the way, it seems fair to assume that for the more experienced players in particular, this was more of a winding-down exercise after a hard season. The football, according to Rougvie, was for some of the guys very much secondary!

"It was some squad, the likes of big Willie Young, Arthur Graham, Andy Geoghegan, Billy Pirie, all those reprobates . . . Duncan Davidson and Billy Williamson, Eddie Thompson and Drew Jarvie. Honestly, they just went off their heads! I was there just to make up the numbers but I ended up playing all the games because the boys went off on one and Jimmy (Bonthrone) couldn't control them, they were out bevvying all the time and half of them weren't fit. I was rooming with Duncan and I don't think he ever slept in his own bed once the whole time we were away. That suited me because I love my food and I was ordering two breakfasts from room service and eating them both!"

By now Doug was roaring with laughter as the memories from what must have been a tour of carnage kept flooding back.

"Billy Pirie had emptied the bar on the flight over to Tehran, he just couldn't get enough drink. Remember Jim Hendry? He should never have been there, he had TB, and all you could hear from his room every morning was the sound of Ronnie Scott (the physio) slapping his back trying to get the phlegm out of his lungs. The keepers Bobby Clark and Andy Geoghegan had this pact that they would play half the games each, but Andy kept faking injuries and Clarky had to play every match! It really was fantastic, brilliant, I had my eighteenth birthday in Newcastle, and I just loved every minute of it."

Back to Aberdeen, back to reality, and it was to be almost eighteen months before Doug made his competitive debut for the club, as a substitute for Jarvie, in a 2-0 home win over St Johnstone. He remains convinced he marked the occasion with a goal, "I scored with a header . . ." but the record books all show it was a Billy Pirie double which sealed the match! That was the first game after Bonthrone had quit as manager and by the time Rougvie was handed his first start, a 3-0 defeat at Motherwell three weeks later, Ally MacLeod had taken over.

"Jimmy was too nice and he just couldn't handle the boys. The best thing he could have done was taken Willie Young by the throat and told him he was sacked . . . [Young had thrown his shirt to the ground in disgust after being substituted against Dundee United a month earlier before storming from the stadium. The centre-half never played for the club again] That would have killed it, but he didn't and big Willie was trouble, he could have caused an argument in an empty house."

The contrast between Bonthrone, the quiet and serious coach, and MacLeod, the ultimate showman, could hardly have been greater.

"MacLeod was one of these boys who knew nothing about football, but was fantastic, a great motivator. He was like Jim Leishman, he could take players and put them in position and get the best out of them. He got the whole place buzzing again, and although you sometimes looked at him and thought 'he's a numpty' you can't argue with what he did. He was a success for Aberdeen."

MacLeod also brought in players who would make an impact, Stuart Kennedy and Dom Sullivan among them, and when he left for the Scotland job his successor Billy McNeill continued strengthening the squad with the additions of Gordon Strachan and Steve Archibald. It was an exciting time at Pittodrie, and while Doug was still something of a bit-part player, he had a feeling something special was brewing.

"You could see the squad coming together and it was with the bulk of those players that Fergie went on to win the league."

Alex Ferguson's arrival was the catalyst for the glory that followed, and it also saw Rougvie getting the chance to establish himself in the first team squad, but the big man admits he did have a few concerns initially, stemming from an earlier meeting with his new manager.

"Dunfermline had been having an injury crisis so I had got called up to play against Falkirk reserves and Fergie was playing up front for them. I was just a big daft boy and every time he got the ball I was savaging him, giving him a doing, and he never came out for the second half!"

Ferguson clearly did not hold a grudge, and after Willie Garner broke a leg in a Cup Winners Cup tie against Marek Dimitrov and Alex McLeish was injured a few weeks later, Rougvie was given his first extended run in the side, making a total of 26 appearances in that 1978-79 season.

"I know that the Chairman had wanted Fergie up there years before, as assistant to Jimmy Bonthrone, but Jimmy didn't want that as he thought it might upset some of our players he'd had run-ins with. It was great when we did get him though, we knew what he'd done with St Mirren, and we immediately bought into that attitude of his that he wanted to be a winner."

Before they became winners, the manager and the players had to sample the bitter taste of defeat. Fergie guided the team to the League Cup Final in March '79, Rougvie's first appearance in a major final at the national stadium, but it would be a day to forget for the towering centre-half.

Duncan Davidson had headed the Dons into the lead an hour into what had been a bad-tempered and towsy occasion. In all, half a dozen players were booked as Rangers came from behind and, capitalising on an arm injury which left Aberdeen keeper Bobby Clark seriously handicapped, scored twice in the final thirteen minutes to lift the trophy. By then the Dons had been reduced to ten men, Rougvie having been sent off after an 'incident' with Rangers striker Derek Johnstone.

It was a devastating blow at the time, but all these years later Rougvie can smile at what happened while still maintaining his complete innocence.

"Wee Davie Cooper was on the ball and I went and whacked him – he was amazing, he was one of those players who'd just bounce right back up again – and I got booked, no complaints. We were one-nil up and they were struggling, really struggling, and they pushed big Derek up front from centre-half. The ball was played out to the left and I was standing around the halfway line and he backed into me and just fell down, and Ian Foote the referee came up and showed me the red card. It didn't surprise me at all. I just wondered if they were in the same Lodge!"

Rougvie was laughing as he said that, but he clearly believed the official could not wait to send him off.

"I told him I'd done nothing, that he couldn't have seen anything and that Derek had dived, and he just told me to get off. Big DJ still swears I hit him and we've spoken and laughed about it many times, but I know what really happened, I know I never touched him."

Despite the fury he felt at the time, Rougvie is fairly sanguine about the episode now.

"Diving wasn't invented by the foreign players who came over here, it always happened. I didn't hold any grudges, but we did have some battles after that, we were always fighting on the pitch. It was brilliant and the big man gave as good as he got!"

The following season saw the big breakthrough for that Aberdeen side, Rougvie a regular starter as the Dons were crowned Premier Division champions.

"It was fantastic for the club, for all of us, but especially for Clarky (Bobby Clark) who'd been there all that time. When you saw just how much it meant to him, that was when I realised what we'd done. It really was special."

Rougvie was fast becoming a cult hero even then with us fans, he was more skilful than he ever really got credit for, inevitable perhaps given his size and strength, and if one of his smaller team-mates was unfairly challenged the cry, 'Dougie's going to get you!' would ring round the stands as a warning to the perpetrator. He revelled in it all and loved noising-up opposition players and supporters, as evidenced by his warm-up routine at Celtic Park where he would do his stretching and jogging directly in front of the notoriously hostile 'Jungle', the area in the North Stand populated by the most vociferous home fans.

"Look, I was always quick – they were never going to catch me, so I was safe enough! It was all about winding them up, all part of that mentality we had going down there, that we could go there, do what we wanted, and win the match."

The next few seasons were a whirlwind of success for the big Fifer as he added another Scottish title, three Scottish Cups and the coveted Cup Winners Cup and European Super Cup to his roll of honour.

Despite his fearsome on-field persona, off the pitch Doug can be quiet and unassuming and his assessment of that night in Gothen-burg was typically understated and to the point.

"Great, just great . . . we gave them a right doing."

I wondered whether the success meant even more to him than most of the others given that he had been so long with the club and had experienced some seriously disappointing times along the way, but he dismissed that. It was special for all of them.

He left Pittodrie in the summer of 1984 as part of the first wave of departures, the great side beginning to break up. Rougvie says the signs were there, but that the club did not want to address them.

"We went on a decline because they weren't prepared to replace the players, old Dick [Donald, the Chairman] wasn't wanting to go and spend money, and they had a provincial attitude. They were quite happy to have the youngsters coming in and to sell the likes of Archibald, Strachan and McGhee rather than spend the cash, get some even better players in, and push on."

Like all his colleagues from that time, Doug also remembers how difficult it was to get any kind of a wage-rise out of the club.

"We were on sweetie-wrappers, we really were. It was ridiculous. The first time I asked the manager for a pay-rise I was told to fuck off! Fergie learned a lot about man-management from his time with Aberdeen, how to handle players, and that prepared him for the big job he went to. That team shouldn't have broken up when it did, he had the power to keep that team together and the Chairman would have backed him because he was making so much money for the club at the time. Maybe he just wanted to keep us hungry."

Dougie also recalls Ferguson offering incentives to convince players to re-sign.

"He used to dangle carrots in front of you. When I signed my last four-year contract he told me that he knew I wasn't getting a big wage or a big signing-on fee, but that if I signed it I would get a testimonial two years into it. Two years later he comes up to me and tells me I'm not getting a testimonial and he refused to give me a raise. Basically, he chased me away. I was on £225 a week and needed to get the appearance money and a win bonus to make it up. You had to be fit, you had to be in the team and you had to win to get a decent wage. I was twenty-eight years old and I was struggling to pay the mortgage."

By then Rougvie had been contacted by Chelsea, something Ferguson had got wind of, and he slaughtered the player both privately and in the media.

"He called me a mercenary and told me to fuck off. So I did!"

Rougvie had always wanted to sample English football, and with the Blues newly promoted to the top-flight, west London seemed an ideal place for the defender to embark on a new chapter of his career.

"There wasn't a big difference in terms of the weekly wage, but I got a £25,000 signing-on fee which was a fortune to me at the time."

While that was a very different Chelsea from the present vintage, there was a vibrancy about the club following their return to the

First Division, and the squad was packed with well-known names, the likes of Kerry Dixon, Joey Jones and Nigel Spackman, and boasted a healthy Scottish contingent with David Speedie, Pat Nevin and Kevin McAllister on the books.

"There was also big Joe 'kick the ball the way you're facing' McLaughlin who loved himself! I really enjoyed it and I had a good relationship with the fans, but it was a difficult time for the club and that was when Ken Bates put the fences up."

Rougvie recalls the night when the Chelsea Chairman decided drastic action was required. The Blues had lost the first leg of their 1984-85 League Cup semi-final 2-0 at Sunderland, and were attempting to claw back the deficit in the return.

"We were 1-0 up on the night when they scored. We were pounding them and wee Clive Walker broke away twice to score and with our fans realising that was it, we were going to get beat, it all kicked off. The first I saw was a fan on the pitch carrying a great big pole charging at the opposition supporters. The match was still going on at that stage, I was playing left-back and getting ready to defend a cross when a policeman on a big white horse came galloping past me. It was a nightmare, riots everywhere that night, our fans just went crazy!"

Video footage confirms that it was an astonishing and horrific night. More than one hundred people were arrested and forty, including police officers, injured as the hooligans rampaged across the pitch and dismantled the stadium, ripping out anything they could use as artillery.

Doug spent three years at Stamford Bridge before setting off on his travels in 1987, beginning a somewhat nomadic period which would take him from the south of England to the north of Scotland, and a few points in between. It all began with a season at Brighton.

"I went down there as captain and we had a great year getting promoted from the old Third Division, but I had a falling-out with Barry Lloyd, the manager, and he savaged me, and I was out. I followed Ian McNeill to Shrewsbury, worst thing I ever did. He told me to join him and he'd make me assistant manager, but he never had the power to do that and the board blocked it. I only stuck around there for four or five months."

From Shropshire, Dougie headed back to London and signed on for Fulham, then battling for promotion from the Third Division.

"Fulham was fantastic, Ray Lewington was in charge and Jimmy Hill was the Chairman, and I signed a two-year contract just to get away from Shrewsbury, but although I loved it down there I knew I needed to get back up the road for the family's sake. Leaving Brighton was the big mistake really, I would have settled in that area, there were plenty teams around and I could have kept playing until I was forty, easy. Instead, I came home and there were hardly any choices."

He saw out the 1988-89 campaign at Craven Cottage before returning to Scotland and finally getting the chance to play for the team which had rejected him as a kid, Dunfermline. But it was not to be a happy homecoming.

"Ooh, that was one of my worst moves ever, honestly. They're a weird lot, that Dunfermline! Iain Munro was the assistant manager and we never really got on. There was one game in which he tried to blame me for giving away a free-kick and we fell out at half-time, I was chasing him around the dressing room and big Leish [Jim Leishman] had to keep us apart."

Later that season Leishman moved upstairs at East End Park and Munro replaced him in the manager's office, which was never going to be good news for Dougie.

"Iain was a really good coach, switched on tactically, but he was never going to play me after that. It's fair to say we had a clash of personalities. Big time!"

Next stop on Rougvie's wanderings was Montrose, where he was appointed player/co-manager alongside former Pittodrie team-mate Chic McLelland. Once again it was a move which did not work out entirely as Doug had hoped.

"That was a bad move, that one," he recalled, shaking his head, a familiar theme developing.

And yet it began well enough with the pair guiding the Angus side to promotion to the Scottish First Division for just the second time in the club's history. As a part-time outfit their elevation was brief, it lasted only one season, and Dougie says he was thwarted in his efforts to try to improve their chances of a quick return to the second tier.

"I wanted to sign Stevie Cowan [the former Aberdeen, Motherwell and Hibernian striker]. Now at that stage Stevie couldn't run, but he could score, and we needed a natural goalscorer, but Chic wouldn't agree to it. We played some nice football, but we couldn't get the ball into the net and by Christmas the Chairman, Brian Keith, sacked the both of us and brought in Jim Leishman. The only good thing about that was Leish went and spent all Brian's money!"

Dougie was out of the game until the following summer when he got a call from Steve Paterson, then the young manager of ambitious Highland League side Huntly.

"I had to decide whether I wanted to get back into playing again, but I thought 'I'm only thirty-seven, I've got heaps of fitba left in me' so I signed up and I loved it there, really enjoyed it. I was still fit as a fiddle, really took to it and I got a load of medals."

Indeed he did. Huntly embarked that year on a period during which they dominated Highland League football, winning the title in five successive seasons. The first two of those were won under Paterson before he left for a successful stint with Inverness Caledonian Thistle and the next two were clinched with Rougvie in charge. He looked to be heading towards three-in-a-row in 1997-98 when he fell foul of the new Chairman and was shown the door.

"Forbes Shand had been in charge there for years and he was great, just left me to get on with the job. No interference. But he stepped down and a lad Hendry [former youth coach Mike Hendry] took over and he was trying to do my job. As you might expect, I told him where to go. We were going for a fifth Highland League title in a row and that had never been done before, and this boy's trying to sign players, trying to pick the team. He was renegotiating contracts with players I was wanting rid of and eventually I told him 'You do your job and I'll do mine'. Well, he did his job – he sacked me!"

Huntly appointed Phil Bonnyman as his successor and went on to tie up that record-breaking championship while Doug moved on to a short-lived and frustrating time at Cove Rangers.

"Alan McRae [Cove Chairman] wanted to get the guys to play for nothing, to play as amateurs, but the boys are never going to travel all around the Highland League unless you're going to weigh them in. You either want a team that's going to win things, or you don't. I had to get a proper job in the real world, it wasn't fair on my wife any more, and in the end I knew something had to give, and it was the football."

In his mid-forties Dougie went back to college to complete his studies for an HNC in Electrical Engineering. He had begun working as a draughtsman with the Wood Group a few years previously, now he realised he had to take that career more seriously.

"It was the only way I was going to make any money."

When he had first left school Doug had taken a job as an apprentice mechanical technician at Rosyth Dockyard and had given it up when he signed for the Dons, but he had been keen to further his education and the club had allowed him day-release to continue studying the subject at the Robert Gordon's Institute of Technology. That was soon halted when Alex Ferguson took over as manager.

"Fergie said to me, 'What do you want to be, son, a fitba player or a fucking engineer?' and he stopped me going, so I went over his head to Chris Anderson [then the Aberdeen FC Vice-Chairman] who was high up at Robert Gordon's and he told me, 'Can't help you, son' so that was it."

Two decades later Rougvie finally returned to his studies, and after a number of years with Wood Group he became a contract worker, finding employment with a range of companies across the North Sea oil and gas sector as an instrument designer. He admits it is all very different from life as a professional footballer, but has its benefits.

"I was working for Petrofac and they opened a place in Dubai. They were asking for volunteers and I fancied it, so I spoke to my wife Brenda over the weekend and by the Monday we'd decided we were going, and within six weeks we'd put our stuff in storage, rented out the house and we were off. We loved it there, really embraced the lifestyle, best thing we ever did. The sports facilities were first-class; tennis, golf and swimming, and they love their football, so I was still able to get a game every week."

The Rougvies spent three years in the emirate, longer than they had anticipated, before the work dried up and they had to return home in May 2011. Big Dougie clearly relished that episode of his life, but seemed happy enough to be back in the north-east. He was in good spirits when we met and he is still doing what he enjoys most, playing the game that made him a Dons legend.

"I love the 'fives'. Obviously there are things I can't do anymore, I've had to cut out the twenty-yard sliding tackles, but I can still run around, and I still love the competitive side of it. I'll keep going as long as I can – I'm only fifty-five and I've got plenty left!"

As one of the first of that Gothenburg squad to arrive at the club Doug had seen more of the bad times than some of his colleagues, and there was little in the early to mid-1970s to suggest that the Dons would go on to conquer the continent. He appreciated every-thing he won at club level and took great satisfaction from winning his one and only international cap for his country, against Northern Ireland in December 1983. The game itself must have felt almost like a club fixture for Rougvie as Leighton, McLeish, Strachan and Weir also started. Mark McGhee came on as a substitute and Willie Miller would have featured but for injury. The Scots lost 2-0, but the result did not lessen the big man's pride. He was simply thrilled to have been picked.

"One of my proudest moments . . . that was just fantastic! I had always been a Scotland fan, had always watched the games, but I never thought I'd ever get the chance to play. I don't think the west coast press were happy that it was essentially an Aberdeen select, and I suffered a bit and got some criticism, but I wasn't bothered, I knew I'd played no' bad that night. I never got asked back and that was unfortunate, but at least I got that cap and nobody can take that away from me."

There are countless examples of football players who wasted their talent, who should have managed so much more in their careers thanks to their God-given natural ability, but who perhaps lacked the drive, the mental toughness to fulfil their potential. There are perhaps fewer who have done the opposite, who through sheer bloody-mindedness and an unwavering self-belief have wrung every last drop out of their time in the game. I have always viewed Doug Rougvie as one of those and admired him greatly for what he achieved.

"I was a centre-half playing full-back and there aren't many players who can do that successfully. I was never going to break up those two [Miller and McLeish] so that was my way of getting into the team and I was determined to stay there. I was mobile, I had a good engine to get up and down the park and I had a good touch. And in the end, I didn't do too badly, did I?"

CHAPTER FOUR

NEALE COOPER

DINAMO TIRANA 0-0 ABERDEEN
Wednesday September 29th, 1982

By the time the second leg against Dinamo came round Aberdeen were suffering something of a wobble.

A 1-1 draw away to St Mirren, former Don Ian Scanlon equalising after Mark McGhee's opener, was acceptable enough but Dundee United had travelled north and handed out a 3-1 cuffing in the League Cup quarter-final first-leg and Rangers had recorded their first ever Premier Division win at Pittodrie, their 2-1 success leaving the Dons floundering with just three points from their first four league matches.

Now the team faced a trip into the unknown.

Albania at the time was a rigidly Communist state, closed off to the West by the dictator Enver Hoxha. It was hardly the kind of place to appeal to a group of young Scottish footballers and it was to be a real culture shock.

It is a trip that stands out among the many undertaken throughout his career by midfielder Neale Cooper.

"None of us had ever been to any of those countries. Going to Albania was like going to the moon. We took our own chef, our own food – Fergie and Archie took no chances at all. It was such a deprived place with so much poverty; people were trying to buy our clothes off us in the hotel lift. Neil Simpson is tighter than a dead-heat, he loves his money, and he came in at one point with a huge handful of local currency, boasting about the exchange rate he had just got for his dollars. When we pointed out there was nothing he could buy and he wouldn't be able to take the money back out of the country he was absolutely gutted!"

John Hewitt's most vivid memory is that of arriving in the country in the first place.

"As we came in to land you could see all the trenches where soldiers had clearly been dug in with machine-guns. The airport itself was just a wooden shack and they kept us there for hours before letting us through. We then piled on to the coach, I say coach, it was more like a Doric Construction works bus, and it was absolutely filthy."

The game itself was played at the Qemal Stafa Stadium, an open bowl with a running track round the pitch. It held just under 20,000 and the ground was close to capacity at kick-off time. It was a sweltering hot evening, the temperature around 95 degrees, and the Dons went into it with just that single goal advantage, but Cooper was not overly concerned.

"It was quite a hostile atmosphere, but we felt comfortable going into it. We were always so well prepared. I always knew the guy I was playing against, whatever the game, because the manager and Archie would have done their individual dossiers. It was never heavy duty, but it was just enough, and it didn't matter whether it was Dinamo Tirana or Bayern Munich, you always had the information you needed."

Team-mate John McMaster remembers the tie with the Albanians as the hardest Aberdeen faced during their run to the Final.

"That was the toughest of them all, they were a hard wee team and we had to be at our best to get through, but we played well and we were professional enough to see it through."

The match ended 0-0 with the Albanians rarely, if ever, threatening as the Dons closed the game down and snuffed out any danger right from the start. Cooper knew it was a job well done.

"It was a tough place to go, it wasn't the most glamorous of ties, but the manager had by then instilled this belief into the players and we just went out there and got the job done. No doubts, we were quite certain we would get the result we needed."

"By then I was quite comfortable playing in these matches. I had made my European debut at Anfield and that was something else. We were 3-0 down to Liverpool, I was sixteen and sitting on the bench and Fergie told me to go warm up. I came on for big Doug Rougvie and I was just looking around the pitch at all the stars: Clemence, Dalglish, Souness, Hansen and the rest. Incredible! They walloped us 4-0 in the end, but a couple of years later I had the experience and I had the belief and it was totally different. You really felt like you belonged out there."

Neale Cooper was born in Darjeeling in the West Bengali state of India on November 24th, 1963 where his father managed a tea plantation. Douglas Cooper was more of a rugby man and it wasn't until the family relocated to Aberdeen five years later that young Neale had any real exposure to the sport which was to bring him fame and glory and become a life-long passion. Douglas and his wife Anne opened a post office/delicatessen in the well-to-do Bieldside area just outside the city but tragedy was just around the corner. At the age of just thirty-nine, and only a week after opening the shop, Douglas died of a massive heart attack. Neale was just five, his sister Shirley nine. Anne was left to bring up their young family and she was to become a driving force behind Neale's football career. No-one was prouder when he was signed by the Dons, joining the club straight from Hazlehead Academy.

Having been a ball-boy and fervent Aberdeen fan it was a dream come true and it wasn't long before the teenager caught the eye of his manager.

"I used to live in Airyhall and got the number 11 bus to Pittodrie every day and Fergie would drive in that way from Cults and I would be hiding behind the bus stop, because if he saw me he would pick me up and I would end up getting stick from the lads. But on the days he did get me, he was great company – I loved listening to him talking about football, but wasn't so keen on listening to Terry Wogan on Radio 2. What was great about him was that it didn't matter how old you were, if you were good enough you got a game."

And young Cooper did not have long to wait before that came to pass.

"Late one Friday afternoon I was tidying up his room – that was part of my job being on the ground-staff – and Fergie walked in and said, 'Right Neale, put the Hoover away, you're playing tomorrow.' I knew Alex McLeish was injured, but I never imagined I would be chosen to replace him; I had never even trained with the first team. I raced home to tell my mum and she wouldn't believe me. I still wasn't sure that it wasn't a wind-up the next day when I turned up at the Ferryhill House Hotel for the pre-match meal and then the manager read out the team, 'De Clerck, Kennedy, Rougvie, Watson, Cooper . . .' and that was when it hit me."

Cooper played in central-defence with the already vastly experienced Willie Miller guiding him through the match and got a deserved round of applause when replaced late on by Dougie Bell having played his part in a 2-0 win over Kilmarnock, a 24th successive league match unbeaten for the Dons as they attempted to secure back-to-back league titles.

Centre-half was Neale's favoured position, one in which he featured regularly for Scotland at various age-levels. He played there in the FIFA World Youth Championship in Mexico in 1983 where the young Scots eliminated the hosts, topped their group and lost out narrowly to Poland in the quarter-finals. Such had been the level of his performances that he was named in the 'select team' at the end of a tournament brimming with future global superstars such as Dunga, Bebeto and Marco van Basten.

He was being tagged by pundits as 'the new Beckenbauer' and yet . . .

"I couldn't get a game at centre-half at Aberdeen because of Miller and McLeish!"

It had however become clear that Neale's talents could not be ignored. Alex Ferguson had decided he had to have him in the team, but how and where? The answer came as something of a surprise to the teenage Cooper.

"The manager has told me this – he wanted me to play, so he decided to turn me into a 'midfield assassin'. He said he wanted me in there with Neil Simpson and with Gordon Strachan and Peter Weir on the wings, and I thought, that's not bad company to have out there! My game definitely changed, I'm not an aggressive guy, but I became an aggressive player and that's where Fergie is so clever, he can make you do things that don't come naturally, but which benefit you and more importantly benefit the team. It's almost as if he brainwashes you!"

"I would go out there and I was never scared. I'd go steaming in to tackles with guys like Roy Aitken and Murdo McLeod; Tommy Burns, one of the hardest boys I ever played against; Fitzpatrick, Abercrombie at St Mirren, God they were hard boys, but Fergie's message would be 'No fear!' and I would go out there and take them on, believing I could do it."

"Fergie's philosophy was simple; he made no bones about it. Big 'Simmy' and I were there to protect Weir and Strachan. We were told to win the ball and give it to them. Job done. I was in my element, I just loved it!"

Hardly surprising that Neale was enjoying life at that time. Here was a teenager playing football for a living, playing for the team he grew up supporting. Not only that, the team were winning and the city in general was on a high. Although this was long before footballers' salaries soared through the stratosphere, he was still earning good money, and decided to invest some of it in his first flat.

"It was in Great Western Place, but I never told the manager I had bought it, and about six weeks later he walked past me and growled, 'Office!' I followed him in and he pointed out that I had been seen coming out of a flat and he wanted to know what was going on – he had his spies everywhere. When I told him it was mine he said 'Get rid of it. Today!' and that was that. I had to move back into my mum's in Airyhall and it was two years before I was allowed to move back out again. Even then I had to ask his permission."

Looking back, Neale feels it was all part of growing up both as a player and as a young man. There is clear affection and warmth as he recalls those days under Alex Ferguson, but there were times back then when it could be hard to accept.

"We were bullied at times, and he knows that. He was a hard man, very hard, hard . . . but fair. Some players could react to it and some couldn't and the ones that couldn't, he saw them as weak, and they just wouldn't last."

Cooper was to be one of those who could cope and following his debut in October 1980 he made four further starts that season, deputising once more for McLeish and three times for Miller. Two of those games were at Celtic Park and Ibrox, Aberdeen beating Celtic and losing to Rangers, and they provided him with further experience and know-how.

1981-82 was to be Neale Cooper's big breakthrough season and it began with him wearing the number 4 shirt in a League Cup sectional tie at home to Kilmarnock on August 8th. Fergie had created his midfield 'assassin'. In total he started forty games throughout the campaign and got his first taste of European football, lining up against Ipswich Town and SV Hamburg in the UEFA Cup. He also got his first winner's medal as an Aberdeen player.

The Dons finished their Premier Division campaign as runners-up to Celtic for the second year in a row, Billy McNeill's side clinching the title on the final afternoon with a 3-0 win at home to St Mirren. Aberdeen meanwhile were destroying Rangers, a John Hewitt hat-trick setting up a 4-0 half-time lead, and while their championship dream was ended, the players took great confidence that day ahead of the sides' meeting at Hampden the following Saturday in the Scottish Cup Final.

Neale was never a prolific goal scorer during his time with Aberdeen, netting a total of 10 in 220 starts, but he scored his most memorable one in his first major final that sunny afternoon at the national stadium.

John McDonald's diving header had put the Glasgow side ahead, but Alex McLeish soon cancelled that out, curling a shot into the top corner from the edge of the box. As was so often the case in the Dons' finals around that time, the game went into extra-time and Aberdeen totally dominated. Mark McGhee and Gordon Strachan netted in the first period and it was left to Neale to apply the finishing touch.

"The Rangers keeper that day was big Jim Stewart, a lovely guy, and I still slaughter him about this every time I see him. I was running through and he came out and kicked the ball against me. It hit me on the chest but I had no idea where it had landed. Next thing I'm in front of the Rangers end, no goalie, and the ball at my feet. There I was, seventeen, a huge Dons fan, an open goal and a wall of Rangers supporters in front of me. It was just a case of, bang, get in there!"

The 4-1 score-line was a humiliation for the Ibrox side, the second heaviest defeat the club had ever suffered in the Scottish Cup Final, the worst being a 4-0 loss to Celtic in 1969, a game which ironically all but ended Alex Ferguson's playing career with Rangers.

It was on the other hand a huge breakthrough for the Dons, confirmation that the team was getting stronger all the time and a reinforcement of the message Ferguson had been drilling into his players on a daily basis. He was convinced they could become the country's dominant force and his men were beginning to believe him.

Looking back three decades later, Neale has no doubts where to place that Cup Final in his list of achievements.

"You talk about Gothenburg, but for me that was my biggest thrill ever with Aberdeen. There I was, just a kid, my first ever Scottish Cup Final and we won it. Fantastic."

The day became even more memorable as the celebrations continued at the luxurious Gleneagles Hotel in Perthshire.

"We stayed at Gleneagles that night and Burt Lancaster was there, he was in Scotland filming the movie *Local Hero* and he landed in his helicopter just as we got back. All the boys got their photos taken with him and it was just wonderful, a beautiful summer's night, we had won the Scottish Cup . . . it was just perfect, and from there it just grew and grew."

Indeed it grew all the way to Gothenburg and the most important match ever played by Aberdeen Football Club. Cooper was nineteen-years-old and room-mate John Hewitt, his best friend then and now, just twenty. Neale started the match, John was on the bench, but would of course become the central figure in the drama that was to unfold on that never-to-be-forgotten night.

"We were lying on our beds that afternoon and I turned to him and said, 'Johnny can you believe it, here we are, two Aberdeen boys and we're about to take on Real Madrid. It's just bonkers!' "

"It was like a fairy story for us. I was up against Uli Stieleke, the West German internationalist, but Fergie had told me not to worry about him, said that he was rubbish! It was ridiculous of course, but that's what the manager did, he talked down the opposition and talked us up until we were so hyped we believed we could achieve anything. He always used to tell me Jim Bett was rubbish when he was with Rangers and then he went and signed him, and when I asked him why, he told me Jim was brilliant, which he was. It had all been a wind-up."

All the players' wives and girlfriends had been invited along for the trip to Sweden, but when Cooper asked his manager if he could bring his girlfriend he was given an emphatic refusal.

"He told me that I had a different girlfriend every week and that there was no way I was getting to bring one with me, so I asked if my mum and my big sister Shirley could come instead. He said that would be fine and it was really special that they were there to share in the moment."

After the trophy had been presented and the celebrations with the fans were over the players returned to the vast dressing-room deep under the main stand. It was then Neale sat amidst the mayhem and in a quiet moment of reflection his mind wandered to someone who had not been there.

"I just had this massive feeling of grief. I sat there and burst into tears just taking in what we had achieved and the fact that my father hadn't been able to see any of it. I would have loved for him to be part of it all, but my mum was great, so supportive. She went to all the games and used to hate it when people were shouting at me . . . I would have thought she would have got used to that over the years!"

After a trophy-laden seven years at Pittodrie, Neale was sold to Aston Villa in the summer of 1986 for £350,000, but it was to be an ill-fated move almost from the start.

"I felt I had become something of a target in Scottish football. I was always getting booked and the suspensions were getting longer and I just felt I needed a change. After I signed I asked the manager Graham Turner who our first game was against and he told me, 'Celtic in a pre-season friendly at Parkhead.' I couldn't believe it, I had just escaped from there and now I was heading straight back into it. There were a number of black guys in the Villa team then, the likes of my mate Mark Walters, Garry Thompson and Tony Daley, and they were a bit concerned about what kind of reaction they might get, so I told them just come out with me for the warm-up and we'll see who gets the most stick! They couldn't believe the reception I got, but that was just the way it was, and then during the game Roy Aitken, who's a great lad, was kicking lumps out of me. What a welcome home that was."

But that was just the precursor to a string of bad luck that wrecked Neale's time in Birmingham. He tore his groin in another pre-season friendly against Leeds United and was out injured for months. His house got flooded and his car was stolen on three separate occasions.

"One time the police called to say the car had been found and when I got there the doors were all open, the windows kicked in and everything stolen. Everything apart from an Aston Villa shirt which the thieves had left lying on the back seat – they were clearly Birmingham fans!"

Turner was sacked before Cooper had even kicked a ball for him in a competitive match and his replacement, the former Celtic boss Billy McNeill, lasted just eight months, at the end of which Villa had been relegated to the Second Division. Next up was the future England manager Graham Taylor who made it clear right from the start that Neale's days at Villa Park were numbered.

"He told me that he had been to watch me a few times in Scotland and that I was a bit of a 'naughty boy' and that he didn't want such players in his team, and that was that. I did get a few more games, but then I hurt my foot and needed an operation and I never played for the first team again."

It was while he was trying to regain full fitness in the Villa reserves that his career took an unexpected twist. The Rangers management team of Graeme Souness and Walter Smith watched Neale on two occasions playing for the second string and offered him the chance to revive his career at Ibrox. He had already turned down the chance of a move back north to Dundee United, fearing that he might not be able to adapt to Jim McLean's autocratic style of management, but this one felt right.

"I drove up for talks and not knowing Glasgow at all I turned off the motorway and saw a big football stadium in the distance. It was only when I pulled up alongside that I realised it was Celtic Park. I had to ask for directions to Ibrox and you can imagine the response I got!"

Neale says he hit it off right away with Graeme Souness and really liked the Rangers manager. It was made clear to him that he was being brought in as a squad player, but was fine with that. His major concern was his Aberdeen connection.

"That was a bit scary. For us as Aberdeen players it wasn't the Celtic games we looked forward to – the games against Rangers were the biggest ones in our lives and I don't think that's changed to this day."

One of those matches was the infamous encounter in October 1988 when an over-the-top challenge by Neale's former team-mate Neil Simpson seriously injured Ian Durrant and put the Rangers player out of football for almost three years. Neale has over the years been accused of stoking up the hatred that day, but he refutes the accusation, saying that he was simply trying to play his own game.

"There had been a few tackles flying around that day and the Aberdeen fans were very hostile towards me, but I could understand that. There I was going back up to Pittodrie but wearing a Rangers jersey."

The Dons won 2-1 that day, but the hostility towards Neale was hardly eased when he chose that match to score his only goal for the Ibrox side. In the midst of all the tension however there was still one moment of light relief.

"I came off the park at half-time and ran straight into the Aberdeen dressing room. It was the first time I had been back to the ground and I just naturally went in there. All the boys were growling at me and telling me to 'get to fuck' while Graeme Souness is looking round the Rangers dressing room asking, 'Where's Neale?' Unbelievable!"

"I'm an Aberdeen boy, an Aberdeen fan, but I had a great time with Rangers. It was a wonderful club, wonderful people and I thoroughly enjoyed it. The religious thing never came into it – having been born in India, I was probably the first Hindu to play for Rangers!"

Injuries were beginning to take their toll on Neale, perhaps an inevitable consequence of having played so many high-profile and demanding games as a teenager, and he left Ibrox two years later having started just 17 matches. He had a brief spell with Reading and then finally got back to playing regular football again with Dunfermline in the Scottish First Division, helping them to promotion to the top flight in 1996 before answering the call from Ross County. The Dingwall club had been admitted to the Scottish Football League two years earlier and were setting their sights high.

Chairman Roy MacGregor contacted Neale and laid out what they would be expecting.

"I went up for the interview and Roy made it clear he wanted to be in the First Division within four years, and we did it. I was player-manager to start with and that was really difficult, next to impossible. We had lost our first seven games on the bounce and I was driving up to Dingwall on the Monday morning wondering what on earth I was doing there. My old manager at Dunfermline, Bert Paton, called and said, 'Aye Coops, it's nae as easy as ye think, eh?' and he was dead right. I subbed myself in one of the games and could hear the voice loud and clear from the main stand, 'Cooper, that's the best decision you've made since you got here!' You had to laugh, but it wasn't easy at times."

He was already facing calls to be sacked, his fledgling managerial career in danger of being snuffed out almost before it had properly begun. And then, suddenly, he found his feet and the team began winning. A 2-0 victory away to Forfar on September 14th, 1996 was his first as a manager and County lost just two more games over the next three months, irritatingly both were against Highland rivals and near neighbours Inverness Caledonian Thistle.

They finished third that season, missing promotion only on goal difference, and again the next year, the margin this time a single point. In 1998-99 County surged to the Third Division title a full 13 points clear of their closest challengers and the following year, thanks to league reconstruction, a third place finish was good enough to see Cooper's side elevated to the second tier of Scottish football.

He established County in the First Division over the next two years and shocked everyone in the game when he announced his resignation in November 2002 in the wake of another defeat at the hands of Caley Thistle.

"I had worked so hard with the players, I had done everything I could in training to set them up, and within a minute we were one down, five minutes later it was 2-0 and I felt I was getting battered.

Honestly, at half-time I just wanted to put my jacket on and get out of there. We played a bit better in the second half, but were well beaten, and afterwards I sat in my car feeling totally lost. I drove back down to Aberdeen because I wanted to see my mum and my sister, and the next morning I called Roy and said, 'I've had a lovely time but enough's enough.' I didn't have long left on my contract, we got that sorted out and I walked away with some fantastic memories. Six years is a long time, especially in football."

Neale took some months out to recharge his batteries, but by the next summer was ready to return to the game, his career taking a surprise deviation as he swapped the north of Scotland for the north-east of England, replacing another former Aberdeen player, Mike Newell, as manager of Hartlepool United, then in the Second Division of the Football League.

The season began with a five-match unbeaten run, there was a memorable 8-1 thrashing of Grimsby Town, and on the final Saturday of the league campaign Adam Boyd scored a late equaliser away to Swindon Town to secure a place in the play-offs. After a home draw with Bristol City, Cooper's side were ahead in the second leg only for City to score twice in the last two minutes to snatch victory.

The next season in the renamed League One was a similar story, with Hartlepool again finishing sixth to make the play-offs, only this time Neale was not there at the end. United had lost their penultimate game 3-1 at home to Walsall and Cooper's shock departure was announced the following Wednesday. It has generally been reported that he quit, but Neale is adamant that was not the case.

"The directors called me in and said they felt it was better if I left. They never gave me a reason, I've not had one to this day, they just said that they felt I wasn't happy and should go. I loved it there, I was absolutely devastated, and to this day whenever I go back I just get the most incredible reaction from the fans. I can't go on to Facebook any more, because as soon as I do, I just get swamped by people from Hartlepool."

As is the norm in football, various rumours swept the town, but Neale says they were all unfounded. As he left the boardroom reeling from the news, he was in for another shock. Walking past the door to the next room he heard his assistant, Martin Scott, already being interviewed by a television crew.

"I couldn't believe what I was hearing. There was Martin telling the reporter how he'd always wanted to be Hartlepool manager, how it was a dream come true. It was really hurtful. Funnily enough, I'd noticed Martin was well dressed that day, wearing a suit and tie, and had been winding him up about it. I had even asked him to come into the meeting with the directors, but he'd said no. At that moment I realised why."

Hartlepool drew their remaining match against play-off rivals Bournemouth and went one step better than the previous season, but lost the final 4-2 against Sheffield Wednesday. Martin Scott was sacked six months later, having won just 11 of his 39 games in charge and United were relegated to the bottom tier of the English game.

Neale's next stop was a short one, at Gillingham. The club had dropped out of the Championship at the end of season 2004-05 and had implemented severe financial cutbacks which, unsurprisingly, had an effect on results. With the team struggling in the league, an FA Cup exit at the hands of non-league Burscough was the final straw and he quit in the November of that year.

There followed almost a year out of the game before Cooper accepted the role of first-team coach at Peterhead under Steve Paterson, taking over as manager himself in 2008. His first season in charge ended in a play-off defeat against Airdrie United and the next year Peterhead narrowly missed out, finishing fifth. Season 2010-11 was, however, a struggle, and with the side bottom of the Second Division and in the midst of a seventeen-game run without a win, Neale left Balmoor in March. Peterhead's relegation was officially confirmed soon afterwards.

When I met him for this book, Neale was house-sitting for his sister and discussing employment opportunities outside the game.

In fact, I dropped him off in the city centre after the interview so that he could attend one such meeting. Within a few weeks his working life was turned upside down as he made a surprise return to one of his former clubs.

Hartlepool had begun the season well enough, but a poor run of results had seen them plummet down the table. Mick Wadsworth was sacked and just after Christmas 2011 Neale was back at Victoria Park. He enjoyed a few decent results in what was a highly competitive League One and gradually lifted the team back to mid-table safety, thoroughly enjoying just being involved in the game once again.

As he looks back on his career, the one thing missing for Neale Cooper was a full Scotland cap. He made a few squads, but injuries at key times and the outstanding level of competition for a midfield berth ended his dream. It is not something that concerns him though, Neale says he is more than happy with what he achieved.

"I've got a lovely haul of medals and they're stored away safely. They mean so much to me. We won in Gothenburg, I won four Scottish Cups and the league titles with Aberdeen, and I won a League Cup and a league medal with Rangers. I had a great time and I loved every minute of it."

CHAPTER FIVE

PETER WEIR

ABERDEEN 2-0 LECH POZNAN
Wednesday October 20th, 1982

Just three days after returning from Albania, Aberdeen were back on league duty and for much of the game at home to Motherwell it seemed as if they were about to drop yet more valuable points. The Icelandic defender Johannes Edvaldsson had opened the scoring midway through the first half and the newly promoted Lanarkshire side were still in front with over an hour gone. The euphoria with which we had entered Pittodrie that day was dwindling as Alex Ferguson replaced John Hewitt with Steve Cowan, and with his first touch of the ball the substitute had levelled the game. The records variously show the attendance that day as between 8,000 and 9,000, an indication perhaps that the north-east public was already taking success for granted, and those of us inside the stadium were readying ourselves to leave when the winner came from a most unlikely route, a Willie Miller overhead kick in the 89th minute.

Dundee United duly sealed our League Cup exit, winning the second leg 1-0 at Pittodrie the following midweek with a Paul Sturrock penalty, but the Dons' title challenge was regaining momentum. Strachan, Simpson and McGhee all scored in a 3-1 win at Celtic Park during which the home captain Danny McGrain was red-carded, and on a freezing cold afternoon the next week Peter Weir provided the only real warmth with a twenty-yard rocket to beat Dundee and make it three league wins on the bounce.

That set the team up nicely for their next European challenge at home to the Poles, Lech Poznan, and a chance to reach the quarter-finals for the first time, something the manager was desperate to achieve. In his programme notes Alex Ferguson spoke of his relief at having been able "to attain a good, detailed dossier on Poznan" and challenged his players to go out and prove they represented "the highest grade of football in Scotland, the UK and Europe".

The Poles may not have been the most glamorous of opposition, but the Aberdeen fans had by then got a real taste for continental action, and 17,425 of us provided the atmosphere while the players went out and did what they generally did back then, put on a thoroughly professional performance.

Throughout my years going along to Pittodrie I stood (before the stadium became all-seated) and then sat in various parts of the ground. That season the South Stand was my area of choice, a huge cantilever structure built just a couple of years previously and which, for the big matches, proved really quite atmospheric. It was during that campaign that the 'Here We Go' chant became popular and it would ripple round from the Beach End and through the South Stand increasing in volume as more and more joined in. That evening however, after a noisy start to the match, there were spells of near silence as our attacks were repelled time after time by a Polish rearguard action.

It was a game totally dominated by the Dons, one in which, on the occasions we did break through, we kept hitting the woodwork rather than finding the net. Black and Strachan in particular were denied, but Mark McGhee finally broke the deadlock shortly after half-time, peeling away at the front post to meet Weir's corner and looping a header just under the bar, and within two minutes the winger himself got on the end of Strachan's low cross to side-foot home from seven yards and secure a more realistic scoreline.

Peter was by no means prolific – he averaged around a goal every six games during his Aberdeen career – he was more often than not the creator rather than the finisher, but he did tend to score in big matches and he remembers that goal against Poznan as being particularly important.

"We hadn't known that much about Poznan, apart from the information handed out by Fergie and Archie, and you know what it's like on those big European nights – you lose a goal and that could be that. We were all over them, we forced corner after corner, but we couldn't score and you had to stop yourself from becoming too frustrated. Eventually Mark got the first and I scored just after, and to be honest, given the team we had then, we knew they were never coming back from 2-0 down."

Had that match been a few years earlier, Peter would have been in the stands rather than on the pitch. Despite being born in Johnstone and brought up in Barrhead, he was a committed Aberdeen supporter, his love for the club sparked by the 1970 Scottish Cup Final. I had been at the semi-final that year, a 1-0 win over Kilmarnock in Perth, and that was the game that had got me hooked. My mother had however ruled out any prospect of her nine-year-old son going to Hampden and I was on the number 24 bus heading home after a shopping expedition when the conductor yelled out that the Dons had beaten the mighty Celtic 3-1 to win the Cup. While I enjoyed a little private celebration on the top deck as the bus wheeled round on to George Street, Peter was immersed in a somewhat more raucous occasion at the national stadium.

"My dad was in the travel business and he was given two tickets for that Final in the Aberdeen end. I just loved it, Derek 'Cup-tie' McKay and Joe Harper were the big heroes, they scored the goals that day and that got me started. When I was thirteen or fourteen I stopped playing football myself for a few years and went everywhere supporting the team. I would get the 8.10am train from Queen Street Station, or the bus that left from George Square, and head up to Pittodrie as often as I could. I used to go into the Dons Shop in Nelson Street and then off to the game, and, of course, travelled all round the west coast following them as well."

When he did get back playing again Peter signed up with Neilston Juniors and soon caught the eye of the scouts. Both Dumbarton and St Mirren were chasing him, but it was the Paisley club who won the race for his signature. Their manager at the time was Alex Ferguson.

"I was working as a greenkeeper at the time at Fereneze Golf Club and then at the Caldwell Club at Uplawmoor, and I was hoping to get a right few quid for signing on. Fergie offered me £100 take it or leave it – I took it, but it was weeks before I saw the money."

Peter's time with Alex Ferguson was short-lived as the manager was sacked soon after, leaving Saints fans to ponder 'what if . . .?' His replacement was Jim Clunie, who quickly put Peter on a full-time contract, and his debut came at the start of the 1978-79 season in a shock win at Ibrox.

A late starter to the professional game, he soon began to make an impact and after just sixty appearances for the Love Street side and having earned the first of what would be six caps for Scotland, he got his dream move to Pittodrie in a record-breaking £330,000 transfer deal which saw Ian Scanlon moving in the opposite direction.

"The deal was being done in Perth and I was supposed to meet Alex Ferguson at the Scone Hotel while Ian was to meet Ricky McFarlane the St Mirren manager at another hotel, but lo and behold, there was a mix-up and I ended up meeting Ian. So the two of us are sitting there exchanging notes and I can't believe the money he's going to be asking St Mirren for – he ended up making more out of it than I did even though I was supposed to be the main part of the transfer!"

Scanlon had been a firm fans' favourite and it took Peter some time to win over the Dons support.

"There was a lot of pressure on me because I struggled a bit to start with and the fans were getting on my back."

That's certainly true, I know because I was one of them, but he would soon prove to be a more than adequate replacement for

78

'Scan', playing a major role in the successes that lay ahead. The big breakthrough came in September 1981 when the Dons knocked the holders Ipswich Town out of the UEFA Cup.

The first leg was at Portman Road and I was at Kenny Johnston's flat to listen to it on the radio – live televised matches even then still being something of a rarity. Franz Thijssen put Ipswich in front just before half-time, but the Dons hit back to spark huge roars from the pair of us which had the upstairs neighbour knocking down in complaint. It was John Hewitt who snatched our goal in the 1-1 draw, firing home Alex McLeish's knockdown from Peter's corner.

"They had some team back then. There was Thijssen and Muhren, Paul Mariner, Alan Brazil, Osman and Gates, and big Terry Butcher. Players I had watched on the telly and here I was, still just a few years out of the juniors, going up against them."

For the second leg Pittodrie was, naturally enough, sold out. The club had been running a voucher system for a few years, handing them out at league matches, and they had to be produced before you could buy a ticket for the big games. A vibrant black market grew with vouchers being sold for considerable sums, but I was never tempted. Those vouchers were like gold dust, the guarantee of being there on those marvellous occasions, and not to be given up for any money.

Having been kept abreast of the first leg by Northsound Radio, Ken and I were among the 24,000 shoe-horned into the old stadium for the second leg and it was to be one of the most memorable matches ever staged there.

As we sat in eager anticipation, little did we know that across on the far side of the stadium Archie Knox had his ear pressed against a grille in the home dressing room listening to Bobby Robson telling his players just how superior they were to their opposition. Neale Cooper says he could hardly believe the scene.

"It was bizarre. Archie's standing there shouting, 'Do you hear that? He's telling them let's get right into these Scottish boys, show them who we are. He's slaughtering us!' and that was just what we needed, we went out on to the pitch really riled up."

Peter agrees those overheard comments played their part, but remembers being really confident beforehand anyway.

"I had told a couple of the boys that I really fancied that if I started the game well I could give Mick Mills (the Ipswich captain and England full-back) a real doing, and that was how it turned out."

Indeed it did. Gordon Strachan put us in front with a penalty only for John Wark to level from the spot before half-time after the pumped-up Cooper felled Eric Gates. Shooting towards their favoured Beach End in the second half the Dons ran riot. Two jinking runs and a low finish with either foot resulted in two goals for Peter and as we spilled from our seats in joy, bodies it seemed strewn all over the stand, he might have had a hat-trick.

"In the last minute we were awarded a penalty and it just shows you how things were different back then, it never crossed my mind to say 'hey, I'm taking it to get my hat-trick', instead I just watched on as our regular penalty taker wee Gordon stepped up . . . and Paul Cooper saved it!"

As we raced back up Merkland Road hoping to get home in time to see the highlights on the television, Peter headed back out to the Bridge of Don for a 'wee party' with his parents and sister, who always travelled up for the big European matches. It turned into a late night, and there had not been much sleep taken when there was a knock on the door the following morning.

"There were reporters there and a TV crew, all wanting in to get photos and interviews, and my mother couldn't believe it. I could hardly believe it myself, it was the first time I'd had such attention, but it was great."

Weir's penchant for important goals became evident in successive Scottish Cup semi-finals. He skidded in the winner against his former St Mirren team-mates in the Dens Park replay at the end of that first season, and then headed the only goal against Celtic at Hampden Park a year later.

"I very rarely played as a substitute [in fact, just 17 times in his entire Aberdeen career] but I came off the bench that day, shut my eyes, and nodded it in at the post. That was really special, scoring for my team at Hampden to reach another Final."

It was a final Aberdeen would win, and it came just ten days after an even more significant victory, against Real Madrid in Sweden. Peter was immense that night, teasing and tormenting his Spanish opponents. He more than played his part and contributed to the winning goal, but just not as directly as he has been credited for down the years. Weir won the ball in his own half and fed Mark McGhee whose left-wing cross found John Hewitt's head in front of an open goal. The TV commentators got it wrong at the time and that mistake has been repeated on countless occasions since.

"A few years ago, when I was working with Celtic," recalls Peter, "I was asked to do a presentation at a school and I was introduced as the guy who had crossed for the winning goal in the Cup Winners Cup Final. I just smiled and took the applause and believe me, I wish I had a tenner for every time down the years someone has congratulated me for that great cross in Gothenburg."

But within a relatively short space of time the squad Weir was a huge part of began to disintegrate.

By the time Alex Ferguson left the north-east to begin his spectacularly successful revolution with Manchester United, five of the Gothenburg heroes had beaten him to the exit door: Rougvie, Strachan and McGhee in the summer of 1984, Neale Cooper and Eric Black two years later. And for those who remained it was becoming painfully evident that things were never going to be the same again.

My recollection from the time is that while we mourned Fergie's departure we simply assumed little would change. In his final full season he had at last filled the only blank space in the trophy cabinet by winning his first League Cup, beating Hibernian 3-0, and then secured a fourth Scottish Cup with a similarly dominant victory over Hearts.

But behind the scenes, with Ian Porterfield the club's surprise choice as successor, cracks were beginning to appear.

"He was a nice man, but he didn't have the experience to deal with the sort of players he was now having to manage. The training wasn't the same, standards slipped and the players started to slacken. If you let players away with it they will take liberties and that's what was happening. Some of the more experienced guys like Willie and Alex called a couple of meetings and stressed how we had to get back to doing things the right way, but it was too late, and by that stage my days were numbered anyway as the manager had brought in a younger left-winger in Gary Hackett."

Peter found himself on the bench more and more often, dropped into the reserves even, and the final straw came when he was told he would be starting in the penultimate match of the season at home to Rangers – the game that would see Graeme Souness clinch his first Scottish title – only to find out he had again been named as a substitute.

"I went home that night and decided my time with Aberdeen was at an end and early the next week put in a written transfer request."

It took a few months before he got his wish, his last game for the Dons being a 2-1 win away to Dundee on December 5th, 1987. Of the starting line-up that afternoon only Weir, Leighton, Miller and McLeish remained from the Gothenburg team.

There had been rumours that Peter was on his way and I remember as a cub reporter with Northsound approaching him on the steps outside Pittodrie to quiz him on a potential move to Leicester City. He politely declined to comment and made for his car and that was the last I saw of him in Aberdeen.

He had a week-long trial with Leicester to prove his fitness – his ankle had been troubling him for months – and signed for David Pleat in an £80,000 deal. City were at the time struggling near the bottom of the old Second Division, an ultra-competitive league that season including the likes of Manchester City, Leeds United, Aston Villa, Ipswich and Birmingham City.

"It opened up a new life for me, going to all these grounds I had never been to, and we had some decent players like Gary McAllister,

Ally Mauchlen and Mike Newell, and two guys I had played against in those Ipswich games, Paul Cooper and Russell Osman. We were at the bottom of the table in the January when I signed, but we put together a fantastic run – we only lost two or three games – and finished up mid-table."

Peter began the following season in good form and was enjoying his football, but feeling a little homesick when word reached him there was interest from two clubs hoping to entice him back to Scotland: St Mirren and Aberdeen.

"George Adams was doing a bit of work for the Dons at the time and had watched me in a couple of games and I was doing well, but Aberdeen never got in touch and St Mirren did. David Pleat was very understanding and said he would let me go rather than have an unhappy player on his books. I flew up to Paisley and met with my old mate Tony Fitzpatrick, who was by then St Mirren manager, and he persuaded me to join up. That night I was staying with my mum in Barrhead and I got the call to say that Aberdeen wanted me, not as a left-winger, but as a sitting midfielder, and that would have suited me down to the ground as my legs were going a bit at the time. I never did get round to speaking directly to the Dons boss Alex Smith because I had given my word to Tony and went to the ground the next day to sign for St Mirren."

Peter says he has very few regrets looking back over his career, but believes that was his biggest error.

"I made a mistake there. I quickly realised that I should have gone back to Aberdeen and I'm left wondering what might have happened had I done so."

It never really worked out for Weir back at Love Street, an old ankle injury flared up and curtailed his first team appearances, and it was while turning out for the reserves that he was approached by a man he had idolised as a Dons fan, and who was offering him an escape route from Paisley.

Ally MacLeod had utterly revitalised the club in the mid-1970s and Peter had been among the crowd at Hampden in November '76 when Aberdeen beat Celtic in extra-time to lift the Scottish League Cup. The following year he was the popular choice to take over as Scotland manager, but crashed and burned amidst the mayhem of Argentina 1978 and returned to Ayr United, where his managerial career had begun. There followed short spells with Motherwell and Airdrieonians, but by now MacLeod was back at his spiritual home, Somerset Park, and he wanted Peter to join him there.

"He offered me a full-time contract and Tony was happy enough to let me go. Ally may not have been quite as sharp as he had been in the past, but he was still a wonderful character and I really enjoyed my time with him. After about eighteen months, Ally left and was replaced by George Burley, my old international team-mate, and I helped him settle in, but my ankle was really playing up by then and at the end of the season I was forced to retire."

After forty games and one goal for Ayr, Peter Weir hung up his boots in the summer of 1992 with no idea what he was going to do next.

Tommy Burns and Billy Stark, then the Kilmarnock management team, asked him to do a bit of scouting, but that was never going to pay the bills and when I next caught up with Peter to interview him for a BBC Radio Scotland documentary marking the 10th anniversary of Gothenburg, it was at an unlikely venue.

"I bought a newsagent on Carmunnock Road right in the shadow of Hampden Park and what an experience that was. The hardest bit was getting up at four o'clock every morning, showering and shaving, and getting myself across to the south side of Glasgow."

The shop was just a few hundred yards behind the goal in which Peter had scored in that Scottish Cup semi-final. On big match days he could clearly hear the roar of the crowd.

"I stuck it for two years and one day out of the blue a gentleman came in and asked if I would be interested in selling the shop. He offered me a price and I near bit his hand off and I couldn't wait for the call from my solicitor to say the cheque was in the bank. It was some experience, but a hard life."

Peter's contacts in the game came through for him and he continued doing scouting and match reports for Tommy Burns, who had moved on to Celtic. He kept involved in the game, but needed a full-time job and his next stop was nearby Glasgow Airport.

"My job was delivering suitcases that had been mislaid and then turned up later. I drove all round Scotland and believe it or not, I loved it. In the winter it could be murder, but in the summer it was a great job and I ended up all over the country, going to islands I had never even heard of. It was hard, sixteen hours a day at times, and after about three years I felt I'd had enough."

He had been doing some coaching under George Adams at Celtic Park, taking responsibility for the under-16s, and then when George moved across the city to head up Rangers' youth programme at the Murray Park complex, joined him full-time to coach and look after the under-17s.

It was a rewarding time for Peter, he loved working with the youngsters and his side at the time was all-conquering, but he was given a reminder of just how tough it can be to make a living from the professional game.

"I thought that most of those boys would go on and make it. The reality is that only John Fleck and Ross Perry got kept on and even they have struggled to make a serious impact."

Unlike many of his former Dons team-mates, Peter has never gone into management, but he did have the chance in December 2005. George Adams had taken over as Director of Football at Ross County and following the departure of John Robertson there was a vacancy in the manager's office. George had no doubts about who he wanted to fill the post.

"Peter Weir is a top, top guy. His coaching ability is second to none; he's excellent with the kids and is a very good man-manager. He's strong on development and discipline, and he's great at encouraging players. I really can't speak highly enough of him and I was so disappointed when he turned down the job. Wherever I go in football in the future he would be one of the first guys I would want on board."

Peter had initially been interested, so much so that he drove to Perth to watch County draw 1-1 with St Johnstone at McDiarmid Park. He had been impressed by what he saw, reckoned the club had some excellent players, and agreed to head up to Dingwall for their next match against Stranraer to check out Victoria Park and the training facilities.

"There was a terrible snowstorm and the match was postponed so I didn't go up. It gave me a few days to think it over and I came to the conclusion that I'm happier working with kids, management really isn't for me. To be honest, I'm not sure I could have coped with players the way some of them are today and I just wouldn't have got the same enjoyment out of it."

The following year Peter landed his perfect job when Willie Miller brought him back to the club he loves. He is in charge of Aberdeen's youth development programme in Glasgow, covering teams all the way through from under-10s to under-17s, working with local scouts to unearth talent across the west of Scotland.

"I'm out every night of the week and at weekends. I work closely with our five or six coaches and spend time with each of the age group teams every week. Competition is fierce for the better players; it's our job to try to persuade them to sign full-time with Aberdeen. The problem is getting to them in the first place. It's not like it was back when I was a kid, now the youngsters are attached to senior clubs from a very early age and it's getting less and less likely that you're going to unearth a diamond playing for his boys club."

"Even if you get them on board and you work with them for a couple of years, there are no guarantees, and it's difficult getting them the level of football they need. We've had to let kids go because they're too old for the 19s, but not quite ready for the first team. We desperately need reserve-team football again, a place for these kids to keep on developing, otherwise guys like me –

remember I was twenty-one when I started playing professionally – are going to be lost to the game."

Whether there are kids out there who possess the potential to become the sort of player Peter was is open to debate. Even if there are, it seems highly unlikely any of them will match his achievements, particularly with a club the size of Aberdeen. While all the Gothenburg side reflect on what they did with a great degree of pride, the Cup Winners Cup triumph was especially significant for Weir, a Dons fan who lived the dream.

And while recalling his memories of that team and that era the sparkle in his eyes and the smile on his face made it clear that win over Real Madrid remains just as special to him now as it was back in May 1983.

CHAPTER SIX

NEIL SIMPSON

LECH POZNAN 0-1 ABERDEEN
Wednesday November 3rd, 1982

Having carved out a respectable 2-0 advantage from the first leg against Lech Poznan, the Dons had successive away encounters against Kilmarnock and Hibernian to deal with before they could contemplate the trip to Poland.

They kept their challenge for the Premier Division title alive with a routine 2-0 success at Rugby Park, Strachan and Rougvie linking up to allow Eric Black to head home the opening goal in the second minute, and John Hewitt sealing the win with his sixth goal of the season midway through the second half.

The following Saturday was somewhat less straightforward. On a wet and windy day, with puddles forming on the Easter Road pitch, Hibernian were hanging on to a second-half lead given to them by Gary Murray who had directed the ball past debutant Dons keeper Bryan Gunn from close range. Aberdeen were piling on the pressure, but looked to be heading for a third defeat in just nine league matches, when substitute Andy Watson crashed a long range effort off the crossbar. Wave after wave of attacks finally paid off in the 90th minute when Doug Rougvie fed Peter Weir and the winger squeezed home an overdue equaliser. The 1-1 draw was hardly ideal and left us trailing both Celtic and Dundee United in the championship race.

United were to be Aberdeen's next opponents, a crucial match, but both had European business to take care of first. Jim McLean's men had the easier task, a 3-1 win in Norway over Viking Stavanger allowed them to cruise through to the third round of the UEFA Cup, courtesy of a 0-0 score-line at Tannadice. The Dons meanwhile were preparing for another trip behind the Iron Curtain.

Alex Ferguson named a strong eighteen-man squad for the Polish adventure which included McGhee, Black, Rougvie and Kennedy, all of whom had been injury concerns, and Jim Leighton, who had recovered from a bout of flu. Two goals for the reserves at the weekend earned striker Andy Harrow an unlikely call-up. The big guns were all there for what seemed certain to be a demanding test, including a young midfielder who was fast becoming one of the first names on the team sheet, twenty-year-old Neil Simpson.

'Simmy', as he quickly became known to fans and players alike, had every attribute required to function superbly in the boiler room of that Aberdeen team. He was tall and muscular, had incredible stamina, was strong in the tackle and was also developing a handy knack of scoring important goals from well-timed late runs into the opposition penalty area.

He was someone we had been well aware of for a number of years thanks to the leadership qualities he had shown in the reserves and with Scotland at the various age levels. The week before the first leg against Poznan he had put in a Man of the Match performance for the under-21s at Tynecastle, scoring the opener against East Germany – a stunning 20-yard half-volley – and helping to set up the second in a 2-0 win. Ricky McFarlane, who was in charge of that squad, labelled Simmy "an excellent player," as he paid tribute to the midfielder's contribution.

Plaudits were something young Neil must have been accustomed to with his career on a decidedly upward curve. Born in London, but brought up in the village of Newmachar, ten miles north west of Aberdeen, he was spotted playing for Middlefield Wasps and joined the Dons on an 'S' form, making his debut as a sixteen-year-old substitute in a 7-1 League Cup thrashing of Hamilton in October 1978. He had been expecting to be farmed out to a Highland League side that season, a successful path taken by a number of Aberdeen players back then, but the management decided he might be better served playing for the reserves, and it was in a 'bounce' match at Stirling University that he really grabbed the manager's attention.

"I scored a hat-trick that afternoon, a left-foot shot, a right-foot volley and a curler into the top corner. Fergie was at the game and he promised afterwards I'd be included for the League Cup tie and that's what happened."

Simmy replaced Doug Rougvie in midfield during the rout of the Accies, and was even able to live out a fantasy.

"I'd always had a dream of playing for the Dons and setting up a goal for Joe Harper, and I managed to do it that night, which was just unbelievable."

He was indeed living the dream. Having grown up a fervent Aberdeen fan, Neil admits he found it mind-blowing to be rubbing shoulders with some of his heroes, but he did not allow himself to be overawed.

"It was amazing going into the ground and there would be Harper and Willie Miller and lots of big names, but I never let it faze me, I just got on and did my own thing, kept my head down and worked hard. There was another young lad there at the time called Alan Duguid and he always said that I was different from him, I could cope with being there and he couldn't, and you need that if you're going to make it."

Sadly Alan never did make the grade at Pittodrie, indeed his fall from grace was perhaps complete when he lined up in the same works team as I did, joining me as a colleague in the Clydesdale Bank after leaving the Dons. Alan had the talent, but not perhaps the mental toughness required. Simmy certainly did, and he needed it, as it was to be a long time before he next featured for the senior team.

"I was getting into the first-team squad after that Hamilton game, but not onto the pitch. We were due to take on Hearts just before

Christmas and Pat Stanton had told me I would be on the bench and that I'd definitely play the following week against Morton. I was thrilled, but the next day I woke up with my neck all swollen; I'd got mumps. That wiped me out for a couple of months and then I got German measles straight after and that was the whole season a write-off."

He was fit enough to head out to Italy that summer to play for Andy Roxburgh's Scotland Under-17 side, and the following campaign continued his apprenticeship in the Aberdeen reserves without ever getting called up to the top side. Indeed, it was not until December 1980, more than two years after his debut appearance, that Simmy got another look in, and it came on a day I remember well.

It was December 20th, 1980, and on the back of a home win over Rangers which had kept us clear at the top of the table, the Dons were in Glasgow to take on Partick Thistle on a bitterly cold day. As we entered Firhill one vendor, who was selling the traditional 'macaroon and chewing gum', made the mistake of putting his tray on the ground and was forced to chase after it, cursing loudly as it slid down the frozen walkway towards the turnstiles. As we huddled behind the goal, our mood was not helped by a soft penalty awarded to the home side and duly converted by Kenny Watson. There were cheers soon after when the towering Walker McCall bulleted home a headed equaliser and we should have won the match, but Gordon Strachan failed to convert an equally debatable spot-kick in the second half. It was during that half that Simmy was afforded his introduction to Premier Division football in place of Willie Garner, but he could do little to influence the outcome and a 1-1 draw was little cause for celebration as we piled back out towards the supporter coaches.

The area around Firhill has been heavily developed in the years since that match and is now quite well appointed. Back then we had to negotiate a waste ground to reach our bus, a waste ground teeming with detritus that very quickly became potentially lethal ammunition in the hands of the locals. Under a hail of bricks, bottles and God knows what else, we raced for cover. The coach driver was not for hanging around, but as he pulled away a quick head count revealed we were one man down. That man – whose name I no longer remember – had been hungry and had left a little early to visit a nearby chip shop. Now he was running down Maryhill Road behind our bus, fish supper clasped tightly to his chest, dodging all manner of missiles. He was finally hauled onboard when the bus was forced to stop at a red traffic light. As he scrambled onto the front, a number of us were surveying the scene from the back and recoiling in horror as one of our assailants, a teenager of no more than fourteen, raced towards us with what appeared to be a full bottle of whisky. His intention was clear, and when he was no more than ten feet away he hurled it straight at the window against which we were pressed. Or at least that was his plan. Somehow he managed to miss the bus entirely and the bottle arced gloriously over it, smashing with some force on the roof of the car in front. The driver of that vehicle quickly got out and as we pulled away our last image was that of the man exacting vicious revenge on the kid, who had clearly been so stunned by his inaccuracy that he had forgotten to run away!

If only the players knew what we fans sometimes had to go through in our support of the team!

Neil missed the next two matches, a home win over Celtic and a draw against United, but was handed the best New Year present he could have hoped for, his first start against St Mirren at Love Street on January 3rd, 1981. John McMaster had been missing long-term through injury, and when Gordon Strachan picked up a knock at Tannadice, which would ultimately end his season, the door opened for Simmy. He missed just one of the remaining sixteen games of that campaign.

"I was playing wide right most of the time. I didn't mind because it got me a game and it was a great experience, but I was getting stick from the fans for not getting up and down the wing and firing crosses in. I didn't bother trying to explain that I was hardly the tricky winger type!"

He also scored his first couple of goals for the Dons in back-to-back 3-1 wins over Partick Thistle and Morton and the following season racked up more than thirty appearances, firmly establishing himself in Alex Ferguson's plans, and collecting his first winner's medal in that never to be forgotten Scottish Cup triumph over Rangers.

"It was my first trophy and everyone was really quite emotional, especially the younger boys, as we'd never experienced anything like that before. It was a great moment for me, as a fan, playing for my club and winning at Hampden with all the family there. It was really, really special."

It was that victory that set Aberdeen on course for Cup Winners Cup glory in 1982-83 and by the time the run kicked off Simmy had already tasted continental competition, having started in both legs of the previous season's UEFA Cup encounter with SV Hamburg in addition to substitute appearances against Ipswich Town and Arges Pitesti.

He played in every match during the campaign which culminated in Gothenburg, scoring his first European goal in the demolition of Sion, and by the time the trip to Poland came around Simmy felt battle-hardened and all set for the challenge. The manager had convinced his players they were ready for anything and no-one at Pittodrie was prepared for the adventure to end against Poznan.

"Archie had watched them, we had the usual in-depth reports on all the players, and of course we'd already played them in the first leg. I don't think any of us set off thinking at all negatively, we knew this was a tie we should get through."

On gathering at the airport players posed for the obligatory photographs showing them drinking coffee/having breakfast/chatting with staff/holding up passports (delete accordingly!), the staple diet for the *Evening Express* ahead of the Dons' European ties. Of more interest that night was the manager's comments, as he made his intentions clear. He would stick with the system which had worked so well in Albania in the previous round, with Strachan and Weir stretching the Poles on the flanks and Mark McGhee operating as a lone striker. The boss told the *EE*'s Alastair Guthrie, 'It is a marvellous opportunity for the club to reach the last eight in a European competition for the first time in its history. We have the players who can defend a two-goal lead . . . and if we can get a goal then I'll be really confident.' Not for the last time in his illustrious career, Alex Ferguson had assessed the situation perfectly.

Fortunately the Polish winter had yet to bite, and Guthrie reported it to be a mild autumnal day, one which would suit the Dons players much better than the previous away tie in the sweltering heat of Albania.

Poznan had considered switching the match to the larger Warta Stadium, but instead kept it at their own Bulgarska ground and a crowd reported variously as anything between 25,000 and 35,000 turned up. The Poles had hoped to make it an intimidating atmosphere, but the Dons nipped any such notion in the bud with another disciplined and professional away performance.

The *Evening Express* from Thursday, November 4th, 1982 tells me Aberdeen were never in any serious trouble during the match, but that is not how I remember it. The game kicked off in the afternoon and my only way of keeping across events was to have a small portable radio in my inside jacket pocket with an ear-piece hidden as best as I could. Fortunately I was not serving on the counter that day, but whatever work I was supposed to be doing probably suffered as much as I did listening to the crackly coverage. Everyone knew what I was up to, but just in case anyone was in any doubt, the roar I let out when we scored shattered the peace inside the bank and totally gave the game away.

That goal came just short of the hour mark. Weir delivered an inswinging right-footed corner, McGhee made a trademark near post run and head-flicked the ball over Polish keeper Plesnierowicz and Dougie Bell stepped in to deflect it into the net from no more than six inches out.

Gordon Strachan nearly extended the advantage late on, finding the net at the end of a slaloming run through the home defence, only to have it ruled out by the Turkish referee. It mattered not, by then the Dons had comfortably won the tie and impressed the onlookers, including Polish national team boss Antoni Piechniczek, who told the *EE*, 'Aberdeen have some of the finest players I have seen anywhere this season. Their defence was excellent and I don't think Lech came near to scoring.' Those sentiments were echoed by Alex Ferguson who praised the efforts of his back line, particularly right-back Kennedy who returned after a month out and strolled through the match.

Neil remembers it simply as a job well done.

"We were pretty much in control out there. They were big and strong, but we managed to play around them and when Dougie scored we all knew that was it. They pretty much gave up after that."

The draw for the last eight of the competition was still five weeks away, but the following morning Ferguson was licking his lips at the prospect. The Dons would be paired with one from this list: Austria Vienna, Barcelona, Bayern Munich, Inter Milan, Paris St Germain, Real Madrid or Waterschei. More about that in the next chapter.

That 1982-83 season was Neil's most productive as he played in 51 games, scoring 10 goals along the way. It was also the season in which he made the breakthrough to the full international side, earning the first of five Scotland caps in a 0-0 draw with Northern Ireland in the Home International Championships at Hampden.

"The good thing back then was that the under-21s travelled with the big team, so I'd become used to mixing with some of the star names at the time, and there were always three or four Aberdeen players around anyway. At first it was just great being with the senior squad, but after I'd been with them loads of times and not been picked to play it did start to get a bit frustrating. You'd look at guys who were getting a game and think 'I'm just as good as them'. Then you had the emergence of Paul McStay, there was Jim Bett,

Souness . . . it was almost impossible to get into that team, you just had to take your chance when you got it."

Neil started against Northern Ireland and came on as a substitute, replacing McStay, against Uruguay a few months later. His third cap was won the following year in the Stade Velodrome in Marseille.

"I remember coming on for Gordon Strachan and I did well that night, and the papers gave me a good write-up following that, noting me as one for the future, but it never happened, one, because the standard of the other players was excellent and two, because of injury. For example, there was a World Cup qualifier against Iceland (the Scots won 3-0 at Hampden in October 1984) and I was being lined up to play but I tweaked my thigh doing shooting practice. Every time I was out injured, someone else seemed to overtake me. I remember Murdo MacLeod being called-up one time, and he ended up with twenty caps and I got five. The competition was so fierce and while I would never have got the cap totals that the likes of Willie, Alex and Jim got, I could certainly have got into the twenties."

After a three-year absence Neil returned to the national team in May 1987 and played in successive seasons against England.

"That was great, the one at Hampden in particular (a 0-0 draw) because I played well that day and set up Charlie Nicholas for what should have been the winner, but he hit the bar. And then I played at Wembley the following year and I enjoyed that, but that was to be my last cap. I started the next season really well with Aberdeen and I got called up for the World Cup qualifier in Norway [Scotland won 2-1 in Oslo] but I got injured in a European tie against Dynamo Dresden the week before, Roy Aitken was called up instead, and that was it."

Despite the frustrations Simmy loved his involvement at the various international levels and believes the early days in particular contributed to his development both as a player and as a person. In total he played around thirty times at the younger age groups.

"Great experiences . . . I'd never been abroad before I got into the Scotland youth teams at sixteen, seventeen, and I ended up going to Italy, Germany, Holland, Las Palmas, Monte Carlo . . . all those trips, and it just opened up a whole new world for me. Funnily enough, playing in Europe seemed to suit me and I had some great performances playing against Lothar Matthaus, Ruud Gullit . . . hardly touching the ball sometimes, but marking them and learning. They went on to become world-class players, but at that time I was on a par with them. Andy Roxburgh was manager at youth level and his organisation, his enthusiasm, was different class and that all helped me when it came to playing the big European ties at club level."

Simmy continued to be a major part of the Aberdeen team throughout the early to mid-1980s, winning successive league titles in the next two seasons. Injuries did however begin to take their toll; 1986-87 was a virtual write-off and he missed more than half the matches in the two campaigns that followed.

Reflecting on the sudden onset of a catalogue of injury problems, Neil wonders now if they all stemmed from a car crash he was involved in during December 1985.

"Before then I had no problem with sciatica, my back, my hamstrings, nothing up until then, and from the January onwards they all began to kick in. I'd suffered whiplash in the accident and could hardly move my neck. We all wondered about over-training, overplaying when we were so young, but I do think now – and I've never mentioned this before – that all my injury problems arose from that crash."

As his appearances dwindled, so too inevitably did his goal return and after being a potent threat bursting from midfield in the early part of his career, Simmy managed to score just three times in his last five seasons, his final goal for the club coming in a 3-1 win over Morton at Pittodrie in August 1987, John McMaster netting the consolation for the visitors.

One game Neil did feature in during the 1988-89 season was to have a lasting and damaging impact on his career and that of the

Rangers midfielder Ian Durrant. Games between Aberdeen and the Ibrox side had long been tempestuous, and tensions were as high as ever when Rangers rolled into town on Saturday, October 8th. As described in Chapter Four, the sight of former Don Neale Cooper in a Rangers shirt hardly dampened down feelings among the home support and he was to have a close view of an incident which continues to make occasional headlines to this day.

Cooper slid in and won the ball fairly in a challenge on John Hewitt just outside the visitors' penalty area. He then tried to sidestep Robert Connor, but the Aberdeen man impeded his progress, prompting referee Louis Thow to blow for a free-kick to Rangers. By then the ball had rolled a few yards, and not hearing the whistle, Cooper gave chase. Realising his team-mate Durrant was getting there first Cooper checked his run. At that moment Simpson arrived and caught the Rangers midfielder with an over the top challenge which caused Durrant's right leg to buckle horribly. After lengthy treatment the Rangers player was somewhat bizarrely given a piggy-back off the pitch by physio Phil Boersma. Neil was shown a yellow card.

Cooper, a close friend of both men, still has vivid and painful memories of that moment.

"Simmy is one of the nicest boys on the planet and that was totally out of character. I have to admit that at the time I had no idea how serious it was. It was just horrible."

Neil had realised it was a bad tackle, but did not fully appreciate the backlash which would follow and it was only when he was leaving the stadium that evening and was collared by a group of journalists seeking a quote that it began to dawn on him just what the repercussions might be. The national headlines over the next few days did not make good reading for the midfielder, and after a meeting with his manager Alex Smith the following week, Simpson's emotions got the better of him as John Hewitt recalls.

"Simmy locked himself in the toilets and he was breaking his heart, he wouldn't come out. That wasn't Simmy. He was hard, but he was fair, and everyone in the game who knew him knows that. As a player, he was never the same after that challenge."

The Monday morning's *Press & Journal* had made little of the incident while noting that Simpson had been 'fortunate to escape with only a yellow card', but by the time the *Evening Express* rolled off the presses, it was all kicking off. Commenting on quotes given by the Rangers manager to the national media, Alastair Guthrie's story, under the banner headline 'WHAT A CHEEK: Hit-man Souness's amazing outburst is sheer hypocrisy', suggested the club may take legal action following 'near hysterical reports' and 'outrageous comments in an English-based tabloid'. The paper also reported that Neil had been 'dramatically dropped from the Scotland World Cup squad to play Yugoslavia' but that national coach Andy Roxburgh had said the decision had been taken "before the weekend's activities", a claim most observers found hard to believe. He went on to describe the loss of Durrant as a "staggering blow".

Ian Durrant lost three years of his career and sued Simpson for damages. The case was due to be heard in Edinburgh in February 1993 with Neale Cooper as the key witness.

"I was at Dunfermline by that time and due to give evidence and it was just awful. Neil Simpson was one of my best friends, and having got to know him while at Rangers Ian Durrant was one of my best friends. I was getting ready to go through there and it must have been no more than an hour before the case was due that I got a call to say it had been settled out of court. That was a big relief."

Neil has never spoken publicly about the incident and told me . . .

"Lots of people have had their say about what happened that day. Obviously I have my own thoughts, but I'm just going to keep them to myself. I don't think it benefits anyone for me to start talking about it all these years later."

I have known Simmy for almost three decades, but was not about to use that friendship to try to squeeze a few headline-making quotes out of him. It was a horrible time for the midfielder and it continued to haunt him for years after; I could absolutely understand why he did not want to comment and potentially reignite the controversy.

While the injury undoubtedly affected Durrant's playing career and earning capacity, he did at least battle back following his lengthy lay-off. He eventually returned to the Rangers side, later moved to Kilmarnock and even reclaimed a regular place in the Scotland team, without ever quite recapturing the form he had shown as a youngster.

Simpson on the other hand saw his career peter out. He played fewer than sixty matches between then and his retiral in 1993, forever stigmatised by one single challenge, albeit a shocking one. The fact is that for the vast majority of his career Neil was, as John Hewitt described, the archetypal 'hard but fair' player, an assessment backed up by the facts; during thirteen years in professional football he was never once sent off.

Ian Durrant suffered dreadfully and was the innocent victim, but Simmy certainly paid dearly for that one moment of madness.

In 1989-90 the Aberdeen side was being reshaped by Alex Smith and Neil was no more than a bit-part player. It was however perhaps fitting that having been part of a team which had temporarily halted the Old Firm's domination of Scottish football, Simmy bowed out by facing the Glasgow giants in his last two matches for the Dons, a 0-0 draw with Rangers in April and a farewell 3-1 success at Celtic Park in the final league game of the season the following month.

"I'd played three reserve matches after being out injured and then played in those two games, Willie Miller also played against Celtic and we were trying to prove our fitness for the Cup Final. I did well that day, and the following week I absolutely burst a gut, I've never tried harder in training, as I tried to get into the team at Hampden."

Sadly there was to be no fairytale ending for the midfielder, he was forced to watch on from the main stand as the Dons beat Celtic 9-8 on penalties after a 0-0 draw.

"I was gutted. Alex Smith gave me the old 'come for a walk' line a couple of hours before kick-off and took me to the dugout and told me I'd missed out. I was supportive during the game, obviously I wanted to see the team win, but I never went to the party afterwards, which I should have, and I've always felt guilty about that. I just went back up the road. It would just have meant so much for me to have signed-off by winning another trophy."

Simmy knew his time was up, but he hoped his years of loyal service might be taken into account.

"I said fine, but I want either a free transfer or a testimonial . . . and I got neither."

A possible move to Ipswich never materialised, and it had seemed as if Neil was about to relaunch his career in Greece, but typically of how things were going for him around that time, that deal also fell through.

"Panathinaikos had come in for me and I was due to fly over for signing talks, so I'd gone into town to get some toiletries for the trip and by the time I got home there'd been a phone call telling me it was off. They had the three foreigner rule then, one of theirs was supposed to be going to Switzerland, but that deal collapsed and that meant there was no place for me."

By the time he eventually left Pittodrie for Newcastle United in a £150,000 deal in summer 1990, Simmy had amassed eight winner's medals and guaranteed his place in the Dons Hall of Fame. He had hoped the move to Tyneside would reignite his career, but his time in England was to be disappointing and short-lived.

"Newcastle was a disaster . . ." he grimaces, shaking his head, "right from the start. I had the flu, I wasn't well and had to go to the doctor. He took blood to do some tests and my arm became swollen and I needed to get that treated, so it was at least six weeks before I even got to play for the reserves. Mark McGhee was there and Roy Aitken, and potentially it seemed like a good move, but it just never worked out."

In the end he was to feature on just four occasions for manager Jim Smith.

"I eventually got to play against Port Vale in the League Cup, then I came on early as a sub against West Ham down there and did well. I thought I'd be starting the next game against Middlesbrough, but I was on the bench and the next week I came on against Bristol City, pulled my calf muscle, and never played again."

Newcastle were in the second tier of English football at the time, and having just missed promotion the previous season, Smith was under pressure. When he was sacked Ossie Ardiles took over and the decks were cleared.

"I had another two years on my contract and I could have sat on it, but the reserve team coach Derek Fazackerley said I'd be better trying to find a club, that I could still play at a high level. I spoke to Joe Jordan about a possible move to Hearts, but that didn't materialise, and then Tommy McLean phoned me, and with nothing else on the table I decided just to head back to Scotland and try to get a regular game with Motherwell. There was a spell then when I hit reasonable form and felt I was getting back to something like my best, and we had some good games and I enjoyed it. There were no trimmings at Motherwell, but it was a good club to be at."

Neil scored the last goal of his professional career at Fir Park in a 2-0 win over Airdrie in October 1992. I always remember watching the pictures coming into the studio that day and seeing the utter disbelief on his face and realising that he could not decide how to celebrate!

"Davie Cooper had a penalty saved and I ran in and tucked away the rebound and it was a case of 'what do I do now' because it had been so long since I'd scored (over five years in fact!). I had a good time at Motherwell, the banter with the boys was really good and Davie was fantastic."

Cooper had won the hearts of Motherwell fans after his surprise departure from Ibrox, and become more open and engaging with the media. I once sat interviewing him and Neil in the Fir Park dressing room and left with tears of laughter running down my face, and his death from a brain haemorrhage in 1995 came as a desperate shock to all who knew him.

"He was a great guy, full of life, and I got on really well with him. He used to come up and do some quiz nights here in Aberdeen and everybody loved him. When I heard he had died it was just awful. Really, really sad."

Simmy had two years in Lanarkshire and that was to be the end of his playing career.

"Tommy McLean had told me about six weeks before the end of the season that I'd be getting a free transfer, in fact he asked me if that was ok, maybe there was an opening there for me to negotiate, but by then I'd had enough and I said that was fine. The constant battling against injury, trying to come back all the time, it was quite draining and I just didn't want to keep going through it all over again."

He was just thirty-one years old.

Although Simmy had played almost 400 games as a professional footballer, he had peaked early, his glory days coming between 1982 and 1985, a three-year period during which he had collected a staggering eight winner's medals. As he sat with me almost three decades later he reflected with pride on those achievements, but his eyes really lit up and the smile broadened when he suddenly mentioned a long-gone, but fondly remembered, tournament which was once a fixture on the Scottish football calendar: the Tennent's Sixes.

The Sixes was born in 1984, initially played at Falkirk's Coasters Arena before moving for a year to Ingliston and then on to the SECC in Glasgow where it continued to be fought out until 1993. Hard as it may be to believe now, the Premier Division teams fielded all but full-strength sides and the players certainly took it seriously. The Dons won the event back-to-back in 1986 and '87 and Simpson revelled in it.

"We always put out a good side, first teamers alongside young boys like Paul Wright, Ian Porteous and Joe Miller, and it was great getting wired-in, crashing into the boards. I really enjoyed that. Hearts thought they were good, they always took it seriously, so it was great beating them and I loved winning those finals. It maybe wasn't the highlight of my career, but it's a fantastic memory."

When he left Motherwell Simmy headed home for Aberdeen and thanks to a suggestion from his cousin, city businessman Ricky Simpson, joined Cove Rangers where he played occasionally and took on the roles of assistant manager and Commercial Director.

"I really enjoyed the commercial side of things actually. The wages weren't great, but when you hit a certain level you got 50 percent commission and I got to that pretty quickly. It was going really well, but then I got the offer from the SFA and that seemed a good way to get into coaching."

That offer in 1993 was to become a Regional Development Officer with the Association. Neil was based in Elgin, but his beat covered the whole of the north-east of Scotland and he was constantly on the road.

"It was all about fostering and developing grassroots football, coach education for adults, helping the Highland League clubs and generally promoting the game. There were six of us covering the whole of the country and I enjoyed it, it was a really good grounding."

He did that job for eight years before getting the call to come home, returning to Pittodrie as the Dons' Head of Community Coaching.

"It was a similar remit, but this time concentrating efforts on the club rather than the more widespread way I had been doing. I was looking after the community programme, but there was also a cross-over with the youth programme, and if I came across some good kids then I'd recommend the youth guys to take a look at them."

Neil's next step was to become Assistant Academy Director to the highly-respected Lenny Taylor, the man who had unearthed the likes of Eric Black, John Hewitt and Neale Cooper, kids who became

Gothenburg legends, and then to take over the top job when Lenny retired in summer 2011.

It has meant Neil spending less time on the training pitch and more time in the office.

"As part of my previous job spec I spent three years helping Neil Cooper with the under-19s, but in this job you couldn't be out there because there's just too much happening. You have meetings all the time with parents, with the SPL or SFA. I do miss being out there, but I try to keep my hand in doing some sessions with the youth coaches, and we've got a good team in the youth programme; we're beginning to see the fruits of all the work we've put in. Lenny and I went down to Manchester United to see how they do it and I remember Fergie saying there's no shortcut, you can implement all the schemes you like, bottom line is it's all down to hard work, that's what gets you results."

Neil says he gets great satisfaction in watching the kids step up to the first team and getting called-up to the various international squads.

"I think the standard of player we're producing is better than it's been for the last ten, fifteen years. We're now focusing more on technique. As a youngster I learned technique myself, doing keepy-ups, playing against a wall, but somewhere along the line the kids stopped doing that. We're making sure they all get the right education and the right environment in which to progress."

Simmy has been immersed in coaching for two decades now, but he did have a brief, a very brief, taste of football management. When Mark McGhee was sacked in December 2010 he and Neil Cooper stepped into the breach, taking charge for one game before the Brown-Knox era officially began. It was at Tynecastle and the Dons were thrashed 5-0!

"Everything was brilliant that week . . . up until the match! The players were outstanding, they couldn't have done enough to help. We prepared them well, we organised them and they were all up for it. We'd worked on set-pieces and Zander Diamond almost scored from one of them right at the start, heading just over the bar, but then you lose a goal in five minutes and you could just see them all going 'here we go again'. I had no illusions, no thoughts that I was going to become manager or assistant manager, but I did enjoy the experience until the match kicked off, then it became the worst day of my life. Honestly, it could have been another nine [a month earlier the Dons had suffered a club record 9-0 reverse at Celtic Park], it was horrible."

It seems certain that will remain Neil's only taste of football management as he sees his future in the coaching side of the game, and as a true Dons fan and legend, he hopes to produce the players that will eventually wear the red shirt with the same pride he showed during the 1980s.

"That's the aim and I hope the boys we bring through will get the chance, even in a small way, to enjoy what we did as players. You know, when we all get together, that group of lads, it's like nothing's changed, it's as if we're still in that dressing room slaughtering each other, having a laugh and just getting on with the job. Great banter, it was hilarious at times, and the camaraderie went a long way towards helping us achieve what we did. It was great, it really was."

One month after recording and writing-up my interview with Neil I had the privilege of hosting the inaugural Aberdeen FC Player of the Year dinner at the city's Exhibition Centre and while all the winners were warmly applauded and celebrated, the biggest cheer of the night came when I announced the recipient of the Special Recognition Award, given to an individual deemed to have provided outstanding service to the club over a period of years. That individual was Neil Simpson and as he stood on the stage, chants of 'Simmy! . . . Simmy!' reverberating around the hall, it struck me there could have been no more popular or worthy winner.

I also revealed that Neil had been awarded his long overdue benefit match and it was no surprise when a few months later it emerged that Alex Ferguson had agreed to send a Manchester United XI north to play in the game. Fergie has never forgotten his players from that time, the young men, Simmy included, who brought him and the club such success and who secured arguably the most notable of all his many achievements that night in Gothenburg. The 21,000 capacity crowd which packed into Pittodrie to see the Dons beat United 2-1 was a fitting tribute to a true club legend.

CHAPTER SEVEN

ERIC BLACK

BAYERN MUNICH 0-0 ABERDEEN
Wednesday March 2nd, 1983

For the first time in Aberdeen's history the club had European football to look forward to after Christmas, but while there was great excitement over who we might get in the last eight, there was also an awareness that domestic matters had to be taken care of and the Dons were embroiled in a three-way battle for the Premier Division title with Celtic and Dundee United.

United already knew their UEFA Cup fate, having been paired with Werder Bremen, and the two north-east sides had been left to fly the flag for Scotland, Celtic having lost to Real Sociedad while Rangers were being humiliated 5-0 by Cologne.

The Tannadice side were unbeaten in the league and they were to be the next visitors to Pittodrie. The encounter would be one of the most memorable of the entire season.

It was a cold, dull day which perhaps kept the crowd down to a less than impressive 14,000, but all of us who were there were treated to a special ninety minutes.

Richard Gough gave United an early lead and we feared the worst. Jim McLean's side had conceded just three goals in their opening nine matches and it was never a good idea to let them take the lead. In addition, United had already beaten us three times that season. What followed was quite astonishing.

Neale Cooper grabbed a swift equaliser, and then to uncontained euphoria, certainly where I was in the South Stand, cult hero Doug Rougvie bundled in two almost identical goals from corners. Three-one at half-time, Eric Black headed home to make it four with twenty minutes to go and Gordon Strachan notched the fifth with a thing of beauty. Drifting towards the shell-shocked United rear-guard, the wee man looked up and gently stroked the ball through a defender's legs and into the far corner of the net past a bewildered Hamish McAlpine. Alex Ferguson later marvelled at Strachan's effort, labelling it, "a right old-fashioned goal, he just passed the ball into the net".

It had been a brilliant afternoon and the bonus was that the match was to be featured on that night's *Sportscene* – back then you actually got highlights on a Saturday night! I recorded it on my clunky old VCR and watched that tape on countless occasions down the years.

The win over United maintained Aberdeen's unbeaten run and there was a real momentum building. Between the end of September and the middle of March the Dons lost just one league match, but could not shake off the Tannadice side or Celtic.

Highlights during that spell included a 1-0 win over Rangers at Ibrox, Eric Black heading the winner from a Peter Weir cross; an astonishing 3-0 victory away to Dundee United on January 3rd in which Simpson, Weir and McGhee all found the net (at that stage United had conceded sixteen goals in eighteen league matches, half that total lost in just two games against the Dons); and a 2-0 beating of Rangers at Pittodrie in which the visitors lost it and had John McDonald sent off for headbutting Dougie Bell amidst scenes of mayhem.

In the middle of a hectic domestic fixture list came that long-awaited news of Aberdeen's quarter-final opponents. The draw was made on Friday, December 10th, 1982 and the early edition of the *Evening Express* managed to squeeze the story into the 'stop press' strap down the right side of the front page. Covering no more than one inch, it read: 'DONS FACE GERMANS Aberdeen to play

109

Bayern Munich in the quarter-finals of European Cup-Winners' Cup, Dons away in first leg'. By the later editions it was a back page headline: 'IT'S BAYERN MUNICH . . . A cup cracker as Dons draw the pride of Germany' with Alex Ferguson declaring himself delighted to have avoided Barcelona and hoping, "the experience the present team have had against top West German sides in the last few years should help us meet this great challenge". The following day's paper quoted Bayern manager Uli Hoeness as saying, "I would have preferred to meet Barcelona or Inter Milan rather than Aberdeen." It was a high quality last eight in the competition, the other ties being Austria Vienna v Barcelona, Inter Milan v Real Madrid and Paris St Germain v Waterschei, the Belgians the only side without a European pedigree of note.

Another crucial match came against Celtic in Glasgow on February 12th. The Dons were one point behind Billy McNeill's men having played a game more, and knew defeat would be hugely damaging. With the Bayern tie just around the corner, the Bavarians, in the form of Hoeness and his Hungarian coach Pal Csernai, were there to spy on Aberdeen, and were given plenty to think about.

Charlie Nicholas gave the home side the lead, but the Dons were irresistible thereafter. Eric Black scored twice in the closing minutes of the first half to turn the game on its head, and completed a famous hat-trick midway through the second. The 3-1 win sent Aberdeen top of the table.

"My main memory of that game is that despite scoring three goals, I got bollocked by Fergie in the dressing room afterwards. I can't remember why, to be fair I got shouted at after most games, and it didn't bother me that day; that was very, very special."

Eric Black achieved plenty in an all too short playing career, but that day was very special indeed, so notable that three decades on no-one has been able to emulate it in a competitive fixture.

I drove the 350 mile round trip down to meet Eric on one of the worst days of the year, through driving rain, wind and flooding, to the Academy of Light in Cleadon, Sunderland's training complex.

Having stopped just over the border to pick up a bottle of water and a newspaper, I returned to my car and threw the *Sun* down on the passenger seat. It flipped open to the back page which read BRUCE ON THE BRINK, Steve Bruce being under considerable pressure following a run of poor results which had left his team fighting a relegation battle. Fortunately he and, more importantly for me, Eric were both still in a job when I arrived and were sitting round a table in the canteen with the rest of the coaching staff. Just twenty-four hours later Bruce had been sacked and Eric left in interim charge of the first team. He was manager for just the one game, a vital away match against Wolves, and Sunderland led 1-0 midway through the second half when they were awarded a penalty. Sebastien Larsson missed and the home side went straight up the park to equalise through Steven Fletcher. The striker scored again shortly afterwards to secure a 2-1 victory, Sunderland's season being summed up in those nine gut-wrenching minutes at Molineux. Black left two days later as Martin O'Neill began a new era at the Stadium of Light.

He had joked with me about giving up the game and setting up a coffee shop near his Midlands home, so when he was named a few weeks later as Steve Kean's assistant at Blackburn Rovers I texted him pointing out he would have to delay the grand opening. His reply was typically realistic, "Possibly just a short delay!"

Of all the 'Gothenburg Greats' Eric Black is the one who has retained his youthful good looks more than any of the others (some were never that fortunate in the first place) and he seemed a picture of health as we shook hands, despite still being in daily pain from the chronic back problems which ended his career ridiculously prematurely. I had always got on well with Eric, and having not seen him for the best part of a decade, it was wonderful to catch up. As we chatted over a bowl of soup his disillusionment with the modern day footballer became apparent, and he despaired of the attitude of a number of those young men taking home fortunes on a weekly basis. Having agreed that we had both become grumpy old men, we turned our attention to his criminally short, but nevertheless hugely successful, playing career.

He was born in Bellshill and initially brought up in and around Glasgow, before suddenly being transported to the wilds of Alness in the Scottish Highlands at the age of twelve when his dad got a construction job in the oil industry. Eric settled quickly into his new surroundings and immersed himself in playing as much football as he could, graduating through school and county level to be picked for the North of Scotland select in their annual match against Aberdeen in 1978.

"It was normally a whitewash each year, but we had a good team and beat them 5-1. The Dons goalkeeper Bobby Clark was looking after the Aberdeen side and he asked me afterwards if I fancied going down to Pittodrie for a trial, which I did. That went well and I signed an 'S' Form and turned professional when I became sixteen."

That was in October 1979; little did Eric know how meteoric a rise he was about to experience over the next few years. Before he was out of his teens Black had won two Scottish Cup medals and the European Cup Winners Cup, he had faced up to some of the biggest names across the continent and scored against most of them.

His first Aberdeen goal came in his first game, the opener in a 1-1 draw with Dundee United on October 31st, 1981, and it was scored in a way which would become all too familiar for us Dons fans throughout that period. I vividly remember him scoring that goal and the buzz that went round the stadium that day – this boy looks a bit special!

"It was a cross from the right from Gordon [Strachan] and I just pulled away at the near post, climbed into the air and flicked it back across goal with my head and the ball floated in at the back post. It was really exciting and I was just pleased that I had got off to a good start, which is important in anyone's career."

Eric had got off to a flier and he would go on to start a further eleven matches that season, making five more appearances as a substitute and scoring four goals. He was on a steep learning curve, but getting superb support from those around him.

"We had good players at the club and an exceptional manager, an exceptional coach in Archie Knox. It was just a good group of people with an insatiable desire to succeed and the atmosphere within the club was really positive. I had nothing to compare it with obviously, I just thought that was how it was – you turned up, played a game, got shouted at a bit and won a trophy every year!"

With thirty years hindsight now under his belt Eric appreciates just how special the club was back then, and having amassed years of experience in coaching and management, understands a bit more about what Alex Ferguson was doing and how he coaxed and cajoled his players into scaling those unimaginable heights.

"It was all about that positivity, about gathering a group of good players with the right attitude, of getting that balance between the younger guys like me and the older heads who had the experience and know-how. They were good professionals to follow and to set standards."

Black was reaching those standards almost from the off. He made his European debut in a UEFA Cup tie against a Hamburg side captained by Franz Beckenbauer, and scored the first goal in a 3-2 home win, and when the Cup Winners Cup run began the following August it was Eric who sparked the rout of Sion, directing a header inside the keeper's right post with just five minutes played. Little did he, or we, know then what he had started!

As Eric and his team-mates lined up in the tunnel at Munich's Olympic Stadium, their opponents were a 'who's who' of world football at the time, virtually all of them West German internationalists. The big names were Paul Breitner, a man who had scored in two World Cup Finals, and Karl-Heinz Rummenigge, voted European Player of the Year in both 1980 and '81.

"The players we were up against were legends when I was growing up, and we realised that this was the big one, but I never felt overawed going into any game. Maybe it was just because I was younger and I got dragged along with it, but I always believed we could get a positive result anywhere."

There were 35,000 there that night, and while the Dons fans were vastly outnumbered, they made their presence felt, buoyed by a first-rate professional performance by their team. Alex Ferguson had decided against risking Gordon Strachan, who was on his way back from injury, so Dougie Bell was handed a start, his ball-retention skills deemed perfect for such an occasion. Defending solidly, Aberdeen eased their way into the match and began to counter-attack, coming closest to opening the scoring in the 16th minute when Peter Weir jinked past two defenders on the left angle of the box and fired a low right-foot shot which goalkeeper Muller scrambled wide for a corner. Jim Leighton was called into action diving low to his right to clutch the ball on the line after Nachtweih tried his luck from twenty yards and shortly afterwards he repelled a Breitner free-kick. They were to be two of just a handful of saves the Dons keeper was forced to make, and he remembers being convinced it was going to be a successful night.

"That game was the best performance I was ever involved in; I just had the feeling that we were never going to lose a goal over there. We defended like hell at times – we had to – but it was a fantastic night."

With Willie Miller prowling in and around his penalty box, snuffing out the German threat, and Alex McLeish imperious in the air, Leighton was well protected, and the Dons remained dangerous on the counter, their best chance arriving shortly before half-time when Neale Cooper chipped a pass forward from midfield, allowing Mark McGhee to gather and accelerate past Grobe. He was forced a little wider than he might have wanted, but still got in a low angled shot from eight yards. Muller dived despairingly and got the fingertips of his right hand to the ball sending it inches wide of the far post. That was as close as Aberdeen would come to breaking the deadlock, in the main their task was to blunt the home attack, and that defending began with McGhee and Black, who were leading the line.

"It was an extremely hard-working performance. We must have covered a few kilometres that night trying to stop them play and preventing them from creating chances. It wasn't just backs to the wall; we did have possession and control of the ball, but didn't make many openings ourselves. Looking back, it was a phenomenal result to get a 0-0 out in Munich."

That scoreline was seriously threatened on only a few occasions after the interval, Leighton diving to turn wide a Rummenigge shot from twenty yards and then gathering a close-range header from the same player. As the Germans grew desperate, Klaus Augenthaler strode up from the back and with just four minutes remaining fired in a well-struck thirty-yarder. Jim Leighton flew to his right to clutch the ball, and that was just about that, the only other minor irritation coming when Rummenigge attempted an overhead kick and removed one of Willie Miller's front teeth with his boot.

It was a tactical triumph for Alex Ferguson, who later proclaimed himself "very proud" of the team effort. He acknowledged that Bayern "are one of the biggest clubs in the world" and that the Germans would come out all guns blazing at Pittodrie. He did however issue this warning, "We will be ready for them though" and indeed they were, more of which in the next chapter.

Eric went on to score the opening goal in the semi-final first leg against Waterschei, and of course in the Final itself against Real Madrid. Ten days later he netted his 19th goal of that season, the winner, four minutes from the end of extra-time, in what had been a largely undistinguished Scottish Cup Final against Rangers. Having collected another winner's medal, Black was in the dressing room about to pop open a bottle of champagne when the door burst open and the manager crashed in. He had just berated the team in a live television interview, branding their performance a disgrace, and now he was not about to hold back in private.

"Let's just say the TV interview gave you a flavour of what was said in the changing room. I know it wasn't a great performance, far from it, but given the circumstances I thought we might have been cut a bit of slack. The manager was absolutely furious and he made that abundantly clear, it had been unacceptable, not up to the standards he set. That was the most sombre dressing room I have ever been in after a victory – we had just won the Scottish Cup, and after he walked out the place was in silence."

Ferguson apologised individually to all the players the following day.

"I have to admit there were times when I didn't like the manager, or Archie or Teddy Scott, the things they did and said to us, but looking back I realise it was because they were all so driven, all so determined to succeed."

And succeed they did.

Eric went on to score in the following season's Scottish Cup Final as well, in a 2-1 extra-time victory over Celtic, and he collected back-to-back Scottish Premier Division championships in 1983-84 and 1984-85.

During his four full seasons playing in the first team he started 138 games and came on as a substitute on twenty-five other occasions, scoring 65 goals. He ended his time at Pittodrie having won eight major pieces of silverware, but was denied a ninth in controversial circumstances, Alex Ferguson leaving him out of the 1986 Scottish Cup Final triumph, a 3-0 thrashing of Hearts, after the player had made it clear he saw his future elsewhere.

In spring of that year Black had become aware that a number of English clubs had expressed an interest in acquiring his services, but that Aberdeen had not shared that information with him. His contract was running out and direct approaches were made to the player, offering the kind of money he could only dream about at Pittodrie. The one that appealed most was made by AS Monaco, but there were strings attached.

"I travelled down to Monaco and agreed a five-year contract, but the deal was dependent on them getting Arsene Wenger from Nancy."

Wenger was at that time less than two years into his managerial career and had made an unremarkable start with the club from the north-east of France, but he had impressed the powers-that-be in

Monaco and had been earmarked to replace Lucien Muller. He was aware of Black and wanted him on board, but Nancy refused to let him go and it would be another year before Wenger ended up at Stade Louis II. That was too late for Eric, and his dream move to the Principality fell through.

"I've never spoken about this before, but I'd had a good look around, viewed apartments, and taken the contract home with me. Four days later I got the call saying that Nancy were hanging on to him and that my deal was null and void. I'd already burned my bridges at Pittodrie and was left wondering what to do next."

Fortunately there was no shortage of suitors and among the sides bidding for his services were Cologne, St Etienne and Metz. Eric went to meet the managers and decided the one he liked most was Marcel Husson at Metz, so he signed on there. The club would later become famed for its youth academy, producing world-class talent such as Robert Pires, Louis Saha and Emmanuel Adebayor, but in the mid-1980s it was largely unknown, and Black's decision came as a major shock to Dons fans.

"Suddenly I found myself in north-east France. I'd never even heard of Metz at that time, but I never regretted the move. It was a good time to be there, the national team were European Champions, there was a lot of money being poured into the league and the overall standard was good."

The back problems which had begun when he was still a teenager were by that stage beginning to take a toll however and curtailing his ability to perform week in, week out.

"To be honest, my back was in bits. I was training for a couple of weeks, playing two or three games, and then having to rest up. Despite that, I was top scorer by Christmas that first season, but then had to have a double hernia operation and it just became a catalogue of injury problems after that."

Eric was still able to add to his medal haul, winning the French League Cup in 1986. A 6-3 win over Bordeaux in the semi-final was followed by a 2-1 victory over Cannes in the final, both matches in extra-time, a familiar follow-on from his Cup successes with Aberdeen. An even more memorable occasion came in June 1988 when Metz won the French Cup for just the second time in the club's history.

"That was a fabulous experience. It was the most important Cup competition in the country and we had a good team, a great bunch of lads, four or five of whom I still keep in touch with to this day. To win a trophy like that in another country was amazing; maybe not quite up there with Gothenburg, but running round the Parc des Princes with the Cup was very special indeed."

Metz beat Sochaux that day, Eric scoring past future Hearts goalkeeper Gilles Rousset in a 1-1 draw to set up a penalty decider. Rousset actually netted for Sochaux in the shoot-out, as did two more men destined to spend time in Edinburgh, Stephane Paille and Franck Sauzee, but Metz ran out 5-4 winners to spark those scenes of celebration in the French capital.

That was to be the last major highlight in Eric's stellar career, one which brought him ten winner's medals in the space of six glorious years. The injuries were becoming more and more problematic, with his back in particular causing him severe distress.

"I had been in traction for two weeks when I was seventeen, just lying there staring at the roof, but we never got to the root of the problem, never established when it had happened. Obviously the medical back-up then was nothing like as sophisticated as it is now. I had a double fracture at the base of my back, something that was only discovered later, so that clearly didn't help. Because of the back I was compensating in my movements and that put a strain on my stomach and led to the hernia operations. Had it happened now, I'd have had the scans, got the treatment and probably been back playing within three months fully fit again, but hey, that's life."

As his condition worsened, Black was training less, and as a result playing less. He was "popping pills" to try to alleviate the pain and they were upsetting his stomach, so he required further medication to offset the bouts of sickness. Eventually he decided enough was enough and walked away from professional football. He was just twenty-eight.

"At that stage I was high and dry. I didn't have a clue what I was going to do next."

What he did was pack up and return to Scotland with his wife Nina and young children, four-year-old Jonathan and baby Danielle. For the next six months he oversaw the building of a house just outside Alness with the intention of making a new life for his family in the Highlands.

Out of the blue he got a call from Ross County, then still a Highland League side, offering him a role in what might loosely be termed their 'commercial department' and he took on that job for the next few months working with the local business community to try to attract investment. It was then that national team manager Craig Brown got in touch and Eric was a handed a more natural role within the game.

"The SFA were starting up their community coaching programme and Craig wanted me to head up the project in the Highland region. I met him and quickly agreed, and that meant I was travelling all over the north and across to the islands. I was everywhere, driving around with a bag of balls in the back of the car. I remember arriving at one wee school in Skye at 8.30am. The teacher lived on the premises and she took me in and gave me a cup of tea and a biscuit, the fire was going and I was sitting there waiting for a dozen kids to turn up. Of course, they were all different sizes, aged from four to ten, and I'm thinking 'where did it all go wrong?' but it was great, it got me active again and back into football."

From there Eric got involved in coach education in Inverness, working with amateurs who ran teams around the area, and eventually Craig Brown asked him to join the SFA's Technical Department in Glasgow on a full-time basis.

"I thought I was back up north for good, but it was a great opportunity and one I couldn't turn down, so it was a case of up sticks and move again. That was in 1993 and it was most enjoyable.

I was working with the youth teams with Ross Mathie, getting involved in the numerous coaching courses, and at the same time working myself to accumulate the coaching badges and certificates I needed. I was there for around four years doing various jobs, up to and including taking the under-21s on a couple of occasions, and then came another unexpected call."

That call was from the former BBC Scotland football commentator Jock Brown, who had recently been unveiled as the new General Manager of Celtic in a move which had stunned Scottish football.

"I went as Academy Director, which ruffled a few feathers as you might imagine, and the rest was just continual ruffling!"

The relationship between Brown and manager Wim Jansen deteriorated rapidly, so much so that despite winning the title and ending Rangers' run of 'nine in a row', Jansen walked out immediately after clinching the Championship. It was not a happy time for Eric to be at Celtic Park, as he was caught in the crossfire.

"I was right there every day. After Wim left, Kenny McDowall and I took the first team through pre-season and then just one week before the season kicked off Jozef Venglos came in. Jock asked if I would be interested in becoming assistant manager and I said that was up to Jozef, who didn't know me from Adam. We met, had dinner and he was happy for me to take it on, but it was under difficult circumstances."

Dr Venglos lasted just a single season before Kenny Dalglish made an emotional return to the club as Director of Football, bringing with him rookie manager John Barnes.

"I met with Kenny down at Turnberry, got on ok with him, and that led to a meeting with John at which he offered me the job as his assistant."

The new managerial team got off to a flier winning twelve out of thirteen league and cup games, the only defeat coming at Tannadice, but Rangers' form was even better and they were ahead in the SPL title race. Henrik Larsson suffered a horrific leg break in a UEFA Cup tie in Lyon and without their talisman the rot began to set in. By

120

February 8th, 2000 Celtic were ten points adrift in the league and that night suffered the most embarrassing defeat in the club's history, meekly exiting the Scottish Cup at the hands of First Division Inverness Caledonian Thistle.

Celtic trailed 2-1 at half-time and that led to an amazing dressing room bust-up between Eric and the club's top scorer Mark Viduka.

"I'll never forget it. I'd not been happy with a few things he had done and told him so in no uncertain terms and he got up and started coming across the room towards me. Fortunately Olivier Tebily and the fitness coach jumped in and hauled him away, otherwise he'd have killed me. After that he just took his gear off and got in the bath, and then the rest of the guys turned against him for downing tools. I don't regret doing what I did; I've done it a few times since when it has been needed, but it was a horrible night."

Without Viduka and with the home fans getting increasingly hostile towards their manager, Caley Thistle scored again to complete an astonishing 3-1 victory. As their players cavorted around the pitch afterwards in joyous celebration, around a thousand Celtic supporters gathered outside to call for Barnes to be sacked. They got their wish less than forty-eight hours later.

Eric was offered the chance to return to his role as Academy Director, but decided that having seen off three managers, the time was right for him to go as well.

After a couple of months out of work he was contacted by Terry Butcher, who was involved in setting up a player recruitment company, Inside Soccer, with the agent Murdo MacKay. Eric went to watch a few matches with them and was taken on full-time. It meant he was still around the game and allowed him the freedom to indulge in a bit of broadcasting, joining us regularly at the BBC as an intelligent and insightful pundit, but he admits he was never totally at ease with the role as agent.

"I was never comfortable in that whole environment, just did not like it, and I felt really awkward at times, but I stuck at it as I didn't want to let big Butch down. The business did ok for a year or so, but then just wound down naturally. I had previously knocked back a couple of offers, including one to join Hearts, but then the Motherwell job came up and I jumped at it."

That was in October 2001; Pat Nevin was Chief Executive at Fir Park at the time and looking to replace Billy Davies. He sounded Eric out, arranged a meeting with ambitious club owner John Boyle, and the deal was done. Black brought Butcher as his assistant, with Chris McCart and George Adams completing the backroom team, but admits he was on a massive learning curve.

"It was my first managerial job of course, and I was as naïve as they come and ill-prepared too, but I wanted to do it, was up for the challenge and it was a great experience. I learned a hell of a lot in a short space of time and was settling into it and then bang, the club went into administration!"

Eric had been in charge for just six months when Boyle, claiming his ownership of Motherwell had cost him £11 million, took that drastic step. Nevin immediately resigned, as did Black, and nineteen players were later made redundant by the administrator.

"Looking back now, maybe I was a bit hasty, but I had promised new contracts to players I was looking to build the team around, and suddenly there were no contracts for anyone. They had been agreed and they were whipped off the table. John Boyle may have been right to do what he did, but he couldn't convince me of that at the time, and I felt I had to walk."

Eric was only out of the game for a few weeks when, as so often during his career, he received an unexpected telephone call, this time from Gary McAllister's agent Struan Marshall. He had already rejected offers to move abroad again, including one from Hong Kong, and not sure about relocating his family down south, had turned down the chance to become Davie Moyes' assistant at Preston. But this one was more attractive. McAllister had been appointed Coventry City manager, but wanted to keep playing and needed someone to be in the dugout while he was on the pitch.

Eric was to be that man. The pair formed a good bond and worked well together, but Gary's wife Denise was battling breast cancer and in December 2003 he stepped down to spend more time with her and their young family, leaving Eric in charge.

Black brought in Archie Knox as his assistant, but it was to be another short-lived stint. According to the official Coventry City website, Eric was popular with the fans, steered the team well clear of relegation and brought an exciting brand of football which led to a number of high-scoring wins. It had been anticipated he would be handed a long-term contract, but the Coventry board instead appointed Peter Reid, and Eric was on his travels again.

"Steve Bruce called me and asked if I fancied meeting him for a coffee. I didn't know Steve at all, but was happy to have a chat, and drove across to meet him at his flat in Knowle, just outside Birmingham. I guess someone must have put in a good word for me – to this day I don't know who – but Steve offered me the job as his assistant at St Andrews and I've been with him ever since."

Or at least he had been until less than a day after we met to record this interview.

He followed Steve from Birmingham to Wigan and then on to Sunderland, seven years spent operating at probably the highest and most demanding level there is in club football.

"We've won nothing, but there have been some incredible memories: keeping Birmingham up and getting them to tenth in the Premier League; getting relegated and then bouncing back up in a year having won thirteen games in a row; at Wigan we had eight points in November but still managed to finish fourteenth and then had a fantastic run the following season as well; and then the big challenge at Sunderland where getting thirteenth and tenth place finishes was no mean feat in itself."

Less than two months after being sacked, Eric was back in the game as assistant to the beleaguered Steve Kean at Blackburn Rovers, very much a case of out of the frying pan and into the fire,

123

and Rovers were duly relegated when rivals Wigan Athletic won 1-0 at Ewood Park in the penultimate game of the season.

His time as a manager in his own right has been limited to those short spells at Motherwell and Coventry, since then Black has been seen as a number two and it is a role he is more than comfortable with.

"I just hanker to be involved in the game. Unfortunately I'm not good enough to pick and choose what I want to do in my career. Let's be honest, if the Arsenal job comes up tomorrow, I'm hardly going to go for that, am I? For as long as Steve wants me beside him I'm happy to be there, if there's no job with him I have to look for something else, either on my own or as a number two. I'm just happy to be involved in football."

Throughout his time in coaching Eric Black has often been linked with the club where he made his name. Managerial vacancies have occurred frequently at Pittodrie during the past decade or so and Eric has regularly topped the supporters' wish-lists, so has he been close to a return to the Dons?

"There have been a few times when I've been close, contact has been made, but I just couldn't take that step. I felt my career in England was going well and while I obviously have incredible emotional links with Aberdeen, I couldn't at the time leave the English Premier League to go up to the SPL, the pull wasn't big enough for me to walk away. But who knows, maybe one day."

CHAPTER EIGHT

ALEX MCLEISH

ABERDEEN 3-2 BAYERN MUNICH
Wednesday March 16th, 1983

The sense of anticipation had been growing in and around the city ever since we had been drawn against Bayern, and now, with the second leg almost upon us, and with that 0-0 scoreline from the away game in our back pockets, it was reaching fever pitch.

To their great credit the manager and players had remained focused and had followed that marvellous victory at Celtic Park with league wins against Dundee (3-1) and Kilmarnock (2-1). They had also made progress in the Scottish Cup. Hibernian were thumped 4-1 at Easter Road, Peter Weir and Neil Simpson scoring in the first half, and after Gordon Rae had given the home side some hope, Andy Watson and Mark McGhee late on in the second. A Simpson goal just after half-time saw off Dundee in the fourth round at Pittodrie and set Aberdeen up for a trip to Firhill in the last eight. Neale Cooper carved out an early advantage, Thistle equalised on the hour mark, and Peter Weir bent in a delicious long-range free-kick to secure a 2-1 success.

One quarter-final taken care of; now for the next one.

The wait had been interminable and I recall arriving early that evening to discover everyone else had the same idea. Queues were already stretching back up into Merkland Road and it took some considerable time to get inside. I was with a few friends and my dad. He rarely went to matches any more, but by cobbling together our

125

vouchers – handed out when you attended league matches – we were able to procure enough tickets to get him in. We selected our seats in the South Stand, level with the eighteen-yard box at the Paddock End and about two thirds up, and I remember thinking it was fitting Dad should be sitting alongside me for what we hoped would be one of the most memorable nights in our club's history.

In a stirring and confident column in the match programme Alex Ferguson made it clear "Aberdeen will not be overawed by the occasion . . . and can enjoy a result that will reflect further credit on the club." Alex McLeish was all too well aware of the fervour ahead of the match, but remembers the manager trying to keep the build-up as simple as possible for the players.

"The one message I remember from Sir Alex was 'you just need to win this game', he kept making the point that all we had to do was score one more goal than them, and that kept us focused. Don't worry about away goals, don't let anything else fill your heads, just win the game."

The first goal of the tie came ten minutes after kick-off. McLeish was harshly penalised for a foul on Dieter Hoeness, Paul Brietner rolled the ball a few yards and Klaus Augenthaler skipped round Black and unleashed a rising twenty-three-yard shot past Jim Leighton's left hand, just inside the post. Pittodrie, momentarily, fell silent.

It took the players a little time to regroup, it also took the fans some time to find their voices again, but gradually the Dons got back into the game, equalising seven minutes before the interval. Mark McGhee sent in a looping cross from the right and Eric Black strained his neck muscles to keep the ball in play at the back post. Augenthaler seemed certain to clear, but decided not to play it first-time, and Neil Simpson came steaming in to force the ball home in front of a euphoric Beach End.

"I don't know why Augenthaler took a touch, but that split-second was just enough for me to get something on the ball and knock it into the net. That was an incredible night, that was the one I felt spring-boarded us into the elite."

Despite having got back on level terms there was much hard work still to be done and the task became even harder on the hour mark when the Germans regained their advantage. Wolfgang Dremmler sent in a cross, Hoeness flicked it on and a stretching Alex McLeish headed the ball out, only for Hans Pflugler to volley the clearance spectacularly into the bottom corner from the edge of the box. Two-one to Munich.

McLeish recalls the manager's reaction afterwards when, in an attempt to keep his players feet on the ground, he was still offering critical advice.

"It wasn't as if it had been a hard-driven cross that I could get any real distance on, I only just managed to get my head to it and clear it as far as I could and the boy lashed it in at the near post past Jim Leighton, but Sir Alex told me afterwards that he thought I hadn't been at my best. It was his way of keeping me on my toes and making me determined to do better next time."

The Dons hit back and very nearly equalised when Peter Weir cut inside on to his right foot and found the head of Eric Black with an inch-perfect cross. The German keeper Manfred Muller dived to grab the point-blank range effort and clutched the ball safely on the line. A sense of resignation began to set in, this was surely going to be another case of glorious Scottish failure, at least that was how I was feeling at the time. Across the other side of the stadium, Alex Ferguson had different ideas. Stuart Kennedy – much to the full-back's disgust – was replaced by John McMaster and Hewitt took over from Simpson.

Time was running out fast when Grobe was adjudged to have handled a through ball just outside his own box and the Dons were awarded perhaps the most important free-kick in the club's history. Gordon Strachan placed the ball, and after a couple of false starts, he and John McMaster both ran towards it, almost bumping into each other, and stepped over the ball. On the German television coverage of the match the commentator actually starts laughing, while our very own Jock Brown's description was, "Well, they couldn't agree

127

obviously . . ." In an instant, Strachan wheeled and chipped the ball towards the back post where McLeish sent a powerful header beyond Muller.

As the first replay was broadcast Brown had changed his tune. "If you think Strachan and McMaster were in any kind of confusion, you're wrong, they were doing this quite deliberately . . . it was a carefully rehearsed piece of tomfoolery" was now his take on events!

McMaster says Gordon Strachan quickly took charge as the pair discussed how to approach the free-kick.

"The wee man says Spammer [John's nickname from childhood] we're going to eff this up. We'd tried it before in matches but hadn't scored and we'd tried different routines and hadn't scored, but that time it worked. Fergie had dreamed it up and we'd been practising it in training all season."

Strachan remains convinced that moment was instrumental in turning the whole match round.

"I believe that cost two goals. They were so confused and annoyed with themselves the Germans that the third goal came from that, they were still shouting and swearing at each other when we got it."

Alex McLeish says the timing was crucial.

"We knew the clock was against us and we needed to get back in quickly or Bayern, with all their experience, would just shut us out. The rehearsed free-kick worked a treat, Bayern were caught out, two-two and it was bedlam. But that wasn't enough and you could see the reaction of John Hewitt, he was in the net getting the ball and running up to the centre-spot, which just emphasised the type of spirit Sir Alex had in that dressing room."

Bayern were rattled. The Germans kicked off but soon lost possession and John McMaster strode forward, still in his own half, and pinged a delightful sixty-yard angled ball deep into the Munich penalty area. Eric Black climbed majestically and powered a header goalwards, Muller clawed it out and down into the mud and

Hewitt, alert as ever, pushed the ball between the keeper's legs and over the line. He had been on the pitch all of two minutes!

Having played his part in the equaliser, McMaster had also made a key contribution to the winning goal.

"They lost possession from the kick-off because they were in disarray and the ball came out to me wide left and I hit a diagonal into the box to Eric and Johnny scores. Even now, sitting here talking about it, I'm getting a spine-tingling feeling."

Those in the stadium witnessed all that unfold; those watching on television caught only the conclusion as the cameras were still showing a close-up of McLeish while McMaster was delivering perhaps the best long-range pass of his career. The only indication they got was seeing Alex's head turn and eyes widen as he followed the trajectory of the ball. The TV director cut back just in time to see Black get his head on it.

"You could sense the whole atmosphere change inside the stadium as soon as we equalised. When John hit that great ball I just concentrated on getting on the end of it. When I got the flick I wasn't sure if it was going in, I couldn't really follow the flight of the ball, and when the keeper knocked it down I just remember it seemed to take forever before Johnny put it in. That was the most incredible atmosphere I ever experienced in my whole career . . . grown men crying all around . . . that will stay with me forever."

John Hewitt has scored the two most important goals in the history of the club. The winner in Gothenburg tops the list, but the third against Bayern is not far behind.

"What the goalie should have done was flip it over for a corner but he parried it down and we were always told by Fergie and Archie to follow things in, so as soon as Eric headed it I was off and if you watch it back you'll see that I got there slightly too early and as the ball breaks, my right foot starts to slip. I only just managed to stretch out my left leg and hook my foot round the ball and fortunately for me it went straight through the goalie's legs."

It was a breathtaking minute both on the pitch and in the stands and after the initial explosion of noise the stadium rocked with the loudest rendition of 'Here We Go . . .' I have ever heard. In the midst of it all I turned to hug my old man, only to find him standing on his seat letting rip. He was never the most emotional of men, old-school in that respect, but in that moment he had lost all inhibition and was carried away on that tidal wave of celebration just like the rest of us.

Bayern simply could not comprehend what had happened, and although they tried to salvage the tie, they rarely threatened in that final quarter of an hour. Karl-Heinz Rummenigge did fashion an opening, finding himself free in the Aberdeen box, but Willie Miller appeared as if from nowhere to block his effort, and that was it.

On the final whistle Alex Ferguson embraced Teddy Scott then danced along the touchline as a mini pitch invasion broke out. As we screamed our lungs out, still unable to take in what had unfolded before our very eyes, the deflated Germans trooped from the pitch as heroes in red hugged and punched the air.

For those players it was a never to be forgotten occasion, perhaps even more dramatic and exciting than the victory over Real Madrid two months later. Neil Simpson says he still gets shivers down his spine thinking about it.

"When you're on the pitch you're sort of taken away from the atmosphere, cut off from it at times, and I sometimes wish now I'd been a supporter and could have watched it all happening. You can't soak it all in because you're so focused on playing the game. I was substituted, luckily enough because that meant Johnny Hewitt could get his goal, so I became more aware of it all then and the atmosphere was amazing that night."

All the players share that sentiment, but perhaps Neale Cooper, in typical fashion, sums it up best.

"It was just . . . a mental night!"

The sixty seconds during which the second and third goals were scored would go down in folklore, the match itself rightly acclaimed as 'Pittodrie's Greatest Night' and Alex McLeish played a central role, both in keeping Munich out and in launching the late comeback.

'Big Eck', as he would become known, arrived in the north-east in the summer of 1978 as a raw seventeen-year-old, another Glasgow boy swept up in the net cast wide by legendary Dons scout Bobby Calder. When he did sign on it came as a huge relief as he feared he had missed his chance.

"I was a late developer, all my friends from the boys club Glasgow United had gone as 'S' forms to Celtic and Rangers or down to England. I was a midfielder in those days, a good team player, but not one to necessarily catch the eye, a bit of a 'steady Eddie'. But I then took a bit of a stretch and got moved to centre-back playing for the under-17s in the Paisley and District League. There was a wee story in the *Evening Times* saying that Aberdeen were watching Glasgow United defender Alex McLeish, and I remember cutting it out of the paper and keeping it, but I never heard anything else. We had a really successful season and were playing in a Cup final at the end of it and it was only then I discovered they had been watching me all the way through and I thought, 'Wow, that's thorough!' "

The man who had initially recommended Alex was John McNab from Greenock, one of Calder's network of trusted spies, and his prompting convinced then Dons boss Ally MacLeod to go and watch the youngster in person. MacLeod attended that final, but might have missed out on McLeish after being fed wrong information.

"He was mistakenly told by Bobby, who hadn't seen me either, that it was the guy from the team we were playing that he should be watching. Luckily Ally said afterwards that quite frankly he liked the look of me and it was only then the mix-up was discovered! The following week Bobby came to the house laden with his traditional chocolates for my mum and a £1 signing-on fee for my wee brother who was only seven at the time, but he needn't have bothered as I just couldn't wait to sign on the dotted line. That summer I went up on the train from Glasgow Queen Street with nine other young hopefuls, among them a certain Jim Leighton!"

The management at the time decided Alex was not quite ready to be thrown into reserve football, then the domain of battle-hardened pros, and instead farmed him out to local junior side Lewis United for eight months, toughening and fattening-up the lanky teenager to better prepare him for life in the professional game.

MacLeod left to take over the Scotland job in the summer of '77 and it was his replacement, Billy McNeill, who was to give McLeish an unexpected call-up to the first team six months later after regular choices Bobby Glennie and Willie Garner ignored their manager's curfew.

"Big Willie and Bobby chose to celebrate Hogmanay against Billy's orders and when I turned up for training on January 1st he was waiting for me in the foyer at Pittodrie. I says 'Happy New Year, boss' and he says 'Happy New Year yourself big man, you're playing tomorrow afternoon!' I was stunned, but he was great, took me out to the training and talked me through it. Trying to get to sleep that night wasn't easy as it was my big chance, the start of my dream coming true."

It was to be a perfect debut for young Alex. His future long-time defensive partner Willie Miller guided him through the ninety minutes, the pair securing the first of countless clean-sheets for the Dons, and Ian Fleming scored with ten minutes remaining to clinch a 1-0 victory over Dundee United.

It was to be the one and only game Alex would play for McNeill, as the Celtic legend was lured back to Glasgow at the end of that season. Next in the Pittodrie managerial hot-seat would be one Alex Ferguson and under the former St Mirren boss McLeish saw his career take off and scale unimaginable heights.

That was to come. In the meantime, the teenager had a big decision to make. At his father's insistence Alex had continued his studies – in fact my first personal contact with him was when

Just 9.6 seconds gone, and John Hewitt scores the quickest goal in Scottish Cup history against Motherwell at Fir Park, January 1982

The Aberdeen squad celebrating at Gleneagles Hotel after beating Rangers 4-1 to win the

Stuart Kennedy completes the 7-0 rout of Sion in the ECWC preliminary round, the popular full-back's only European goal for the club

© SNS GROUP

© SNS GROUP

Hewitt earns the Dons a narrow advantage to take to Albania in the home leg against DinamoTirana

Ticket stub for the return leg in Poland

KOLEJOWY KLUB SPORTOWY
„LECH - POZNAŃ"

ZAPRASZA

NA MECZ RUNDY PZP W PIŁCE NOŻNEJ

Aberdeen F.C.
Szkocja : „KKS LECH" Poznań

KTÓRY ODBĘDZIE SIĘ

O GODZ. NA STADIONIE KKS „LECH"

LOŻA HONOROWA - RZĄD

Peter Weir heads the second goal in the 2-0 win over Lech Poznán at Pittodri

Eric Black scored a hat-trick in a famous Dons win at Celtic Park in February 1983, watched by Bayern Munich spies

Alex McLeish's header evades Bayern keeper Muller to draw Aberdeen level on 'Pittodrie's Greatest Night'

Sixty seconds later John Hewitt hooks home the winner to stun the German giants and send the Dons into the semi-finals of a European competition for the first time in the club's history

The jubilant Dons players acknowledge the fans after a night of breathtaking drama against Bayern

The celebrations continue in the dressing room afterwards

Mark McGhee flicks home Dougie Bell's cross to put the Dons 3-0 up against Waterschei in the semi-final first leg at Pittodrie

McGhee completes the 5-1 rout of the Belgians after a frantic goalmouth scramble

© MIRRORPIX.COM

Eric Black spins to
hook the Dons 1-0
ahead against Real
Madrid in the Cup
Winners' Cup
Final in Gothenburg

The most famous goal in
the history of Aberdeen
Football Club. John
Hewitt dives to head
the winner in the Ullevi
Stadium . . . then wheels
away in celebration

© GETTY IMAGES

© PA IMAGES

ECWC Final match
programme

'The Gothenburg Greats'

Tens of thousands of fans lined the streets of Aberdeen eager to get a sight of the trophy as the open-topped bus slowly made its way to Pittodrie

The first time is always the sweetest – Alex Ferguson's crowning glory as Dons boss

Carnage on the *St Clair* as the ferry makes its way back home from Gothenburg

Mark McGhee at Aberdeen Harbour waiting for fans to arrive home on the *St Clair*

THE SUPER CUP

Aberdeen

Hamburg

SUPER CUP
SECOND LEG
AT PITTODRIE
20.12.1983

THE DON
MATCHDAY
MAGAZINE
SOUVENIR
EDITION
PRICE 50p

Goalscorers Neil Simpson and Mark McGhee with the
Super Cup 'trophy'

Match programme for the
Super Cup Final second
leg against Hamburg

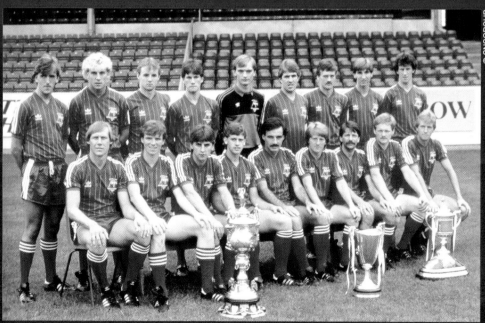

The Dons squad line up for the 1983-84 season with the Cup Winners' Cup trophy flanked by
the Aberdeenshire Cup and the Scottish Cup

we were both night class students at the Aberdeen College of Commerce – and was also getting practical work with a local accountancy firm.

"I'd gone to a school in Paisley for fifth and sixth year to do more Highers and I had enough qualifications to think about doing a degree. My dad, who'd worked in the shipyards all his days, was keen for me to do that, and I'd applied to a few banks for a job when Aberdeen stepped in and offered me the chance to do what I really wanted to do. Ally [MacLeod] was great and they got the college sorted out and I was going three nights a week to get extra qualifications for the accountancy foundation course I was doing. By the weekend I was knackered!"

In addition to the studies, training and playing for Lewis United, McLeish worked every afternoon in the offices of Atholl Scott in the city's west end.

"Atholl was the boss, a great guy and leader, and there was a bloke in there called Norman Gray who is still my accountant to this day and a close pal. He taught me the rudiments of accountancy and auditing books. It was different obviously from training and playing with the boys every day, but I got a lot out of it."

That was to continue for a year or so, but Alex had a decision to make and it was all but taken out of his hands when MacLeod called him back from the juniors and offered him a new, improved deal with the club.

"My dad wanted me to be a footballer of course, but he still had his doubts. I told him I felt I had to immerse myself in the football and he backed me all the way and told me to make the most of it. Billy came and went and I was still on the same deal and then when Sir Alex arrived he gave me a four-year contract and that was it settled."

McLeish was to get his chance early in Ferguson's first season, the call-up coming after Garner broke his leg in a Cup Winners Cup tie in Bulgaria against Marek Dimitrov. He got a run of eleven matches initially and by the end of that campaign had featured in almost thirty first-team fixtures, a number of them not at centre-half, but in the boiler-room of the team.

"I had played most of my schooldays in midfield, which helped, and I always remember a game against Celtic where Fergie had told me just to be a scarf round Tommy Burns' neck, to keep it simple, and it was easy because I had such talented players around me. I just did basic stuff, matched runs and supported the forward players, and it was a good chance for me to get into the team and make my way."

Alex had to quickly find his feet at a club where there was no shortage of strong characters, old pros who had seen and done it all before, and the teenager was keen to soak up as much as he could from the experienced players.

"Guys like Drew Jarvie and Jocky Scott – when I first went I was playing in the reserves with Jocky – taught me a lot. Even Davie Robb was there when I first arrived and what a man he was! As a kid I'm looking around and thinking 'what a world this is' . . . you really had to adapt very quickly."

And he did.

Ferguson's second season was to be epoch-making and young Alex missed just one Premier Division match as the Dons were crowned Scottish champions for only the second time in the club's history, clinching the title by humbling Hibernian at their home ground.

"When we won that first title at Easter Road I was wondering what all the fuss was about because I had just come out of boys' football where I'd been used to winning cups for five years. I was looking around and grown men were crying. The likes of Bobby Clark, who was a mentor of mine and gave me great advice, was in tears. I didn't understand it then; looking back, of course I understand why these guys were so emotional, but at the time it just seemed a natural progression for me."

It was so much more than that. It was Alex Ferguson and his players laying down a marker to the Old Firm, warning Celtic and

Rangers that after all their years of domination there was a new kid on the block, a team ready to take them on head-to-head and, more often than not during that glorious period, come out on top.

"I remember one game against Rangers when the sparks were flying and the banter was flying around the pitch, Gordon Smith saying to me, 'Aye, but you can't beat us when it matters.' When we began to prove ourselves, to win things, I could turn round to him and say, 'Big yin, we can now' and that was really important in the development of that team."

Making the big breakthrough was one thing, following it up was another, and that is why McLeish sees the back-to-back title wins in '83-84 and '84-85 as even more significant than the first one.

"I remember going on a trip with Scotland to the eastern bloc just after the 1980 title win and Danny McGrain saying to me that the next season would be even harder, and he was right. The next two championship wins were very important for that Aberdeen team because it put them right up there with the greats."

The game of football was a very different beast back then and clubs did little to capitalise on commercial possibilities. That was, particularly in the case of the Dons, perhaps a fatal flaw.

"Aberdeen was a rich city, maybe if we'd harnessed the North Sea oil industry and tapped into the financial possibilities we'd have done even more in that decade both at home and abroad. Ten years later I think everyone was looking back and regretting we hadn't taken advantage of that and turned Aberdeen into a real power."

Alex McLeish was the last of the Gothenburg greats to leave Aberdeen, his playing career stretching a full and uninterrupted seventeen years, but he did have a few opportunities to quit earlier, and very nearly joined his old boss at Old Trafford. Ferguson had initially agreed not to plunder Pittodrie for the Dons top stars, but the gloves came off when he judged the club to have reneged on a possible move for young striker Joe Miller.

"He did eventually come back for me when he felt Aberdeen had broken the pact by selling Joe to Celtic, he thought that was the end of the arrangement and we were all fair game. We toyed with things for a month or so and Ian Porterfield [Ferguson's replacement] was open about it and said he wouldn't deny me the chance of a crack in England, but the clubs couldn't agree on a fee."

Ferguson was prepared to pay up to £750,000 but the Aberdeen board were holding out for around £1.25 million and the United boss told Alex he could not go that high because of the player's age. He was then twenty-eight years old.

"Not long after that he signed Gary Pallister for £2.3 million, but he was much younger and seen as an investment for the future. I was disappointed of course, but I wasn't desperate to leave Aberdeen and I didn't have anyone driving me on, no agent pushing me. My dad had died around that time, the family were settled in the city, and I was always of the mind that what will be, will be. I was quite relaxed about the whole thing."

There were other possibilities too. He spoke to Paris St Germain and the French side were keen but already had their quota of three foreign players. They were at that time trying to offload Ray Wilkins – which they eventually did, to Rangers – but not in time for big Alex to sign on. There was even stronger interest from Newcastle United – I remember in my days as a cub reporter at Northsound Radio going round to Alex's house to conduct what seemed certain to be his last interview as a Dons player – but that too fell through when Jim Smith was sacked and Ossie Ardiles took over.

Alex had told me previously that he had heard that the Rangers scouts had been questioned over how they had let him slip through the net as a teenager, but what he had never previously let slip was that he very nearly signed for Celtic in the mid to late-1980s. Twice!

"Davie Hay came in for me one summer, he was really keen to get me, and I met up with him, but it just didn't feel right for me and I knocked that one back. By the next year [1987] I was ready to go, Billy McNeill was in charge by then, and I kind of threw big hints but he never bit, and a few months later after a game in which we'd beaten Celtic he said, 'I should have come in for you, I thought you were done, thought your legs had gone.'"

Throughout his career, Alex was always closely linked with his defensive partner Willie Miller; he talks of a telepathic relationship between the pair, the older man initially helping the less experienced McLeish through matches. After a few years it was much more of an equal partnership with both men assured and comfortable in their respective roles; Alex going in where it hurt – he has the scars to prove that – and Willie reading the game with an expert eye and mopping up everything behind. Their partnership was the bedrock for much that was achieved.

Willie and Alex first played together in that New Year fixture against Dundee United in January 1978 and their swansong as an Aberdeen duo came in a 1-1 draw at Dens Park on November 4th, 1989, future Don Billy Dodds denying them a farewell clean-sheet with a last minute equaliser for Dundee. Eleven days later the pair were in tandem for Scotland in a crucial World Cup qualifier against Norway and when Willie was stretchered from the field after 66 minutes it signalled the end of an era. Miller would play three more matches for the club, but Alex featured in none of them. With their figurehead sidelined the team needed a leader and McLeish grabbed the responsibility with such relish that by the end of the campaign he was voted Player of the Year by the Scottish Football Writers' Association.

"That was a really proud moment because I always felt I was kind of overlooked for those awards because I was a steady rather than spectacular type of player, so that was good recognition of my consistency and, after what happened to Willie, my leadership. I did get nominated a few times for the players' award, and John MacDonald [of Rangers] beat me in a recount for Young Player of the Year in 1980, so it was great to win one."

The award was announced at the start of Cup Final week in May 1990 and while he was delighted Alex also feared, in a typically Scottish way, that having had the good news, bad was bound to follow.

"I was in the papers all week, big smiles with my Player of the Year trophy and I just hoped that wasn't going to come back to bite me . . ."

The game against Celtic had ended in a 0-0 draw and the Scottish Cup Final would, for the first time ever, be decided by a penalty shoot-out. It was 4-4 after the initial phase, so went to sudden-death with Joe Miller giving Celtic the advantage.

"Jocky Scott asked who wanted to take the sixth penalty and I said because I was the captain I'd do it. He said only to take it if I was going to score, and I admitted I wasn't that confident, but that I would do it. He turned round looking for another volunteer, but no-one was pushing themselves forward, so he told me to go ahead."

There were 60,493 fans inside the national stadium that Saturday afternoon, the tension palpable, and the pressure on those taking the penalties almost unbearable.

"I remember walking from the halfway line up to the penalty spot and the crowd were just like cardboard cut-outs and it was just noise, a wall of noise. I was looking around, but I couldn't pick out faces, it was all a blur, and everything going through my head was negative, 'Aye this is where you get egg on your face, big yin, you've been in the papers with your trophy, smiling, doing interviews, now it's pay-back time' and I had to try and steady myself, concentrate and pick my spot, take a good long run-up and hit it accurately."

Which is exactly what he did. Alex's penalty was one of the better ones in what was a nervy shoot-out, as he side-footed it high past Pat Bonner's left hand. As he turned away there was no great joyous celebration, simply a bow of the head and both fists clenched upwards.

"After that the players went to jelly, they were kicking the ground and the ball was trundling in, even big Brian's winner was a trundler. Theo [Snelders] had a brilliant left-hand save from Anton Rogan and gave Brian Irvine the chance and I think by this time Packy was thinking 'I'm going to soar away to my left, or my right' which he did, and the big man just put it down the middle to win the Cup for us."

It would earn Alex the twelfth and last winner's medal of his playing career, and for the only time – with Willie Miller out injured – it was he who led the team up those Hampden steps, he who accepted the trophy.

"That was great. I did feel for Willie, but to be the skipper myself that day was the pinnacle. I hadn't given it much of a thought before, but I knew I couldn't nick Willie's iconic pose with the trophy, so I just gave it the old favourite, a kiss on the Cup and then lifted it with both hands to show the Aberdeen fans. A really special memory, that one."

So too had been his first win in the Scottish Cup back in 1982, another of those landmark occasions for the club as they destroyed Rangers 4-1 in extra-time, Alex having scored the Dons' opener with a marvellous goal, crafted earlier that week during training in Cruden Bay.

"Sir Alex always took us away for a golf and training day in the build-up to the Cup Final, and I curled one into the net during practice, and then during the big game it was even more spectacular, the ball just fell perfectly to me in a similar position and I could see right away that big Jim Stewart wasn't getting to it. It curled into the top corner, the most cultured and technical goal I ever scored."

On top of his success-laden club career and later triumphs as a manager, Alex McLeish also enjoyed many highs as a Scotland player. His total of seventy-seven international caps has only been bettered by long-time team-mate Jim Leighton and Kenny Dalglish. The Celtic and Liverpool great was in the side when Alex made his Scotland debut, in midfield, in a European Championship qualifier against Portugal at Hampden. The Scots won 4-1 and McLeish was a fixture in the squad for the next eleven years.

"When I got that first cap, I thought, 'If that's the only one I get I'll be a proud man', but to go on and win another seventy-six was a real achievement. I played in three World Cup Finals – a great honour when you consider how tough it is to qualify these days. At the time it was hard to appreciate what we'd done and obviously expectation levels grow. We were expected to get out of the group and into the next phase, we never did, and that was a great disappointment for me given the talent we had. Maybe we just didn't believe in ourselves enough."

Alex played for Scotland against all the world's greatest nations, he twice featured against Brazil, in 1982 and 1990, and he was in the last Scotland side to win a match in the Finals, the 2-1 success against Sweden at Italia 90, but overshadowing all those is a game played at Wembley on May 23rd, 1981.

"Peter Withe was the top scorer in England that season, he went on to score the winning goal for Aston Villa in the European Cup Final, and he was up front alongside Trevor Francis [Francis replaced Tony Woodcock at half-time] and Willie and I marshalled them really well that day. It was a good England team, Bryan Robson, Steve Coppell, Glenn Hoddle and Ray Wilkins all played, and we won it with a penalty, Stevie Archibald got brought down in the box and Robbo [John Robertson] despatched it and that was . . ." he pauses and his face breaks out into a huge grin ". . . quite amazing to win at Wembley with all the Scots fans there. That was a real, big highlight."

Younger fans might not appreciate just what an occasion Wembley weekend was in those days. London was invaded by tens of thousands of tartan-clad Scots, and no matter what the English FA tried – a ticket ban was even introduced after the on-field celebrations in 1977 – Scottish supporters got in somehow and outnumbered their counterparts from down south. As the Lions Rampant and Cross of St Andrews flags were waved all around the stadium the players wandered around the pitch soaking up the atmosphere and revelling in a famous victory. Little wonder McLeish holds that match in such high regard.

Alex finally left Pittodrie in the summer of 1994, the last of the 'Gothenburg Greats' to depart, at least in a playing sense. I was at

Turnberry covering the Open Golf Championship for BBC Radio Scotland when the news came through and it was devastating. I had always assumed he would end his career at Pittodrie before moving into coaching and perhaps even management with the Dons. The realisation that he was no longer part of the club really was hard to digest. While there is to this day an emotional attachment between all those guys and the Aberdeen fans, big Alex is perhaps held in the highest regard, partly down to the fact that he is a genuinely decent fellow, partly perhaps because he has always spoken so warmly about his time in the north-east. He believes it may also be down to the fact that he knew when to quit.

"I probably got out at the right time. Willie offered me a new contract, but I knew I was slowing up. My experience would probably have helped Aberdeen that troubled season, remember Jim Bett and Robert Connor also left, and I'm sure we'd have kept them away from the relegation play-offs. What if we'd finished fifth or sixth? That wouldn't have been good enough for the fans and they'd have been criticising us saying we were too old . . . but they finished bottom, and everyone was saying they should have kept us on! I just thought it was a good time to leave."

There had been interest from a couple of English Second Division sides, Tranmere Rovers being one of them, but then out of the blue came the offer to join Motherwell as player-manager and McLeish was off to Fir Park.

"I discussed it with Sir Alex and he told me it was a great opportunity. It wasn't easy to cut the ties after eighteen years, but I didn't want to sour my relationship with the Aberdeen fans, and Motherwell was a good club for me. In the end I only played five matches, but I did a full season with the reserves after that. It would have been demanding combining the roles, but I had good players I could rely on in that defence – John Philliben, Chris McCart and Brian Martin formed a back three – and they deserved their places anyway. Tommy McLean had built that team and I just told them to go out and play, it wasn't broken so there was no need to fix it. I tried to do a 'Fergie' or a 'Jim McLean' on a couple of occasions, manufacturing situations to try to get at the boys, but then I realised there was no need, and for a couple of years everyone was going about with smiles on their faces until that squad disintegrated."

As part of the break-up Rob McKinnon and Paul Lambert were among the first 'Bosmans', leaving Motherwell on frees to join FC Twente and Borussia Dortmund respectively.

"They were a right good team and we played some really good football, but once the big names started going it was always going to be hard to maintain it. I wasn't in any hurry to leave Motherwell, but then the opportunity arose . . ."

That was in February 1998 when Alex was lured to Easter Road by a struggling Hibernian to replace the sacked Jim Duffy. At the time Hibs were five points adrift of Dunfermline at the foot of the Premier Division with twelve games to go, but they never at any stage looked like pulling off an escape, and were relegated to the First Division. Motherwell finished second bottom that season, four points clear of the Edinburgh side.

"There was still enough time, but the rot had set in, there was a malaise throughout the club, and we went down. I still felt it was a good opportunity for me as a manager to rebuild them."

Season 1998-99 saw the newly formed Scottish Premier League kick-off without Hibernian who instead began their campaign in the second tier with a 2-1 home defeat to Stranraer! That result focused minds in the Easter Road boardroom and Alex was given the finances to construct a squad filled with top players. John Hughes was captain of a team which included the likes of Stuart Lovell, Mixu Paatelainen, Russell Latapy and former Champions League winner, and future Hibs legend, Franck Sauzée.

"I had told them the squad we had wasn't good enough to win the First Division without a struggle and that Stranraer result was a real shocker, they'd just come up from the Second Division. We were just too ordinary and we needed players who would make a difference . . . and we got them! I'm a student of world football and I knew all about Franck, and when I heard he was having troubles at Montpellier and that he might be interested in coming, I knew he would be a great signing. We played three at the back with him in the middle and he just strolled it. Latapy I did a bit of diligence on, spoke to Bobby Robson who'd had him at Sporting Lisbon, and he told me he was a great player but would need spurred on at times. I played him in a trial match at Forfar, it was a horrible night, and as soon as I saw him out there not wearing gloves I knew he had a bit of character, and he was brilliant, a genius. And of course big Mixu was streetwise and led the line superbly."

Hibernian went on to romp the First Division by twenty-three points that season, losing only two more matches along the way, and they took to life back up in the top flight without missing a beat, comfortably finishing mid-table in the first campaign and in their highest-ever SPL placing, third, in 2000-01. They had even led the table in the first few months, starting the season with an impressive six-match unbeaten run, and they finished it with a first Scottish Cup Final appearance in more than two decades, losing out to a Henrik Larsson-inspired Celtic.

"That was a really fast-flowing Hibs team, we so nearly beat AEK Athens in Europe, we beat Hearts 6-2 at Easter Road when Mixu scored a hat-trick and 3-1 at Tynecastle where Franck got one with a fantastic strike from the edge of the box. The Cup Final was a disappointment, I always go into every game thinking I can win it, but with Larsson and Co it was just too much for us on the day and they were easy winners in the end. It was my first Final as a manager and it was a good experience."

McLeish's third full season was not quite so enjoyable and Hibs were in the bottom half of the newly expanded SPL, and in the middle of what would eventually become a run of eighteen league matches without a win, when Rangers announced that Dick Advocaat was moving upstairs and that Alex would be their new manager. He took charge of Hibernian one last time twenty-four hours later, somewhat bizarrely in a 1-1 draw against his new team, and then set to work on one of Scottish football's most demanding jobs at Ibrox. Sauzée replaced him as Easter Road boss, while Motherwell denied Alex a Rangers debut win, scoring with a controversial last-minute penalty to secure a 2-2 draw at Fir Park.

It would be over four months before McLeish would taste domestic defeat as Rangers manager and along the way he lifted his first trophy, the League Cup, having beaten Celtic in the semi-final, and only narrowly lost out to Feyenoord in the UEFA Cup. The league championship was a lost cause – Celtic had been eleven points clear when he had taken over – but by the end of that first season McLeish and his team also had the Scottish Cup in the trophy cabinet, thanks to a 3-2 win over their bitter rivals in the final.

Alex was going head-to-head with one of the most experienced managers in the game, Martin O'Neill, and over the piece he came out on top. In the three and a half years they matched up, McLeish won seven major trophies to O'Neill's four, including the treble in 2002-03 when he became only the eighth manager in Scottish football history to secure the domestic clean sweep.

"I've taken on some challenges in my career and the Rangers one was a no-brainer. The hardest part was trying to rebuild while there was no money. At the start it was a little bit surreal because at that time I thought the Old Firm would only be going for exotic managers and that I'd maybe have to go to England, work my way up from the Second Division to get the chance of a bigger club, so to get the call from Rangers was amazing. They had been struggling a bit, but when I looked at the players, the quality in that team, I reckoned it must just be a confidence thing. Dick felt he just couldn't do it anymore, but he was genuinely helpful through until the end of that season. It was a bit daunting looking around that dressing room and seeing the likes of Ronald de Boer, Artur Numan and Lorenzo Amoruso, but they worked with me, we got them smiling again, and it all began to take off. Beating Celtic in that League Cup semi was a big moment."

McLeish won two SPL titles with Rangers, both in nerve-wracking final-day shoot-outs. The first, in 2003, came after Celtic had hauled them in by reeling off win after win in the closing few weeks, and on Sunday, May 25th it took a 6-1 thrashing of Dunfermline, while their rivals were winning 4-0 (and missing a penalty) at Kilmarnock, to clinch the title by one goal.

"I knew exactly what was going on. Chick Young was behind me and he was telling me, all the punters were telling me. At one point a big roar went up and Barry Ferguson, who was running with the ball, stopped and turned to the dugout to ask what had happened. What a day that was . . . emotional . . . dramatic . . . one of the greatest days in Rangers' history."

My recollection of that day would be of an afternoon when the lead in the title race swung back and fore, but in checking my old notebooks I discovered that there was only a ten-minute spell in the second half, when Celtic were 3-0 up and Rangers 3-1 up, that McLeish's men had been knocked off top spot. It was nevertheless breathtakingly exciting and an astonishing way for Alex to win his first SPL title as a manager. His second was to be almost as dramatic.

Rangers were five points behind with four games remaining when Celtic, surprisingly, lost at home to Hibernian. McLeish's side won at Pittodrie the following day and by the season's climax on Sunday, May 22nd still trailed by two points. When Chris Sutton put Celtic in front in the first half at Motherwell the situation looked bleak, and even though Nacho Novo gave Rangers the lead at Easter Road, with just two minutes remaining the title was heading to Celtic Park when out of the blue Scott McDonald spun on the edge of the box and lobbed the ball goalwards. I was at Fir Park that afternoon and it was as if time had stood still. Everyone seemed to freeze as the ball arced over Rab Douglas and when it hit the back of the net the Celtic players and management crumpled. Some forty miles away there was an eruption of noise.

"That was a real spine-tingler. When I heard the Rangers fans roaring that day it was like nothing I've ever experienced. I'd told the boys just to make sure we won our game and I had to reassure them at half-time, hammering home the message that two goals would change it. Wee Nacho got the goal for us and then all of a sudden there was that huge roar . . ." He paused and chuckled, ". . . you couldn't make that up."

The scores as they stood saw Rangers top, just, and a 1-0 defeat suited Hibernian as that would tie up third place for them (ahead of Aberdeen on goal difference). There followed a bizarre few minutes.

"We had the ball at the back and you just never know, a player might slip or something, and I was a bit worried, but Hibs weren't interested. Even when we lost the ball they would just pump it upfield but not chase it. Then came that second roar (McDonald grabbed a second in stoppage-time to make it 2-1 Motherwell) and it was just bedlam!"

Rangers won the SPL title by a single point.

The following season Alex became the first, and so far only, Rangers manager to guide the club into the knockout stages of the Champions League, losing out only on away goals after 2-2 and 1-1 draws with Villareal.

"That was a tough season as we'd brought in a number of free transfers and the likes of Ferguson, Amoruso and Arveladze had left and Ronald de Boer was injured. We did manage a strong end to the league campaign and we played a tactical game in Europe, shutting up shop on occasion, and getting some good results, beating Porto at home and drawing away, and then drawing at home to Inter Milan to qualify. I thought we played a brilliant game out in Villareal taking the lead there [through Peter Lovenkrands]. They equalised and then my life flashed before my eyes when the ball went across and Kris Boyd was on the end of it – exactly the person you would want in that situation – but he never quite got the connection right and we were out. Had he scored we'd have gone on to play Arsenal."

By then it had already been announced McLeish would be departing at the end of the season, Paul Le Guen named as his ill-fated replacement, and for the first time since he left school big Alex was out of work. His unemployment lasted seven months. By then the Frenchman had been sacked and Walter Smith had quit as national team boss to return to Ibrox. McLeish was the new manager of Scotland.

"I wasn't sure if I was ready to come back, but when the SFA approached me I thought that was the perfect job. I wondered if it might have been too early for me, but when they offered it I jumped at it and I knew Walter had done a good job and that it would only need a bit of tweaking."

The Scots were involved in qualifying for Euro 2008 and topped a tough group when McLeish took over. He won five out of six to keep us right in contention, including a stunning 1-0 win over France in the Parc des Princes.

"That was another special, special moment. I'd told the boys beforehand that one day a Scotland team would win in Paris and asked them why it couldn't be them. And we did it! It was nerve-wracking, incredible, but what a night that was and it kept us in the race to qualify."

The crunch match came at home to Italy on the evening of Saturday, November 17th. A win and we would qualify for a major championship finals for the first time in a decade. The country was in a ferment, the excitement at fever-pitch, all of which was punctured by an early Italian goal. Barry Ferguson equalised and we pressed for a winner but, in a typically Scottish way, it all went horribly wrong right at the death.

"We totally controlled the midfield that day against the likes of Pirlo, the boys were magnificent, and Kenny Miller came on and so nearly scored, and then James McFadden might have done it but didn't quite get his foot round the ball and it went past with the goalie stranded. In the final minute the referee gave one of the most ridiculous decisions I've ever seen [Manuel Gonzalez awarded the Italians a highly dubious free-kick from which Panucci headed the Italian winner] and the dream was over."

Later that year Alex attended the draw for the 2010 World Cup qualifiers, but within days he had quit and was appointed as manager of Birmingham City. There followed a four year rollercoaster during which his team was relegated twice, promoted, enjoyed their highest ever Premier League finish (ninth) and won the Carling Cup with victory over Arsenal.

"We couldn't quite keep them up that first year but got them back up at the first time of asking. It was never an easy job and winning at Wembley was sensational. Arsenal were firm favourites but we had a certain game plan, played to our strengths, and I thought deserved the victory. Unfortunately we had a horrific run of injuries after that and I was never able to field that eleven again for the rest of the season, Obafemi Martins and Nikola Zigic missed the rest of the campaign, and the relegation certainly goes down as a black mark."

In the summer of 2011 McLeish stunned the football world by crossing the great Birmingham divide, his appointment sparking furious protest from Aston Villa fans.

"I certainly took on a huge challenge and I knew a lot of people would be against my appointment. I knew rebuilding wouldn't be easy, as Villa had lost a number of senior players, but I thought if we kept the first team intact we'd be ok. Unfortunately we weren't able to do that and it was really tough because the Barclays Premier League is unforgiving."

It was a season bedevilled by serious injury problems and with a host of experienced players on the sidelines Alex was forced to turn to his youth side, pitching in kids who clearly were not ready for a sustained run in the team. Villa, apparently safe halfway through, tumbled down the table and it took a 1-1 draw with Spurs in the penultimate league fixture to finally shake off the spectre of relegation.

Sadly for Alex, that was not enough for club owner Randy Lerner nor the supporters who did not want him there in the first place, and after just eleven months in charge, McLeish was sacked.

Of all the 'Gothenburg Greats' Alex McLeish has been perhaps the most high-profile in the years since, he has certainly been the most decorated, amassing a total of twenty-one trophies during his time as player and manager in addition to managing his country, playing in the World Cup Finals and his haul of international caps. It all began of course with that wonderful Aberdeen team and three decades on he still looks back with a mixture of wonderment and pride.

"It just seems like a fairy-tale, doesn't it? If I sat down with some of the big-name players I've worked with in England and told them about '83 I don't think they'd believe it . . . it just sounds like fantasy . . . but it's not fantasy, it's reality . . . and we did it."

CHAPTER NINE

GORDON STRACHAN

ABERDEEN 5-1 WATERSCHEI
Wednesday April 6th, 1983

After the incredible drama and the emotional drain of that stunning night against Bayern there was perhaps a certain inevitability about the reaction which followed. For a number of years Alex Ferguson had been able to keep his players focused and on track, ensuring they maintained high levels of performance and concentration, but this was a whole new ball game and in the next few weeks Aberdeen's title challenge all but evaporated.

Three days after 'Pittodrie's Greatest Night' Dundee United returned and took the points with a 2-1 victory. Ralph Milne scored a quick-fire double in the first half, lashing vicious shots past Jim Leighton, and was later sent off for kicking Alex McLeish, but the only response the Dons could muster was a Strachan penalty. That same day Celtic lost 2-1 at Dens Park, leaving the three title challengers separated by a single point. Aberdeen were still top and maintained that position the following weekend, but only just. Andy Ritchie (who else?) had Morton in front at Cappielow, but Andy Watson scrambled an equaliser with seven minutes remaining and Eric Black fired in a stoppage time winner. Celtic had drawn their game in hand against Rangers the previous midweek and were held 1-1 by St Mirren on the Saturday, while Dundee United drew 3-3 at home to Hibernian.

On the first Saturday in April Celtic cruised to a 3-0 win over Motherwell and Dundee United disposed of Rangers 3-1 at

Tannadice. On an unseasonably cold afternoon at Pittodrie with snow driving in across the pitch a much-weakened St Mirren side beat the Dons 1-0. Gordon Strachan missed a penalty, shooting wide just before the interval, and Saints won it when substitute John McEachran picked up on a lucky deflection off McLeish to fire past Leighton. With seven league games remaining Celtic had 45 points, United and the Dons 44.

On Wednesday April 6th, 1983 Celtic and Dundee United met in a rearranged fixture at Parkhead, the home team winning 2-0 with second half goals from McGarvey and Nicholas, to open up a three point advantage, but Aberdeen had other things on their mind that night.

The semi-final draw for the Cup Winners Cup had been kind. The Dons might have been pitched in against Real Madrid or the then powerful Austria Vienna; instead they had been paired with un-known Belgians Waterschei.

In the Fergie column in 'The Don' that night the manager made it clear all eyes were on Pittodrie, "The size of the task, as we represent the surviving British club side in any European competition, will not be underestimated . . . I feel sure that it is going to be another magic night for Aberdeen . . . while we all intend to keep our feet firmly on the ground, it is a situation that keeps an invisible tingle among the routines of the day-to-day life in Aberdeen."

That tingle was certainly in evidence as another capacity crowd assembled on what was a glorious evening, and arriving a little later than planned, we were unable to get a seat in the main body of the South Stand, positioning ourselves instead at the rear of the un-covered corner near what I still think of as 'The Paddock'. It was to be a perfect spot to enjoy one of the most sensational openings to a major football match I have ever witnessed.

With less than two minutes on the clock Doug Rougvie dispos-sessed striker Eddy Voordeckers ten yards inside his own half and Dougie Bell collected the ball. Neither he, nor we, knew it at the time, but Dougie was about to have his finest ninety minutes in an

Aberdeen shirt and he set off on a jinking run deep into the Waterschei penalty area. With the visiting defence in disarray he flicked the ball with the outside of his right foot and Eric Black ran it into the net at the far post. 1-0 the Dons and bedlam in the stands. I actually had to be rescued as I fell backwards over my seat and very nearly tumbled down the hill behind. We were still celebrating the opener when, beyond our wildest dreams, it became 2-0. Again Bell was involved, linking up with Peter Weir, and when the winger harried Pier Janssen into making a poor pass on the edge of his own box Neil Simpson latched on to it gleefully, evaded three desperate challenges, and shot the ball low past an unconvincing Podelko. Four minutes into the two-legged tie and we already seemed set for the Final!

Captain Willie Miller, surveying the damage being done in front of him, could barely believe what he was seeing.

"It was Dougie Bell's night. They just couldn't handle him, he was unleashed upon them, did his mazy dribbles and tore them to ribbons really."

John McMaster was an unused substitute that night, but despite being left on the bench, recalls it as an extraordinary occasion.

"What a night, what a night! When the first goal went in Archie Knox turned to me and said, 'Book the tickets', when the second goes in he says, 'Get the plane booked'. After the third it's, 'Book the hotel', and so it went on. Simmy was an animal that night, he just kept running and running, it was just phenomenal."

It was to be another hour before there was any more scoring, and again the Dons hit their opposition with the old one-two. Bell wriggled clear on the left and drove in a cross to the near post, which Mark McGhee stabbed in from close range with his right foot and just two minutes later Mark turned provider, curling over a cross which Peter Weir met perfectly with a flying header to direct the ball beyond the keeper and into the corner of the net.

Waterschei pulled one back soon after, Voordeckers' cross headed inside Jim Leighton's near post by Icelandic international striker

Lars Gudmundsson, but Aberdeen were not finished yet and they wrapped up a 5-1 success with a goal which said much about McGhee's determination to find the net.

John Hewitt passed into the box for Gordon Strachan to set up Mark with a precise cutback. His first and second efforts were both blocked at close range and keeper Podelko managed to claw the ball away, but only as far as Miller. The skipper's effort was again cleared off the line by defender Tony Bialousz, but McGhee, lying on the ground one yard out, managed to spin and finally hook the ball into the net.

It was a comedy cuts ending to an astonishing night.

Gordon Strachan might not have scored against the Belgians, but he was, as ever, involved in almost every attacking move. He was enjoying an incredible period, a time when his game was at its peak and which produced astonishing levels of consistency, both in terms of his overall contribution and his goal-scoring. Having netted twenty in 1981-82, he matched that total in the Gothenburg season and added a further nineteen in the following campaign. Fifty-nine goals in 146 starts over three years; remarkable statistics for a wide midfielder, and testament to his skills and determination, particularly given that his Pittodrie career might have been over before it had properly begun.

Signed from Dundee in November 1977 by Billy McNeill in a swap plus cash deal which saw the Dens Park team pick up around £50,000 plus Jim Shirra, the wee man certainly took time to make the transition.

"At Dundee I just thought it was the norm that you went to the pub on a Thursday afternoon after you got your wages, I think it was about eleven quid, and it was the one time in the week you had money in your pocket. The rest of the time you had nothing. There were four of us shared a bedroom and we literally had no heating on a Tuesday and Wednesday. But it was all about setting standards; on the pitch it was fine, we had guys like Dougie Houston to show us the way, but off the pitch there was no-one to set standards for the young lads. Looking back you think, 'Whoa, could have blown it there', but I was lucky in that I kept training, going back in the afternoons, and I had that base fitness that kept me going."

When the chance came to move up the north-east coast, Gordon did not hesitate.

"It was an opportunity to earn twenty-five quid a week more and I couldn't miss it."

The amounts of money involved back then would stagger some of today's high-earning superstars, especially those operating at the levels Strachan would eventually arrive at. He was given a £2,000 signing-on fee, but quickly realised the sums were not going to add up when he began looking for a house in the city. The same size of property as he had owned in Dundee was fifty percent dearer in Aberdeen and it was outwith his budget.

"I was looking at new houses and the guy asked if I wanted central heating. I asked how much and he said five hundred pounds. Na! He asked if I wanted a garage and I said no need, I don't have a car. I had to go to Billy McNeill and say, 'I can't afford to live here' and eventually Aberdeen helped me out and I bought a smaller house."

Those behind-the-scenes problems may well have contributed to Gordon's failure to shine early on, and unaware of his troubles, the fans began to get on his back. I even recall one fan regularly bemoaning the fact that we had let Jim Shirra go and replaced him with 'this rubbish'. McNeill might also have been having second thoughts, and has joked since that Gordon 'stitched him up', saving his best form for when Alex Ferguson took over.

"I was useless, absolutely useless, and it gets worse because you feel you're letting the guy who signed you down, and he would get angry with me. You lose confidence and it snowballed. When you heard the team being read out over the Tannoy and my name was mentioned the crowd would be going, 'Boooo', when they saw the ball being passed to me it would be the same. But I dealt with it myself, it was a test of character. When it was all going so wrong

Tony Collins tapped me up asking if I would be interested in going to Bristol City, but I thought, no, I'm not leaving here until I prove I'm a good player. Once I've done that, then I'll leave."

Even when Ferguson took over the next season Strachan still struggled initially. The manager tried him in a number of roles, none of which proved successful, until one day it suddenly clicked.

"I discovered a role for myself really. I was standing out on the wing and I decided just to go and float about, see if I can get on the ball. I just thought if I'm going to go down, I'll do it on my own terms. From then it just seemed to click. Things were better off the park too, we had a child then, Gavin – does that help make you better? I don't know."

What certainly seems to have been a driving force was a sense of insecurity, a fear of losing what he had and an utter determination to prove himself time after time.

"I always felt everyone was better than me. No matter who I was playing against, or who was in the reserve team wanting my place, I felt they might be better than me. I worried about that and used that. At Pittodrie it was Dom Sullivan, I always wanted to be better than Dom."

I had taken the train down to the Midlands and Gordon had met me for a bowl of soup and a cup of tea. Of the Gothenburg legends he was among those I knew less well, our paths having rarely crossed despite his time as Celtic manager, and I was surprised to hear him admit to what I took as a lack of self-belief, his playing style having hardly suggested that. He thought about that for a moment, before putting it down more to his single-mindedness, his absolute need to be the best he possibly could be. Those were the attributes which ultimately drove him to unimagined success with Aberdeen, those, and the fear engendered by his new manager.

"I didn't want to go to Nairn to play in a reserve match if I'd made a mistake, I didn't want to go to the worst supporters' club miles away through the snow. He could frighten you into playing well, particularly those days when if you didn't play you didn't get your bonus, you needed to play, you needed that extra money. The fear then turned to respect. I told him a couple of years ago that we'd got to the point where we'd have run through a brick wall for him – we knew he was a nutcase at times, but we also knew there was a decent bloke there and that if we all stuck together we'd win things. And we enjoyed winning games of fitba', we enjoyed winning things, we enjoyed beating Celtic and Rangers."

As we chatted it was becoming clear to me that this was going to be a very different interview from most of the others conducted for this book. A number of his team-mates had excellent recall for games and incidents, could pinpoint feelings and emotions at specific times, others less so. Gordon could remember next to nothing! What he was instead offering was a general overview, a fascinating insight into that astonishing period at Pittodrie. He paused, then his eyes lit up and he smiled broadly, his affection for that team, those guys, shining brightly.

"I wouldn't have missed it for the world. The raw energy in that dressing room was frightening. The raw energy from the players, the manager, the assistant manager . . . honestly, if you could have turned that into electricity you could have powered the whole of the north of Scotland. It was frightening at times, it was exhilarating, it was just incredible."

Was it then, the best dressing room he was ever in?

"Oh, I've been really lucky. I think of the players at Leeds . . . Manchester United was a fantastic dressing room, Bryan Robson and people like that . . . and the lads I've dealt with in management. I still speak to some of the boys from Coventry every week, from Southampton. I speak to Lenny (Neil Lennon) every second week and the lads I was with at Celtic. That's really the legacy for me, I've been involved with some great people, no matter what we've been through. I saw Jim Beglin the other week, he was once going to knock my head off when we were at Leeds, and it wasn't an idle threat! We still laugh about that. They talk today about 'dressing room unrest'. At Pittodrie every Monday morning there would be eight of us wanting to kill Fergie, literally eight of us, but by Tuesday we're laughing and joking about it."

As was to be the case throughout our conversation, he never really answered my question, instead he had me enthralled by his recollections, his genuine enthusiasm for the game, and more importantly the characters he has encountered during his time in it.

I decided to try to focus, to home in on the specifics. What about the championship winning side of season 1979-80, the first big breakthrough into the winner's circle?

"Stressful! I actually missed a game through stress . . ."

Seeing my eyes widen and my jaw drop, Gordon laughed before admitting . . .

"Actually it was haemorrhoids, but we just put it down as 'couldn't make it'. That was really painful. I didn't have a car so my mate had to pick me up and take me to hospital. I was in agony, the nurse gave me the wrong procedure and I didn't make the next game. I'd been having all sorts of problems with the excitement during the run-in, I was getting an upset stomach, I couldn't eat properly and that must have all been part of it."

Typically, Gordon could not remember which match he had missed, but the record books show the only one he did not feature in during those closing months of the campaign was the final one, a 1-1 draw against Partick Thistle in the midweek after the title had been won at Easter Road. He had clearly dragged himself through those struggles before giving in to the relief of finally seeing off Celtic's challenge.

"We just ground out results at that time. We weren't pretty, and then when the goals started flowing against Hibs we knew we were going to do it. That was brilliant . . ."

Then, just as I awaited his detailed recollections of that beautiful, sunny Saturday afternoon down in Leith, he added: "I can't remember anything about it! I phoned big Alex [McLeish] one day when he was having a bad time, and I'd been in the house myself and I'd watched us playing Real Madrid on ESPN Classic. I said to him, 'We weren't a bad team, were we?' I did not realise we were so good. I can say it now because I'm fifty-five, I wouldn't have said it at the time, but we could play. We were fit, we were faster than what I thought. I had a shot at goal and the goalie blocked it with his legs – I don't remember that, didn't have a clue it had happened. First time I've watched the game since. I knew we could take on anybody and I knew we could beat anybody . . .''

Gordon trailed off and ordered another cuppa, allowing me to try to haul him back to that title-clinching afternoon in the capital. Surely he had some memories of that day?

''I remember going to the bingo at night with my mum and dad at the social club just along from Easter Road . . . and I won at the bingo as well!''

Becoming Scottish champions for just the second time in the club's history was a massive endorsement of everything Alex Ferguson was doing, and must, I suggested to Gordon, have given the players genuine confidence they could build from there.

''We started the next season really well . . .''

Indeed they did, unbeaten in fifteen until a first league defeat of the campaign at the start of December, 1-0 to Morton (who else?), the goal scorer Andy Ritchie (him again!), but at the end of that month Gordon suffered an injury that was to rule him out until the following August.

''I tore my stomach muscle against Dundee United and I said to Alex I was in agony, but he just told me to get on with it, that I'd be fine. In the end I was out for eight months, we tried everything, and I only got back after going to Harley Street. Steve Archibald had recommended the guy (Dr Jerry Gilmore) and I was just the second person ever to have that operation. To this day, whenever he's doing ops on people I know he asks them to tell me he's asking for me!''

He returned in time for the start of 1981-82 and began, along with his fellow players, amassing that impressive haul of silverware, supplying us supporters with some of the most thrilling and memorable occasions of our lives, all the way to Gothenburg.

The idea for this book, as I hope you will have realised by now, was to devote each chapter to one of the matches from that ECWC run, interspersing it with a potted life story of one of the stars of that side. For this chapter the star was to be Gordon, but when I asked him about the 5-1 win over Waterschei, he typically – after correctly recalling impressive performances on the night by Simpson and Bell – took me down an unexpected route.

"Despite the big win there was always that wee thing at the back of your mind . . . I remember when we were playing Arges Pitesti (UEFA Cup '81-82) and we were three-nil up from the first leg but two-nil down at half-time in the second game. All hell let loose – that's a good after-dinner story that one, takes about half an hour to tell – and Fergie tried to get me, but knocked over the tea urn, then he threw some cups trying to get me, but hit Willie and Alex instead and I made the mistake of laughing. It was just madness! That one ended 2-2 [Gordon scored the first Dons goal from the penalty spot], but that's always at the back of your mind. We were fine though."

As already mentioned, the wee man has little specific memories of the night in Gothenburg, but does have very firm views on the team and his colleagues from that time.

"It was Real Madrid, for goodness sake, you can't take that away from us. We beat Real Madrid, we beat Bayern Munich and then we went and beat Hamburg over two legs. I think we were the best team in Europe at that time; we proved it. You hear people talking about legendary players these days . . . that bunch of lads, they're legendary players. A manager keeps his team up in the Premier League for two seasons and he's a legend! When I look at a picture of that group I say 'legendary', but when I see them individually I go, 'That's my mate; there's Dingus [Mark McGhee], he eats too much; there's Willie, he's as bald as a coot; big Alex's getting fat . . .' I still think of them as young men."

A spin-off from the incredible success achieved by that team was the inevitable international call-ups for most of them. Four are proud members of the SFA Hall of Fame: Jim Leighton with 91 caps, Alex McLeish 77, Willie Miller 65 and Gordon 50.

"I'm more pleased for the people round about me. I remember playing against New Zealand at the 1982 World Cup Finals in Spain and standing there before the game and looking around and thinking 'my dad's in the golf club watching this with his mates, my mum will be getting nervous now, my wife Lesley couldn't be there because we'd just had a baby, Craig, hope they're all right, but they'll be happy with this' so I wasn't thinking about what it meant to me, I was thinking about how much it meant to all of them."

Gordon left Aberdeen in the summer of 1984, part of the first wave of the post-Gothenburg exodus and after a wrangle over whether or not he had signed a binding agreement with Cologne, joined Manchester United. Was he overawed by the prospect of playing for such a huge club?

"No. I won all the player of the year awards that first season, I scored twenty goals. The next again year I started even better, and then I dislocated my shoulder. Bobby Charlton said to me, 'You're my favourite player' and I'll remember that forever. I enjoyed it there, I loved it, then after Ron (Atkinson) left and Alex came in I was looking forward to that, but I think I'd got to the point where I'd heard it all before, I'd heard all his motivational speeches and they didn't work any more, and I didn't work for him."

Ferguson was happy to let him go and in 1989 Strachan made the short journey to Leeds and an incredible new chapter in his career, helped in no small way by his relationship with his manager at Elland Road, Howard Wilkinson.

"That was fantastic. I had someone there who completely trusted me, who believed in me. It was a partnership and I'm still best of mates with him now."

That Leeds team won promotion from the old Second Division in his first season, finished fourth in the next campaign in the top tier and then won the last English Championship before the Premier League breakaway, edging out Manchester United in a thrilling climax.

"People think that when we did it I must have thought, 'great, one up on Alex' but I never gave it a second's thought, I was so involved enjoying what I was doing."

A number of that Gothenburg squad, Jim Leighton, Eric Black and Mark McGhee included, saw their relationships with Alex Ferguson break down. There are different reasons, some real, some perhaps imagined, why that has happened; it may partly be down to the fact that with strong characters in play, friction is an inevitability. Certainly by that stage Gordon and his former boss no longer enjoyed the close bond they once had.

"It wasn't great, but I was fine with that, we had periods like that at Aberdeen. He wrote me a letter saying that he had released me too early, one or two other things, but it did seem to get worse after we won that league. Lesley used to go and help with Alex's kids, so I found it very strange . . . and then he wrote in his book about me . . . [Ferguson claimed in his 1999 autobiography *Managing My Life* that Gordon 'could not be trusted an inch'] and I never said anything for years because I felt I had nothing to reproach myself over. When he won his first European Cup I called to congratulate him and couldn't get him so left a message with his secretary asking her to tell him I was delighted for him and his family, but she never passed it on, which was unfortunate . . . It's a shame, it's a shame . . . but we're respectful now, I'll meet him and say, 'Hi, how you doing' and that's fine, he's got his mates and I've got my mates."

As his playing career wound down Gordon moved to Coventry to take his first serious steps into coaching, but found it was not so easy to hang his boots up permanently.

"Ron Atkinson and the players asked me to start playing again – I tried my best not to, but I played and we stayed up. Then I played the next again year and we stayed up. Then I packed in again, and we got in trouble again and they said, 'Do us a favour, start playing again' and I did. Then I was the manager and Gary McAllister asked me to start playing again, and by the end I'd helped keep them up six years, two just as a player and four as a coach. In the seventh year

I failed, but the reason was Gary and Robbie Keane had left and we couldn't replace them."

Coventry were not in deep relegation trouble every season Gordon was there, it just seemed that way, but on the occasions they were down at the bottom he would try anything to turn the team's fortunes around.

"I tried a Fergie-type speech once and I walked out the door after and I was like Basil Fawlty, jumping up and down and going 'what have I done? that's not me' and I realised that in management you have to be whatever you are."

Eventually Strachan was sacked, but he was only out of the game for a short while before the call came from Southampton.

"They were second-bottom, but we ended up in Europe, full-houses, eighth in the league. And the Cup Final in 2003, that was just a fantastic day. (Arsenal won 1-0 at the Millennium Stadium in Cardiff) The only bad bit was telling people they weren't going to be playing in it and I had to go round their rooms at eight o'clock in the morning the day before. There were two in particular, the goal-keeper (Paul Jones, who eventually came on to replace the injured Antti Niemi), who handled it all right, and Fabrice Fernandes, who literally couldn't run at training, it was just too much for him, but I had to do that. I wasn't going to tell them in front of everybody, that wouldn't have been right. But that was a fantastic spell, in fact I've still got my house down there."

Less than a year after that FA Cup Final Gordon had quit the club, deciding he wanted to spend more time with his family. He was out of full-time football for sixteen months and when he returned it could hardly have been in a more high-profile and demanding position, replacing Martin O'Neill as manager of Celtic. His reign there got off to the worst possible start, a 5-0 humiliation at the hands of Artmedia Bratislava in a Champions League qualifier. The *Scottish Daily Record* headline blared: CELTIC'S EURO SHAME while the Bratislava daily paper *OE Sport* went with ARTMEDIA BEAT CELTIC TO THEIR KNEES. I was presenting Radio

Scotland's coverage from the Glasgow studio while my colleague Chick Young was gearing himself up, in his role as pitch-side reporter, for one of the more difficult interviews of his professional life.

"It was stiflingly hot that night and the sweat was running down my face, partly from the heat and partly from apprehension! I've had to stick the microphone in the face of plenty managers during my time, sometimes after horrendous and embarrassing results, but that one was right up there. I've known Gordon a long time and felt I knew best how to approach him, but I wasn't prepared for the look on his face that night. I swear he'd aged a decade in those ninety minutes."

Listening to that interview and watching the television pictures which were being beamed back, Strachan seemed, understandably, to be in a state of shock.

"That's when you need the support. The owner [Dermot Desmond] came in afterwards and said, 'You're my manager, I'll tell you when you're useless and you'll only see me when you're in trouble' and I needed that that night. You know, when I'm gone, on my gravestone it's going to read: 'At least this is still better than that night in Bratislava!'"

The following Saturday Strachan watched his new side throw away a 3-1 lead to trail 4-3 at Motherwell, only for Craig Beattie to snatch a stoppage-time equaliser, and later in the season there was further embarrassment as minnows Clyde knocked Celtic out of the Scottish Cup on what was a horrific debut for Roy Keane.

But by the end of 2005-06, Gordon's team had won both the League Cup and the SPL title, the first of three-in-a-row championship wins, a feat previously achieved at the club only by Willie Maley and Jock Stein. His four years at Celtic Park was the most high-pressure and high-profile spell of his career.

"Unless you've had a shot at it don't even think about trying to compare it to anything else. It took me about three weeks to realise that it was like no other job. I had to change my training completely.

At Coventry and Southampton you're working on how to stop other teams, while at Celtic I had to spend ninety percent of the time trying to work out how to break down other team's systems. That was a learning curve and it helps to make you a more rounded coach."

At the time Gordon spoke about how difficult it was to try to lead a normal life, he talked about how his privacy was invaded on occasion, and there was the famous quote in relation to radio phone-in shows about complaining supporters who 'wear tracksuits, devil dog at their side, can of Kestrel in their hand'. But the highs certainly outweighed the lows and it is a period Strachan treasures.

"Oh wonderful, wonderful. Every day now, everywhere I go, I meet a Celtic supporter and they say well done, and it's like an energy that keeps you going."

Gordon told me he gets the same feedback from Manchester United fans, from Coventry and Leeds fans, but probably not from supporters of the team he went on to manage after leaving Celtic, Middlesbrough.

"It wasn't a good move. I wasn't right for them and they weren't right for me. Fifty percent of it was my fault. I signed players that I never did enough homework on . . . incidentally Kris Boyd's not one of them, he's a good kid you know, he's strong, trains like a beast and he loves football . . . but then I look back and I think [Kevin] Thomson got injured first game, so did [Willo] Flood and Rhys Williams and [Gary] O'Neil, and I wonder maybe if I'd just held on a wee while it might have been different. Scott McDonald got injured for a while as well . . . but, it's just one of those things. I do think I was unfortunate, but I'm all right with it."

He paused again, reflected, then added: "I wouldn't like to think that I would just be remembered for that time as a coach, because I'm quite proud of the people I've worked with and how I get on with them. Chris Sutton said a few things in his book, but that's one in fifteen years in management. Look at Roy Keane, he was

164

great when he came, great with the kids, miserable with everyone else . . . but great with the kids, good with the coaching staff, he was terrific. I still speak to him now, one of the few that still speak to him!"

Gordon was laughing as he delivered that sentence, and one thing he could never be accused of lacking is a sense of humour. His particular brand of comedy might not be to everyone's taste, but it led to him becoming something of an internet sensation and a quick search throws up some classics:

Reporter: There goes your unbeaten run, can you take it?
GS: No, I'm going to crumble like a wreck. I'll go home, become an alcoholic and maybe jump off a bridge. Umm, I think I can take it, yeah.

Reporter: There's no negative vibes, or negative feelings here?
GS: Apart from yourself, we're all quite positive round here. I'm going to whack you over the head with a big stick – down, negative man, down.

Reporter: Gordon, do you think James Beattie deserves to be in the England squad?
GS: I don't care, I'm Scottish.
Reporter: If you were English?
GS: I'd top myself.

Reporter: You must be delighted with the result?
GS: You're spot on! You can read me like a book.

It was a tactic he also used as a player.

"It was my only weapon, because I never kicked anybody. I got kicked, but never kicked back. That was my weapon. I certainly got kicked a few times because of my sense of humour . . . sometimes I deserved it!"

But it was as a manager that his witty, at times sarcastic, retorts really came to the public consciousness.

"It's a protection mechanism when people are close to annoying me. I'm like any small, ginger-haired Scotsman, I don't like getting bullied, so instead of going 'fuck off', I'll say something that might throw them off. When I go to meet my maker, if sarcasm is the only problem I've had then I should be all right. I've no' cheated the game in any way, I've no' taken bungs, I've no' harmed anybody. There's two or three things I'm no' proud of, but I've always said sorry to someone I've upset. There are parameters during interviews though. It's like the boy John Barnes with Jim McLean [my BBC colleague John was punched during a television interview in 2000 by then Dundee United Chairman McLean for asking a question about the future of United manager Alex Smith, having been told beforehand not to do so], you have to have that trust, that respect."

Those attributes are core to everything Gordon holds dear. In his career first as a player then as manager Strachan collected in excess of twenty major team or individual honours and as my hour in his company drew to a close I suggested that those successes perhaps meant less to him than the relationships he had forged along the way.

"It's the people, honestly, I just love the people in the game. I'm such a lucky man to have dealt with these characters. People I can rely on and who know they can rely on me. I look back now and I laugh. I can laugh non-stop just thinking about the people and the stories. I've been on the end of some bollockings, some press coverage, but it doesn't bother me one little bit . . . I don't like getting criticised, nobody does, I hate it, because I always worked hard to get things right, as a player, as a manager . . . but it's the people who help you through that. That time at Celtic, I never laughed as much in all of my life as I did with Tommy Burns, you wouldn't believe some of the things Tommy used to get up to! I was in tears at times . . . I gauge it by how much I laugh, that makes it worth it. The dark nights, the lows; I don't really remember them

... but I do remember the fun I've had. Wouldn't have missed it for the world."

And with that my time was up. We headed back up into Leamington High Street where Gordon was due to meet his wife Lesley in a camera shop, photography being one of his major hobbies and something he has used as a release from the demands of professional life. As the three of us wandered back down to the railway station chatting about family life, the weather and the difficulties of motorway driving in this country, I almost had to pinch myself. It seemed a million years away from those Saturday afternoons or Wednesday evenings when I would be in the stands and the wee man with the ginger hair would be carving through opposition defences, creating chances, scoring goals and lighting up the dullest of games. It was a further reminder of just how lucky I have been in my career, how lucky I have been to get to know my heroes, to have the access I have had, to sit with them and listen to their reminiscences about that never-to-be-forgotten time.

That night in April 1983 as I watched the Dons demolish Water-schei I was still working in the Clydesdale Bank, and the very thought of spending time with those guys, chatting to them, inter-viewing them, would never have crossed my mind. What was uppermost in my thoughts back then was how on earth I was going to get to Gothenburg.

The next morning I put my case to my boss, Ken McLauchlin. Fortunately Ken was a good guy, a committed football fan and a close friend of Archie Knox. He was happy for me to book holidays for the second week in May and equally helpful after I explained that I could not actually afford to go to Sweden. At that time, aged twenty-two, I had never been abroad – this was going to be a special trip in so many ways. Eventually we agreed that I should apply for a Personal Loan of £400 to cover the purchase of new carpets and a fridge! It took me two years to repay that loan, but every month when the standing order came out of my account it was another little reminder of that memorable, magical occasion.

The only problem was going to be getting there. One of the main reasons I had never previously left these shores was that I was utterly terrified of flying, so when it emerged that P&O were going to be putting on a ferry, the *St Clair*, to take fans to Sweden, all my prayers were answered. Or so I thought. But by the time I got through on the booking line the ship was full!

CHAPTER TEN

JOHN MCMASTER

Aberdeen had two matches to play between those games against Waterschei, a Premier Division encounter with Rangers at Ibrox and the Scottish Cup semi-final against Celtic at Hampden the following weekend.

The league game began well enough, Alex McLeish marking his 250th appearance for the club with a powerful header past towering home keeper Peter McCloy, but Ian Redford diverted in a cross for the equaliser, and with the Dons pouring forward time after time, Rangers counter-attacked to damaging effect, future Don Jim Bett snatching the winner with just four minutes remaining. While Aberdeen were losing, their championship rivals were winning away from home, Celtic 3-0 at Hibernian and Dundee United 2-1 at St Mirren. The Glasgow side had now opened up a three point advantage over United with just five games left, the Dons, having played one match fewer, were five adrift.

The semi was a scrappy and bad-tempered affair with neither side willing to give anything away. It was not a huge surprise that a single goal was enough to separate the sides, Peter Weir heading beyond Pat Bonner from close range midway through the second half.

Aberdeen might have been toiling in the title race, but they had reached a second successive Scottish Cup Final, and of course there was the little matter of seeing out their European tie in Belgium to reach the Cup Winners Cup Final.

Incredibly, despite the 5-1 first leg stroll, there were still a few concerns floating around. Neil Simpson recalls one fan who was taking nothing for granted.

"There was an old guy, Orlando, who used to come along to all the training sessions, and the morning after the first leg we all came running out and saw him standing there shaking his head and saying in a really downbeat fashion, 'You know that away goal could be crucial.' Fantastic, eh?"

Mind you, Orlando was not alone. Even experienced keeper Jim Leighton was a little worried.

"We were probably as uptight before that game in Belgium as we were for the Final itself just because we'd won the first leg 5-1; can you imagine how we'd have felt if we'd then gone out?"

Willie Miller, took a somewhat different approach.

"You see what I had to deal with?" he told me, laughing, "Negative players all around me! How could he possibly think that? We did all the business here, so that made the second game quite an enjoyable trip because there was no way we were going to lose anything like five goals, not with our defence!"

Willie was to be proved right, but the Dons did suffer their only defeat of the whole campaign in Genk, Alex McLeish getting caught out and standing on the ball, his slip allowing Voordeckers to beat Leighton. By then there was just seventeen minutes left and even big Jim, pessimist though he is, knew they were going to be fine.

"In the dressing room afterwards you could have heard a pin drop. Folk were coming in with champagne and baskets of strawberries – nobody touched them. We had just reached a European final, but because we'd lost the game nobody was celebrating. Fergie tried to gee us up, but no-one was interested."

There were not many Aberdeen fans at the game as most were already saving up for the trip to Sweden, but one of my old schoolmates, Graham Shand, and a few others from The Hawthorn

Bar had decided they were going to make the trip, perhaps rashly booking before the first leg.

"We went by train and ferry using the young person's railcard to keep the cost down and we just drank and played cards all the way. I remember us upsetting a few straight-laced English commuters on the first part of the journey down to London! Outside the stadium we bumped into Eric Black and Gordon Strachan who were injured; Eric spoke to us, Gordon ignored us! The match itself was instantly forgettable."

Apart from actually qualifying for the Final, the other notable thing that night was a knee injury to Stuart Kennedy which, although none of us knew it at the time, would finish the popular defender's career.

"I'd actually been injured in the Cup semi-final win against Celtic, big Roy Aitken caught me late, and I wasn't 100 percent fit for the game in Belgium, but the manager told me, 'Even fifty percent and with your suit on you still won't break sweat in this one' and that massaged my ego and I played. He'd put in a few of the youngsters, but he wanted to keep his back-four intact. The challenge was innocuous, I caught my studs and the guy ran into me – it wasn't even a foul – and although the knee immediately swelled up I had to carry on for the last thirteen minutes. I couldn't push up though, couldn't play my normal game, and the manager even had a go at me for that in the dressing room afterwards!"

That Aberdeen squad was a mixture of personalities and characters, from the battle-scarred experienced hands like Miller, Kennedy, McLeish, McGhee, Strachan and Rougvie to the likes of Black, Hewitt, Cooper and Simpson, the kids who contributed so much. There were the strong dominant figures and the quieter ones, and one of those was Greenock born John McMaster, the oldest of the bunch, and a player who, at least to those of us on the outside, seemed to just keep his head down and get on with the job. No fuss, no hysteria, just a solid, straightforward and richly talented professional.

He was the first of that group to sign for the Dons, just ahead of Miller and Rougvie, but he had to fight all the way and show great determination and strength to get his career underway at all.

John was born and brought up on the Gibshill scheme in his home town, one of eight children. When he was just four his dad, John senior, drowned in an accident while out fishing with friends, leaving his mum, a canteen lady, to feed and care for John, his brother and their six sisters.

Life was clearly tough, but John recalls his childhood fondly and with a smile on his face. The male influence in his life was his uncle, Andy McKillop, who encouraged his love for football, and it was while playing for Port Glasgow Rovers under-16s with Bobby Street, a friend who also signed for the Dons, that John was spotted by local scout John McNab (who would later send Alex McLeish to Pittodrie) who monitored his progress for a year before alerting senior clubs.

"I had been invited down for a trial at Leicester and they had some players then, the likes of Keith Weller, David Nish and Alan Birchenall. Peter Shilton was also there and he'd have us back for extra training in the afternoons. We'd spend three hours firing balls at him and we'd never score! He was just a beast."

The manager at the time was Jimmy Bloomfield, who according to John 'hated Scots', so he was sent back up the road.

"It was Bobby Calder, the old Aberdeen chief scout, who signed me. He came down to the house, gave me £80 to sign on, £12 a week wages. The manager was Jimmy Bonthrone and knowing my background, he made it up to £100 and £20 a week. I'd been on £4 as an apprentice plumber at the yards, so I was loaded! I remember going into Burton's and putting a deposit down on a suit – that was unheard of, a lad from Gibshill having a suit – and I'd go in and pay it up each week."

He may have been living the dream, but it was not all plain sailing for the youngster, away from home for the first time in his life.

"There were times the Aberdeen fans had me in tears, even in reserve matches. I'd be wearing the number 7 or 11, and they'd be crucifying me, telling me to get down the wing. I was never a winger."

John made a few substitute appearances in 1974-75 and was in and out of the team over the next two seasons without ever looking like holding down a regular place. When he was reintroduced to the first team at the start of the 1977-78 campaign it was in that number eleven shirt, as a replacement for Arthur Graham who had been sold to Leeds. 'Bumper' certainly was a flying winger, and I well remember John getting abuse; I may even have doled some out myself!

It was not until he was handed the number four shirt by Billy McNeill – in a 4-0 thrashing of Rangers at Pittodrie in December '77 – that we punters began to appreciate what he had to offer; the vision, the movement and the extraordinarily accurate range of passing with his left foot.

"Big Billy put me into the centre of the pitch alongside Dom Sullivan, Drew Jarvie and with Ian Scanlon outside me, and it all took off from there."

John credits Billy with having a huge influence on his career and feels his relationship stemmed from their first meeting.

"I was the first player to meet Billy McNeill when he came to the club because I always did extra work in the summer to make a bit of cash. I'd married young, Katie and I were just nineteen, and we needed the money. We'd moved around a bit before buying our first flat in Summerfield. It cost £4,400 and the mortgage was £27 a month. Things were tight, so I asked the Chairman if I could work at the stadium during our ten weeks off. He told me to go see Andy Bowie, the maintenance man, and he had me doing digging, concreting and slabbing, I even learned how to reverse a tractor and trailer! I was there when big Billy arrived and I think he realised that I had a good mentality, that I wanted to get on in life."

Billy stayed at Pittodrie for just the one season and so nearly brought success before being lured back to his first love, Celtic. Twelve months on, John was again helping to maintain Pittodrie and again he was the first player to meet Billy's successor, Alex Ferguson.

"He took us all on to a different level, instilling that competitive edge, but the first thing I remember about Fergie was that he looked so young. Billy was different when he arrived, he had real stature, whereas Fergie looked like a wee boy! It didn't take him long to establish himself, mind you."

He continued in midfield throughout Ferguson's first season in charge, and for most of the following campaign, 1979-80, one which ended with the Championship flag flying at Pittodrie and saw John collect his first winner's medal.

"That was the big one, that was the one that gave us all the self-belief. Now we knew we could win things, that we could beat Celtic and Rangers and Dundee United. That really started it all."

He began the next season at left-back for a few matches, then returned to a midfield berth as the Dons put together an unbeaten run, topping the league after the opening quarter. On October 18th John scored in a 3-2 win at home to St Mirren, a result which set the team up nicely for their next challenge, a somewhat more demanding one.

Aberdeen had begun their European Cup campaign with a narrow aggregate victory over Austria Memphis and had been paired in the second round with the all-conquering English champions, Liverpool. It was a game which had naturally fired the imagination of the supporters and one in which all the players were desperate to test themselves against such quality opposition. For John though, the dream was to turn into a nightmare.

"I picked up the ball near the dugouts and went on a diagonal run towards the Beach End, right up to the corner of the eighteen-yard box, but I overstretched and tried to reach the ball with my right foot, which planted on the ground. Ray Kennedy came in and caught me and I went right over on the knee. It was a terrible tackle, he was about two feet off the ground. The physio, Roland Arnott, came on and told me to run about for ten minutes to see how it was, and actually it felt all right, but within those ten minutes the leg felt heavy and within a week they thought my career was over. I got the scans, by then my leg was hanging like a pendulum, and they discovered I'd severed my medial ligament and the cartilage was done as well. Fortunately the cruciate was ok; otherwise I'd have been finished."

John was out for nine months with that injury, and later in his career missed another nine months after having to have his left ankle rebuilt. Such was the bond he had with his players, Alex Ferguson looked after John during that time, keeping him on full bonuses for a large part of his lay-off, and also involving him in coaching young kids around the country.

Aside from the Kennedy challenge in the Liverpool game, John is often remembered for a match played seven weeks earlier at Ibrox. It was a League Cup third-round first-leg tie which Rangers won 1-0, but the following day's headlines were all about a horrendous challenge by Willie Johnston, who was sent off for stamping on John shortly after coming on as a substitute, the thirteenth red card of the winger's career. There are many reports of the incident available online, most suggesting that Johnston stamped on John's neck, throat or head and that he had to be given the kiss of life on the pitch. More than three decades on, the real story can finally be told.

"I slid in for a challenge on the halfway line and Johnston jumped up and he stood on my chest. I never had to be given the kiss of life, that never happened, my family were all panicking when that story started doing the rounds. There was a lot of damage to my chest, I had all the stud marks, but I certainly never needed the kiss of life. The press asked to speak to me afterwards and I said that I thought it had been a disgraceful challenge, that there had been no need for it, but that was all, and they made an issue out of it. John Greig was Rangers manager at the time, he and Fergie were big pals, and he'd asked him to play it down. By the time Fergie got on the bus and told me not to say anything, I'd already spoken to the reporters and he threatened to fine me! He never did. Johnston was lucky big Doug Rougvie never got a hold of him, he was ready to rip his head off. The thing that bothered me most was that Johnston never apologised to me – he said he had, but he never did. I thought he was a bit of a nutcase!"

In 'Sent Off At Gunpoint', an autobiography published years later, Willie Johnston gave his account of the incident and provided an astonishing reason why it occurred.

"I'm not proud of that. It's no excuse but I thought he was Willie Miller. Willie was a great player but he was a hard man and deserved some of his treatment back. Unfortunately I got the wrong player."

John was patched up and continued playing and even exacted the best kind of revenge in the second leg at Pittodrie three weeks later, crashing home a 25-yard angled strike early in the game to set up a Dons comeback completed by a last minute Gordon Strachan penalty which sent the Ibrox side tumbling out of the competition.

While injuries continued to interrupt his career, John did at least manage long runs in the team at crucial times, allowing him to amass an impressive medal haul. 1983-84 was the last in which he was able to make a serious contribution. In the following season he appeared just once, as a substitute in the penultimate league game at Tynecastle, and he missed almost the entire '85-86 campaign, only returning at the end of March. But his timing was perfect, he featured in every match from there on, culminating in another Scottish Cup Final at Hampden Park.

"I had played really well in the 1-1 draw with Hearts in the league, the first ever Premier Division game that was televised, and afterwards Fergie told me, 'Spammer, you're playing against Hearts in the Cup Final.' That was still three weeks away, but what a lift that gave me! He had prolonged my career by moving me to left-back, but in the Final he played me centre-mid on the strength of how I'd played at Tynecastle that Sunday afternoon. Ten minutes in, big Neil Berry whacked me on the ankle and that was me done really, but I made it through to the second half, did my bit, and was replaced by big Starky."

That was Billy Stark and his diving header from a Weir free-kick added to an earlier John Hewitt double and rounded off a 3-0 triumph, earning John one final piece of silverware, his third Scottish Cup winner's medal.

By then he had been awarded a much deserved testimonial match at which 16,500 fans turned up to pay their own tribute. The Dons took on a Billy McNeill Select boasting star names such as Kenny Dalglish, Alan Hansen, Jesper Olsen and Frank McAvennie, and three of John's former Aberdeen colleagues – Gordon Strachan, Mark McGhee and Doug Rougvie.

John last appeared in a Dons shirt on Wednesday, November 19th, 1986. He played left-back in a 5-0 win over Clydebank at Pittodrie in front of 7,301 fans. After almost a decade and a half in the north-east, more than three hundred games and a sack-full of memories, it was time to go home.

"My sons John, Steven and Scott had all been born in Aberdeen and they found it tough to settle initially with the language and the whole religious thing, and I must admit I didn't find it easy going from a professionally run full-time club to a part-time outfit."

John had joined his home town club Morton as player-coach, and went on to devote considerable time to the club's youth set-up, but his first priority was to help the side back up to the top flight of Scottish football.

"I went down there in the February when Dunfermline were eight or nine points clear and the manager Allan McGraw was still talking about winning the league. And we did! We went on a great run and they blew it. In fact that's another winner's medal I should have, but the boss said, 'you've got enough John, I've given your medal to wee Boagy [Jim Boag] because he's not got one, is that ok?' What could I say?"

Morton were beaten on the final day of the season against Airdrieonians, but Dunfermline also lost, away to Montrose, and the Greenock side were promoted by a single point.

That was a happy start to almost a decade at Cappielow helping McGraw to keep the club afloat by producing and selling on young talent like Alan Mahood, David Hopkin, Derek Lilley, Alex Mathie and Derek McInnes among others.

"We were given the mandate by our Chairman John Wilson to sell a player a year. He was fantastic, he bought the club for peanuts, but took on a huge debt, a quarter of a million pounds back then, and he wasn't going to throw money at it. We must have raised one-and-a-half million through sales and that kept the club going. The scouts were never paid, but they got one percent of any transfer fee, and so did we for doing the coaching. It kept the Chairman happy, he wasn't really a football man but he's local and wanted to do something for the community and every home game he'd be in asking how many scouts were there from the big clubs."

Locating and developing young talent was an important aspect, getting the best deal when selling that talent was perhaps even more important, and in Allan McGraw the club had the right man to do just that.

The first player sold by the new regime was young forward Archie Gourlay in 1988. He had been attracting the attention of Newcastle United but boss Iam McFaul was unsure whether to make the move. McGraw invited Newcastle up to Cappielow to play a friendly and to have another look at the youngster, allowing him to put his master plan into operation.

"Allan had hinted to McFaul that Celtic were also interested in Archie. Billy McNeill and Allan were good friends and he invited Billy along to the game. Celtic weren't interested in Gourlay at all, but McFaul sees big Billy up in the director's box and starts panicking, and then after the game McGraw tells him that he's got Billy waiting in his office and that he's ready to make an offer. That was enough, McFaul did the deal and we got £60,000."

The pair worked well together, John doing the coaching and Allan, in between puffing on his ever present cigar, pulling the strings and doing the deals, but by the latter part of their partnership

178

local businessman Hugh Scott had taken over in the boardroom and his controversial spell in charge led to an acrimonious departure. John was replaced by his friends and former Aberdeen team-mates Billy Stark and Peter Weir, and believing they had stabbed him in the back, broke off all contact with the pair.

"I didn't speak to Starky for two years, didn't speak to Peter for about a year. I regret it now, and we patched up our differences. They said it was all down to Scott, that he had stitched them up too and sworn them to secrecy, but that was a bad time in my life."

John's next move was as a coach helping to run the SFA courses at the Inverclyde National Sports Centre in Largs and during that time Drew Jarvie asked him along to assist two nights a week with youngsters training with Aberdeen at Hamilton, and to do some scouting.

"The money wasn't great, I was getting £200 a week, but at least it kept me involved in the game and I did that for a few years. I got into the insurance business, working with the Co-operative, and I then got involved in doing some agency work, joining Scott Hume through a mutual friend in 2007."

Through that John met Dave Leadbeater, then a scout with Middlesbrough, and he got John on board with the Teesside club, taking him with him when he was appointed as Swansea City's chief scout in summer 2010.

"It suited me fine. I got to pick my games and Swansea were happy with that and you know, despite what people say, there is good talent out there, the Scottish game isn't as bad as some would have you think. The big plus is of course the money here; clubs down south can't believe it when I tell them a player's on £500 a week and that makes it so much more affordable for them. But the talent is there and I can't believe some of the rubbish I hear from other scouts, they shouldn't be in the game, they're just imposters."

Never one to enjoy too much free time, John also signed up to do market research for Ipsos MORI.

"Generally that means going out and doing surveys for Scottish Housing. The addresses are pre-arranged and I go along and ask questions about people's situations and their local area, I also do some consumer stuff and it's great, the hours marry in well with the scouting."

When he left Greenock as a sixteen-year-old, John McMaster could not have imagined what lay ahead, that he would become part of the greatest team ever assembled at Aberdeen Football Club. He admits that the 'legendary' status was something that until quite recently he was uncomfortable with, he felt he was simply doing his job to the best of his ability, but he eventually realised it was something to be proud of and has enjoyed the occasions the old squad has reassembled to celebrate notable anniversaries.

"The boys never change. Some have done magnificently in the years since, some have struggled, but when we get together we're mates, comrades. Stuart Kennedy always used to say after matches, 'Right, let's get off this beach, job done' and that became our saying. All it takes is for him to repeat that and we're all smiling and the stories and memories begin to flow. We've heard them all a hundred times before, but that doesn't matter. It's like time has stood still, it's just brilliant."

CHAPTER ELEVEN

GOTHENBURG

ABERDEEN 2-1 REAL MADRID
Wednesday May 11th, 1983

With Cup Final appearances at the Ullevi Stadium and Hampden Park already secured, Ferguson's team had work to do to try to clinch a second Premier Division championship. They had half a dozen league matches still to play and the first of those was a vital one, at home to pacesetters Celtic, who were still reeling from a potentially damaging home defeat against their other title rivals Dundee United the previous midweek, the pair now separated by a single point. A victory for the Dons, who had two games in hand, would make things very interesting indeed.

The Real Madrid manager Alfredo di Stefano joined the 24,000 fans crammed into Pittodrie that afternoon to watch a tense affair settled by a single, somewhat scrappy goal, Mark McGhee's header finding the net after hitting the post and deflecting off Roy Aitken. Aberdeen had stayed in the hunt, but Dundee United were flying and a 4-0 beating of Kilmarnock saw Jim McLean's men hit the top of the table.

Now the Dons were playing catch up. McGhee, Strachan and Hewitt scored in a 3-0 win at Motherwell the following Wednesday and the latter two were also on target in a 2-0 victory at Dens. That same day Celtic won 5-0 at Kilmarnock and United 4-0 at Morton to further enhance their goal difference advantage over Aberdeen.

With the trip to Gothenburg looming, the Scottish League allowed the club to bring forward the following weekend's fixture to give them almost a week free to prepare. That meant playing Tuesday, Thursday and the first of those games all but killed our title challenge.

The trip to Easter Road ended 0-0 with Hibernian, but the points should have been won, Gordon Strachan missing another crucial penalty midway through the first half when Alan Rough saved his spot-kick.

United now had 52 points, Celtic and Aberdeen both 51. The top two shared identical goals records, 84 for, 34 against, with the Dons well adrift in that respect, but they made inroads in their second midweek fixture against Kilmarnock. The match programme carried the slogan "Good Luck In Gothenburg!" and inside, Alex Ferguson, while concentrating on the conclusion to their league campaign, devoted a little space to the trip to Sweden. "We are all, of course, very much looking forward to the occasion when there will be millions of people seeing Aberdeen for the first time through their television. It will be a tremendous night for every Aberdonian and every Scotsman and I know we shall go into the match confident that we can make it a special and memorable occasion to remember for a long time."

He certainly got that right!

There was something of a party atmosphere in the air that night. I do not think any of us believed winning the title was still a realistic possibility, but this was a last chance for us to wish the team well ahead of the Cup Winners Cup Final, and while we cheered and sang, the players routed their visitors. Strachan and McMaster each scored in the first half and later combined for a superb fourth goal, the full-back's raking angled pass finding his team-mate who scored with ease. That was sandwiched by a rare Ian Angus double which completed the 5-0 rout and Aberdeen topped the table, at least for a few days.

While Ferguson and his men got down to the serious business of getting ready for the trip across the North Sea, United and Celtic were in no mood to slip up and routine wins over Motherwell and

Morton meant the Premier Division season would go to the final day with three teams still in with a chance of lifting the trophy.

And so, with the Dons record 'European Song' (written and produced by Harry Barry, printed on white vinyl and performed by a less than melodious first-team squad) riding high in the charts, it was off to Sweden.

Having missed out on the ferry trip, I had to bite the bullet and accept that the only way I was going to be at the Final was by flying, and so early on the Tuesday morning I found myself climbing the steps and boarding an airplane for the first time in my life, the laughs and jeers of my friends ringing in my ears. It was sheer torture. Every slight bump and wobble had me clutching the seat in front, each mini panic sparking joy among my fellow passengers who had very quickly been alerted to the fact there was a frightened 'virgin' on board. The landing almost finished me, although it was as I recall a pretty smooth one, and although I was already getting worked up by the prospect of the flight back home, I determined to forget about it for the next forty-eight hours and just enjoy the occasion.

While I had been forced to fly, my fellow Dons fans were also en-route using just about every mode of transport imaginable. A school friend, Graham Rhind, had attended all the home games during the CWC run with his dad, and he was determined to be in Gothenburg, it was just a question of how.

"I saw an advert in the *Evening Express* for a bus trip to the Final, so I booked on to that with my girlfriend, now wife, Angela. We were picked up in Union Terrace on the Monday and they had fitted bunk beds in the bus so everyone could have a lie down. We drove down to the south of England, got the hovercraft from Dover to Calais, and then stayed overnight at a hotel in Hamburg, which as you might imagine saw a number of the single guys heading out to sample the city's more exotic delights! We had to catch a ferry from somewhere in Norway, but we were over an hour late, and there was a real fear we were going to miss it – fortunately it was still there, they knew we were coming and had waited for us. The two things I most remember from when we finally got to Gothenburg were the fact that everywhere I turned I bumped into people I knew from back home, and the rain!"

As anyone who was there will remember only too well, it did rain consistently throughout and there were rumours spreading like wildfire that the game might have to be called off. Those fortunately proved to be unfounded and I joined the massed ranks of Aberdeen fans trudging across the city towards our Holy Grail, the Ullevi Stadium. Among us by then were those who had managed to book places on the *St Clair*, and what a voyage that was, as Graham Shand recalls.

"We had met in a pub in Market Street and walked down to the harbour where it was just a sea of red and white. Hundreds had turned out to wave the ferry off, the terminal was heaving, and there were lots of people at the breakwater at Fittie and up on the Torry Battery overlooking the harbour entrance. The bar opened as soon as we left – they were selling out-of-date tins of Tennent's Lager and McEwan's Export, but it was still quite drinkable! P&O had put on a band and there was other entertainment, but we pretty much looked after that ourselves and 'European Song' was repeated over and over again. There were a couple of journalists on board, one of whom was even more pissed than we were, and the sea was pretty rough at times, but probably because we'd drunk so much that hardly bothered us. We just wandered around the city after we'd docked, and then back to the boat to get the coaches out to the stadium and the atmosphere was incredible with everyone singing and Dons fans everywhere."

Adhering to the north-east stereotype, Graham has one other memory of the day of the game.

"Everybody was moaning about how expensive everything was!"

As we fans had been going through our little routines and rituals, so the players had been going through theirs, guided all the way by

Alex Ferguson, who left no stone unturned. He had pulled off a masterstroke by inviting the legendary Jock Stein along for the ride and the Scotland manager was not only a calming and reassuring presence, he also added a certain gravitas. Everyone in football knew who Jock Stein was, even the Real Madrid superstars.

We were all looking for a little omen that the game was going to go our way, and Neale Cooper believes he found one when the official party discovered the name of the hotel they were to be based in; Fars Hatt (if you are not from the north-east the significance might be lost on you, but that's Aberdonian for 'where's that').

"We couldn't believe it, far's 'at? It was definitely a sign!"

Assistant manager Archie Knox says the coaching staff tried in the build-up to keep the players as calm and focused as they possibly could, but that was not always easy given the strong characters on show.

"We had our usual quiz the night before and some of the boys were so competitive. [Stuart] Kennedy was the worst, always arguing, and he and the manager were at each other's throats because they both wanted to win whatever they were doing! The routine was just as normal though; quiz, meal, off to bed, breakfast and a walk in the morning, a meeting after lunch and then he would announce the team. Mind you, for that game we had picked the side well in advance."

The side did not include the unfortunate Kennedy.

"After the injury in Waterschei I knew I wouldn't make it, but didn't want to admit that. I was at Pittodrie one afternoon before we left for Sweden and the manager wanted to test me, making me sprint along the pitch from the tunnel. It was agony and by the time I got back the sweat was lashing off me. I still tried to tell him I'd be ok, but he came close to me – I actually thought he was going to hug me! – and said, 'Stop the charade, I'm putting you on the bench', which was great man-management. He then asked how the knee really was and I told him, 'Where do you want to amputate it?' Me being the sort of character I am, I still thought he might put me on if we were winning the game comfortably, and at one stage he sent me out to warm-up. After ten minutes out in that lashing rain I went back to the bench and heard him telling Johnny Hewitt to get ready to go on. When I asked why he'd bothered to send me out he told me, 'I gave you a run out in front of the fans and let them sing your name' and I really appreciated that."

As those of us lucky enough to be in Sweden gathered inside the stadium, fans back home were reading Fergie's final pre-match words in the *Evening Express*: "We have a marvellous chance to do it and I know each player will give his last ounce of energy to win the cup. We intend to play our normal game – and our normal game is to attack. It would be foolish if we were to suddenly try a pattern that's foreign to our nature." He also spelled out that not one of his players would be in awe of the opposition. "If we go into tonight's match as underdogs we will finish up with memories instead of winners' medals. And we are not in Gothenburg to finish as losers."

Real Madrid kicked off, delighted the influential Uli Stieleke had been passed fit, but it became clear very quickly the pitch was going to cause problems for both sides. The Dons were first to settle and a chipped pass from Gordon Strachan allowed Neil Simpson to run and fire a thirty-yard shot just wide of Augustín's left post. Strachan was involved again seconds later, gathering a poor clearance and crossing for Eric Black. The nineteen-year-old unleashed an acrobatic volley from just inside the penalty area and turned away in frustration as the ball rebounded from the crossbar.

"I couldn't believe it, the keeper couldn't have touched it by more than his fingernail, but that was just enough. If only that had gone in, eh? I might have been remembered," smiles Black all these years later.

Such was the ferocity of the effort, the ball had lost its shape and had to be replaced. Eric's big moment had, however, only been delayed.

In the seventh minute Strachan floated over a corner from the right, and in a much-rehearsed move, Alex McLeish arrived late to head powerfully towards goal. The ball was going just wide, but Madrid full-back Juan José lost his bearings and swung his foot at it, slicing it back towards his own goal. His goalkeeper tried to react, but as the ball held up on the muddy surface Eric got there first and hooked it beyond him from three yards out. The massive, 'YES!' which roared out from the stands must have been heard miles away and as we cavorted and hugged the eleven men on the pitch celebrated joyously. It was the start they had dreamed of.

"I knew what the plan was and it was all about anticipating where the ball might land. It spun nicely off the defender and pretty much landed at my feet. I had to readjust a little, but got there, and managed to generate enough power to hook it past the keeper."

Madrid lost it for a spell after that, conceding a succession of free-kicks, but out of the blue, and totally against the run of play, they found themselves level.

It is a moment goalkeeper Jim Leighton remembers vividly to this day. "Almost as soon as big Alex hit the pass back I knew we were in trouble and the ball got caught in the puddle. I had to come out but Santillana got there just before me and I took him down."

Alex McLeish was at that moment distraught, knowing he had given Madrid a wonderful opportunity to get back into the game.

"I hit it blind, Willie and I hit blind back to Jim a million times because of our telepathy, but on that occasion I didn't carry through the advice I'd given to the other players. I was always big on getting the right studs, checking the surface during the warm-up, and I told the guys they'd need to make sure they lift the ball because of the water on the pitch, but because it was a split-second, because I'd done it so often in the past without hesitation, I got caught out. Needless to say, the gaffer blasted me at half-time and I reacted, and there was a barney and Archie had to get between us. I still had another forty-five minutes to go and I went back out just determined not to let him down, not to make another mistake. After the match when, incredibly, I was in the shower feeling a bit sorry for myself, he came over and told me how proud he was of me, proud that I hadn't crumbled, that I had shown good character. That was great man-management."

Had the game been played these days Jim Leighton would have been sent off for conceding that penalty. Back then he was spared, but was powerless to prevent Juanito scoring from the spot, the striker sending the big keeper the wrong way. There was deflation among the massed ranks of the travelling Dons fans, and I certainly remember fearing the worst. The Spaniards took a huge lift from that and were more lively for a spell, enjoying the bulk of the possession without ever looking like scoring again. Willie Miller had to make an excellent interception on the edge of the box, but that was about it.

And then there was a rumbling in the stands. The chanting began in one corner of our terracing and slowly spread, thousands of north-east voices growing louder, first with the traditional, "Aberdeen, Aberdeen, Aberdeen . . ." and then our more recently adopted anthem, "Here We Go, Here We Go, Here We Go . . ." and we just kept singing, and singing. Watching the DVD while researching this book, I was amazed by just how long and how often our voices could be heard. Yes, the equaliser had stunned us for a few minutes, but we were very quickly back on track and so were the team.

Gordon Strachan was everywhere, involved in everything, dragging his exhausted body all around the park, creating one minute, defending the next. Doug Rougvie rattled the Spanish keeper in an aerial challenge. Simmy and Cooper were snarling and snapping at the feet of Stieleke as he tried to pull the strings for Madrid. As the game moved into the dying embers of the first half the intensity dropped a little prompting Alex Ferguson to race to the touchline to berate his players. Just before the interval Johnny Metgod fired in a free-kick from miles out and it flew harmlessly over Leighton's bar. Half time 1-1.

The interval brought the usual chat among the fans and there was plenty bravado. I was not so sure I seem to recall, but as a fan that was my default setting, in fact it remains so to this day. If I do not allow myself to get too excited, too positive, then I won't have so far to fall when it all goes horribly wrong. I think it was the TV presenter Adrian Chiles who said, "It's the hope that kills you," and he is dead right.

The players re-emerged and all had taken the opportunity to replace their sodden jerseys from the first half. The Spaniards had also changed shorts, some even their socks, and that marvellous white strip seemed to gleam impossibly in the floodlights.

There was some early sparring before the Dons began to pick up the pace. Eight minutes in and Gordon Strachan suddenly broke, played a one-two with Mark McGhee and passed wide to Peter Weir. The winger cut inside and blasted an angled shot, the ball deflecting off Metgod and high over his fellow defender's heads. Strachan met it perfectly on the volley, but his shot was too straight and cannoned back off the keeper's legs (that was the effort Gordon mentioned in Chapter Nine, and which he cannot to this day recall).

Sixty seconds later, Weir won a corner which he himself took, whipping it in at the near post in a move we had all seen countless times before. Eric Black was first to react and directed a downward header just inside Augustin's right post. The keeper pulled off a marvellous save, clawing the ball away, but it bounced back to Weir, who crossed again. This time he found Strachan who drove back into the danger area. Cooper and McGhee threw themselves at the ball, but their efforts were blocked and the relieved keeper finally pounced on it.

High on the terracing we were going crazy. I may have had my doubts at half-time, but it was clear the players had remained positive and confident. They were going for the jugular, turning the screw on an increasingly beleaguered Real Madrid defence.

McLeish rolled the ball back for Neale Cooper but his 25-yard effort was easily saved. And then came arguably the best chance of the entire night.

Sixty-three minutes gone and Peter Weir set off on another of his mazy runs from the halfway line. His cross took a deflection off Stieleke and hung in the air at the back post. If there was anyone in that Aberdeen side you wanted to see appear in such a situation it was Eric Black, and there he was. Surely the Dons were going back in front?

"I knew as soon as I saw the ball coming over that I was going to struggle to get it on target. Because of the deflection it was spinning and spinning, I was going to have to get a lot of power in the header, and even in that split second I realised that if I didn't make perfect contact the ball could go anywhere."

He didn't, and it did. Twenty yards over the crossbar!

Madrid began to get rough, adopting a more physical approach to try to stem the succession of Aberdeen attacks. Isidro kicked out at Doug Rougvie who thought about retaliating, but wisely checked his natural instincts. Bonet chopped down Strachan on the halfway line and incredibly escaped a booking.

With the old favourite "Aberdeen, Aberdeen, Aberdeen . . ." pouring from the terracing Strachan and Weir tried the old mixed-up free-kick routine, but Gordon over-hit the cross. Six minutes left. Rougvie sent in a long ball from the right and Eric tumbled over after heading across goal, inflaming an ankle injury incurred weeks earlier against Celtic in the Scottish Cup semi-final. Then a rare Madrid attack. Juanito chipped the ball into the box, Isidro turned away from John McMaster to open a yard of space, but shot weakly at Leighton.

Immediately the Dons countered. From Jim's clearance McGhee laid the ball off for Strachan and summoning extraordinary energy the wee man knocked it past Metgod and ran round the other side of him. With the defender flailing, Gordon drove into the box, Augustín advanced from goal, and Strachan chipped him. This action played out directly below us and for a split second it seemed as if time stood still. We all willed the ball to drop just under the bar; instead it sailed over.

Black had run his race, time to call for 'Super Sub', and with just two minutes of the regulation ninety remaining John Hewitt entered the fray. Real pushed forward in search of an unlikely winner and won a corner. Juanito floated it in, Rougvie headed clear, and the referee blew his whistle. We were going into extra-time.

Neil Simpson maintains the players never lost their self-belief, even though they had failed to break through in a match they had dominated.

"We were the better team that night, by far the better team, and we were determined to win it in extra-time because with penalties, you just never know. It becomes a lottery."

The captain, Willie Miller, shared his optimism.

"Do you get a bad Real Madrid team? You maybe get an average Real Madrid team, in world terms, but it is still Real Madrid. We had to be at our best that night, and we were, we totally outplayed them for just about the entire match, particularly in extra-time."

Madrid threatened first, Isidro getting clear, but slipping and shooting wide as commentator Brian Moore told ITV viewers that the night's big film *The Domino Principle* (no, me neither!) would follow News at Ten. I somehow do not feel its delay was of much concern to the tens of thousands of Aberdeen fans watching back home.

The camera then focused on Knox and Ferguson screaming instructions from the touchline, and you did not have to be much of a lip-reader to work out the manager was shouting, "John, you fucking stay up!" He had only been on the park eight minutes, but Hewitt was himself in danger of being substituted.

"When I got on the manager wanted me to stay as far up the park as I possibly could, alongside Mark, but it was so frustrating, and because I was so full of energy and desperate to get involved, I found myself dropping deeper and deeper. The manager was going crazy with me, he was bawling and screaming, and he did tell me afterwards that if I hadn't followed his instructions he was going to haul me off!"

191

Still the Dons drove forward. After a surging run Simmy drove in a low cross from the left. It seemed certain Neale Cooper would get on the end of it, but the ball held up in the mud and the midfielder crashed to the ground in a tangle with Isidro. We bellowed for a penalty, but it wasn't. Gallego was eventually booked for his umpteenth foul, incredibly the first, and only, yellow card on the night. Weir then sent in an inswinging corner from the right which Rougvie powered goalwards, but the Madrid keeper dived to clutch it on the line.

The Spaniards made a change, Salguero replacing the toiling Isidro, and they came close to snatching the lead soon after. Juanito's corner was flicked on by Bonet and the ever dangerous Santillana let rip with an angled volley. Leighton, standing firm, needed strong wrists as he blocked the ball to safety.

And so on to the final fifteen minutes of play, a period the Scots were to dominate.

Straight from kick-off Peter Weir waltzed through leaving a trail of Madrid defenders in his wake, but his hanging cross was slightly overhit. Next he chipped the ball into the box, McGhee nodded it on and the lunging Hewitt was thwarted only by a despairing save by Augustín. The pressure was mounting, surely it would pay off? It did. In the 112th minute.

The most important goal in the history of Aberdeen Football Club had its origins deep in the team's own half where Peter Weir dispossessed Juanito, ghosted past two opponents and chipped the ball left-footed down the touchline. Mark McGhee gathered, slipped it past a defender, and raced into open space down the left flank. A quick look up, then he delivered an inch-perfect cross which just cleared the straining Stieleke. Keeper Augustín thought about coming, but hesitated, and in that split second history was written. When he did finally make his move it was too late, the ball flew beyond his outstretched fingers and John Hewitt dived to head it firmly into the net from just a few yards out.

There was a brief moment when I had to check he actually had scored, that the ball was indeed nestling at the back of the goal, and then uproar. Sheer, unconfined joy and elation. We were hugging and dancing with strangers, screaming in each other's faces, oblivious to anything other than the fact that our team, our wee team from the north-east of Scotland, was beating Real Madrid in a major European Final and there were just minutes left in the match. I found myself some twenty yards from where I had been standing and my friends were similarly scattered around that terracing. It mattered not. You just became best mates with whoever was next to you. By the time we had settled down play was already well underway again, so I missed the on-field celebrations.

It was only when reviewing the pictures that I saw Doug Rougvie reaching John first and enveloping him in a massive bear hug, the pair then throwing celebratory punches towards the vast Aberdeen support before being swamped by their team-mates. On the television Brian Moore, talking through the replay, was saying, "That's the real Peter Weir and that's the brilliant John Hewitt." The goal was shown time after time and the commentary team never once picked up on the fact that it was Mark McGhee, not Peter, who had delivered the cross. To be fair, even three decades later, they are not alone, as the confusion continues to this day.

"It genuinely hasn't bothered me, it's not something I give a moment's thought to . . ." Mark told me, before pausing and admitting, "There was a time when I used to correct people and I could see they didn't believe it was me who crossed it. Eventually I stopped, in fact I was beginning to feel a bit stupid saying, 'It wasn't Peter Weir, it was me', so I just gave up!"

They were simpler times back then, security was not what it is now, but remarkably ITV had somehow omitted to arrange accreditation for their heavyweight reporter Bob Patience, so he had cooked up a cunning plan with Archie Knox which would get him the access he needed.

"Bob asked me if he could get an Aberdeen tracksuit so that he could float about as if he was part of the staff, so I asked Ted (kitman Teddy Scott) and he said, 'Where are we going to get a fucking tracksuit to fit Bob Patience?' Anyway, we got him kitted out, and he was bulging out everywhere, but he got in. When Hewitt scored that goal I set off down the touchline, I must have been just about at the corner flag, and when I turned round big Bob jumped on top of me. He just about killed me!"

Rather than sit in and defend their advantage the red shirts kept pouring forward in waves. Mark McGhee spun and bundled his way into the box before having his shot saved, then another chance for the Aberdeen number nine, created by Hewitt, but the ball got stuck in a puddle, and by the time Mark got his shot away the keeper had repositioned himself and saved easily.

Again Weir drove forward from halfway, again he was fouled, scythed down by Stieleke, and suddenly Knox was nose-to-nose with the Madrid manager.

"He was giving it plenty so I started giving it back to him. It's only afterwards that you think about it, there he was the great, the legendary Alfredo di Stefano and I'm giving him stick and I've done nothing in football!"

The Dons created one further chance, Hewitt burrowing his way into the box and setting up Simpson, but the midfielder's shot from sixteen yards flew just wide of the left post.

And then came that last minute free-kick drama.

Ángel, in possession, pushed towards the Dons goal down the left and drifted inside. Willie Miller, alert to the danger, moved to challenge, but the ball once again held up in the surface water and as a result the skipper's mistimed tackle was penalised. A free-kick for Real twenty-five yards from goal and a real moment of concern for Jim Leighton.

"If it had been a boxing match it would have been stopped, but they hung in, and that was their big chance. It would have been awful if it had gone to penalties, anything could have happened then, especially with me in goal!"

The drama of those few seconds are described in the Introduction to this book – substitute Salguero eventually blasting the free-kick

194

just wide – and Leighton knows how close Aberdeen came to a gut-wrenching finale.

"I dived full length, I was at full stretch and normally you have a sense of where the ball's going, but with that one I honestly didn't know if it was in, going wide or hitting the post. Speak to any striker and they'll tell you the best sound in the world is that of the ball hitting the net; for a goalie that's the worst sound and that's what I was listening for. Thankfully it whistled past."

"Was it a free-kick in the first place?" ponders Willie Miller. "Well, the referee gave it and I would have been devastated if it had gone in. But it went wide . . . and big Jim had it covered anyway!"

Exactly twenty-six seconds after Salguero had struck the ball the Italian referee Signor Menajali blew the final whistle. The Dons had beaten Real Madrid, we had won the European Cup Winners Cup!

Alex Ferguson was first out of the dugout, but he slipped on the track and fell headlong into a puddle. No-one, not even his right-hand man Knox, was stopping to pick him up.

"We all charged out and I saw him going down, but I never even thought about helping him, I just stood on his back and made for the pitch and I was jumping around and diving on top of all the players."

I cannot begin to pretend that I have any clear recollection of what happened next. I vaguely recall red shirted players cavorting across the pitch, but all around me was madness and noise, joy and emotion. Grown men wept unashamedly, and I was one of them.

The television pictures were cutting from one scene of celebration to another, Brian Moore still crediting Peter Weir with the cross, and eventually the stage was set for the presentation. It was not the all-singing, all-dancing, pyrotechnics and ticker-tape event it is these days, instead a wooden table was dragged across the pitch and the trophy plonked on it. Willie Miller's next problem was getting it out of the hands of UEFA President Artemio Franchi.

"He wanted to lift it up, so I had to sort him out," grins the skipper. "He was all set to take it in both hands and show it to the fans, so I said, 'Hey, that's ours' and I grabbed it off him and held it up in my right hand."

Ah, that iconic pose!

Interviewed just after his captain had collected the silverware, Alex Ferguson told Bob Patience, "It's the greatest night of my life – it was a magnificent performance" before adding with relish, "What a night it's going to be!"

That pledge was carried out, as Archie Knox recalls.

"That was a fantastic night and carried on right through, I don't think I was in my bed for two days. I can remember walking around the Fars Hatt, it was like a castle, and Ted Scott and I were walking round the grounds at half-six in the morning just reliving the whole thing."

Neale Cooper remains convinced the Spanish giants contributed to their own downfall that night.

"They definitely underestimated us, a wee team from Scotland, and the support we had was unbelievable, just phenomenal. It was a fantastic feeling and I had the best night afterwards. My mum and sister were staying in the city at the Europa Hotel and a few of us got a taxi in and when we got there the place was just a sea of red and white. I still meet people to this day who thank me for going along and joining the party."

My own personal celebration was somewhat more muted. We returned to the small hotel we were staying at and after one beer in what was a heaving bar, I went up to my room, lay on my bed in the dark and just let the enormity of what had happened wash over me.

While those of us in Gothenburg celebrated in our own individual ways, unknown to us there was a huge party kicking-off back home.

"It wasn't until later when I saw the television footage," recalls Cooper, "that I realised what was going on in Aberdeen. It was mental. Union Street was packed, people were driving up and down hanging out of cars and waving banners and scarves, tooting their horns. That really brought it home to me, just what we'd done and what it meant to the fans."

The supporters who had been in Sweden returned home with memories that will last a lifetime, it was an utterly unbelievable experience, but amidst all the euphoria there was tragedy. During the game I had been aware of a disturbance some distance behind where I was standing and soon after a young man was quickly hurried away on a stretcher. I got only a glimpse of him, and thought I recognised him, but it was not until I returned to Aberdeen that I was able to confirm it had been a friend, Phil Goodbrand, who had collapsed and died. He was just twenty-two-years-old.

Graham Shand had travelled across to Gothenburg with him on the *St Clair*, and had been standing beside Phil when he had fallen.

"We immediately called the stewards and police over and they got the Swedish Red Cross. They examined Phil and tried to revive him with the help of one of my local GPs who happened to be nearby. As he was stretchered away he was attached to a monitor and it seemed to show a faint heartbeat. Another friend, Alan Davidson, went with him to the hospital. It wasn't until later that night, when we got back to the boat, that we found out he was dead. The first night of the journey home was a sombre affair, we all just sat around in shock and tears and went to our cabins. I got up fairly early next morning to gather my thoughts, lots of people were commiserating with us, and we did join in with the celebrations that evening, albeit in a subdued way.

"P&O handled it very well, they arranged for Phil's body to be returned home, and the Swedish authorities had contacted Grampian Police to inform his parents."

I remember being at the funeral and the utter sense of loss and disbelief. We were all young men, just starting out in life, it was almost incomprehensible that he was no longer among us. The club was well represented, Alex Ferguson leading the mourners, but it was a hugely difficult occasion, particularly of course for Phil's family. Graham still has one regret from that day.

"In hindsight it would have been good for one of us, one of his mates, to stand up and say something, to share a few memories, but we were all a bit immature back then, and no-one did."

I know I couldn't have done it.

Phil was full of fun, a genuinely good guy, always up for a laugh. We all have so many memories of nights out, of playing football, of trips the length and breadth of Scotland following the Dons. His death at such a young age was cruel and devastating, and every May 11th since, while celebrating the team's magnificent achievement, I have thought of him, just as I am sure all his other friends have.

The team returned home on the Thursday to rapturous acclaim, there was an open-topped bus trip through the city and a party back at Pittodrie which naturally attracted a full house. Everyone wanted to see that trophy! The supporters also made their way back in dribs and drabs. We flew back in late Thursday afternoon, the *St Clair* docked on the Friday to be welcomed by Alex Ferguson, Mark McGhee and the Cup Winners Cup, but it took Graham Rhind and his fellow coach passengers a bit longer to return.

"It was just one long party! We eventually got as far as Calais where we were booked into a hotel, but some folk never even made it off the bus. Next morning we had to push it as the lights had been left on and the battery was flat. When we got to Dover I phoned home and my dad told me the devastating news about Phil. I never got to go to the funeral as I'd contracted chicken pox from my brother Brian – sadly also no longer with us – before I'd left for Sweden! I always remember two couples from Kemnay who were with us on that trip. One of the guys had been really quiet all the way there, but after the game he was transformed, and kept shouting 'Magic! Unbelievable!' as he produced bottle after bottle of whisky from his bag. I can't remember when we actually got back home, either Friday or Saturday. It really was one helluva trip!"

These days, such an achievement would spawn special television and radio documentaries and page after page of newspaper coverage. Back then, it was all very different. The local press was of course jubilant, among the *EE* headlines: KINGS OF EUROPE!, ROLLING OUT THE RED CARPET and I KNEW I WOULD SCORE – HEWITT, but the 'Victory in Gothenburg Cup Souvenir' was a four-page black and white pull-out mainly consisting of photographs and no more than 500 words of copy. It was also packed with adverts for local companies such as Telemech, Studio 81 Hair Design and Crombie Mill Shop.

As the reaction to Gothenburg began to very slowly settle down and the reality of what our team had achieved started to sink in, there was still domestic business to take care of, and some sixty-five hours after the final whistle had blown in the Ullevi the players trooped out on to the Pittodrie pitch, applauded by their opponents, Hibernian, and cheered to the rafters by us fans. The explosion of noise when we caught a glimpse of the first red jersey emerging from the tunnel that afternoon was absolutely incredible, and it is to their immense credit that the team somehow put on a show despite the mental and physical exhaustion they must have been suffering.

Ferguson had made two changes, Watson and Angus replacing midfield powerhouses Simpson and Cooper, and the Dons were soon ahead thanks to an Ally Brazil own-goal. Mark McGhee's 27th of the season made it 2-0 before the break and Gordon Strachan's successful penalty conversion was his 20th goal of the campaign. Late counters from Angus and substitute Steve Cowan meant Aberdeen finished their title challenge with back-to-back 5-0 victories, but those three defeats in March and April proved too much of a hurdle to overcome, and the championship went instead to Tannadice. Celtic had come from 2-0 down at Ibrox to beat Rangers on the last day, but United clinched it with Ralph Milne and Eamonn Bannon scoring in the derby at Dens, the 2-1 win enough to make them champions by a single point.

CHAPTER TWELVE

JOHN HEWITT

'SUPER-SUB'

Every member of that incredible Dons side is rightly considered an Aberdeen legend. They all made their own contributions along the way and it was without question a team effort, but when you come out on top in a match like the one in Gothenburg, and it is a tight affair secured in dramatic circumstances, the headlines will inevitably focus on the man who netted the winner.

In this case that player was John Hewitt, the man who will forever more be remembered as having scored the most important goal in the club's history.

I met John one evening at the Atholl Hotel in Aberdeen, an old haunt from my Northsound days, to interview him for this book, and from the moment we arrived it was clear the years have not diminished his status. Countless people came up to chat and to shake his hand, and all round you could hear the whispers, "There's Johnny Hewitt."

Of that Gothenburg side, only Neale Cooper and Eric Black were younger than John. He was just twenty years of age when he dived to head in that goal, his euphoria that night heightened by the fact he was a local lad and lifelong Dons fan.

He had been playing for the boys club Middlefield Wasps when he first came to Aberdeen's attention and has the honour of being Alex Ferguson's first signing at Pittodrie.

"I remember it well. He came up to the house with Bobby Calder – Bobby had the obligatory box of chocolates for my mum – but he didn't have to sell the club to me, I was always going to sign on, although I did have other choices. Dave Sexton was Manchester United boss at the time and he flew up and there was an offer on the table, but I turned it down. I wanted to join Aberdeen."

He made his debut on December 15th, 1979 in a 2-0 home win over St Mirren, "a dream come true", and made one further start and three substitute appearances during the remainder of that campaign as Ferguson slowly introduced him to the first team.

John was chosen for the opening Premier Division match of the 1980-81 campaign, another home win over St Mirren, and then netted his first goal for the club three weeks later in a match which would become a famous quiz question: 'Name the Belgian who scored for a Scottish team in a League Cup tie in England?'

The Belgian was goalkeeper Mark de Clerck, whose clearance had soared over the head of his opposite number Peter Davidson to give the Dons a 3-0 lead in the second leg of their match against Berwick Rangers at Shielfield Park. By then Hewitt had opened his account in equally dramatic fashion.

"It was a corner in front of the main stand and I swung it in. There was a bit of a breeze and it floated right over the keeper's head and into the net at the back post!"

In all, he featured in twenty-eight games that season, along the way getting his first taste of European football as a substitute against Austria Memphis and in both legs of the heavy defeat to Liverpool. Throughout his time at Pittodrie John had the happy knack not only of scoring, but of scoring in big matches, important and notable goals. One such was that winner against Motherwell in January 1982, still the fastest goal scored in the history of the Scottish Cup.

"Stuart Kennedy hit a diagonal ball and I just basically gave chase, I didn't really think I was going to get it, but when the ball broke to me I touched it past the defender and fired it across Hugh Sproat and in at the far post. 9.6 seconds and that was it, although it was a really hard fought victory. Amazing to think that was the goal that really set us on the way to Gothenburg."

Hewitt also scored the only goal in the next round at home to Celtic and his reputation was growing in tandem with his self-belief.

"As a striker there's no better feeling than scoring a goal. Every time I was out on the park, whether I'd started or come off the bench, I was always eager to get into the right positions, to get a chance. It's something you can't really coach, it's a natural instinct you have in you. I was getting on the end of chances, I was burying them, and my confidence grew and grew. I always believed I could score no matter who I was playing against."

The early years of any player's career are vital in shaping him and with Alex Ferguson and Archie Knox guiding and driving him on, John believes he got the best possible tutoring.

"They were so thorough. Archie's coaching was fantastic, better than Alex's, and they worked so well together, training was so competitive, and Archie had all the young boys back every afternoon working on their weaknesses. It's not until you get older and you move away from Aberdeen that you realise how much these guys had done for you and how they'd shaped your professional career."

The important goals kept coming.

John scored the Aberdeen equaliser at Portman Road against Ipswich Town in the UEFA Cup, the 1-1 draw setting the Dons up nicely for Peter Weir's magical performance in the home match. He also found the net in both legs of the tie against the Romanians Arges Pitesti to help keep the run going, and notched the winner in a 3-2 home success against Hamburg, although Aberdeen were eliminated on aggregate by the West German giants. Back on the domestic front he scored eleven goals in twenty-two starts in the Premier Division, including a first half hat-trick against Rangers on the final day of the league campaign, and a week later collected his first winner's medal in that famous Scottish Cup Final humbling of the Ibrox side.

"That was just fantastic for me, a Dons fan through and through, winning the Cup at Hampden and beating Rangers in the way we did. One of my best memories from my time in the game."

Although season 1982-83 turned out to be the most momentous in the history of Aberdeen FC, and the most sensational of John's career, it was, for large chunks, a desperately frustrating one for the striker. He suffered a succession of injury niggles, and eventually had to have his ankle put in plaster. He did not start a league match between October 2nd and March 19th, managing only five substitute appearances during that time, and it was not until the final month of the campaign that he was able to enjoy a sustained run in the team.

But he did, crucially, make it for some of the bigger matches. John scored eleven goals that season, five of them in the Cup Winners Cup run; in both legs against Sion, the all-important single counter against Tirana, the decider against Bayern, and THAT goal in Gothenburg.

"I knew I wasn't going to be starting against Real Madrid because of the injuries and the fact Fergie had a settled team, so it was no surprise when he announced the line-up. I was just hoping I was going to be on the bench and that at some stage I was going to get the chance to get on."

He had to be patient. There were just two minutes of the regulation ninety remaining when he took to the pitch, but with extra-time looming there was going to be ample opportunity for the substitute to make his mark, and after the initial scare of being threatened with the hook, he did just that.

"It began in our left-back position with John McMaster, then Peter had a bit of magic and beat two or three players before clipping it down the line to Mark, but the thing with him was that you were never sure if he was going to cross it or not, because a lot of times he would cut back, and then double back again, so I was always having to reposition myself. Fergie later slaughtered me for not making a front post run as I'd been taught, but I didn't have a marker to lose and I was always on the move, eye on the ball. I was more concerned about whether or not Mark was going to cross the ball early and when he did I picked up the flight of the ball and I could see the goalie was struggling and that there was no way he was getting it. When he did finally make his move it was too late, and when the ball passed his hands it was just a case of letting it hit my head and going into the goal. I couldn't miss!"

That seemed remarkable to me, that John had such a simplistic view of such an important strike. I wondered if during that split second there had been any room for negativity, the fear that he might pass up such a glaring opportunity?

"No. That never crossed my mind. I just had to make sure I watched the ball carefully and judged it. I knew for sure I wasn't missing it."

If John has one regret from that night it is perhaps that he had not rehearsed a more fitting and memorable goal celebration. As it was, he performed a less than impressive limp star-jump before being consumed by Doug Rougvie, and has taken stick for it ever since, but that is a small price to pay.

So, did scoring that never to be forgotten goal change his life?

"In a word, no! Obviously I've gone down in the club's history as the player who scored the winning goal, and that's a marvellous thing, but it never changed my life."

There were nevertheless fringe benefits to what John had achieved that season and he and his wife Lorraine were able to celebrate in some luxury soon after.

"I had got a call from a foreign journalist before the Final, but I'd thought it was the boys on a wind-up – Stuart Kennedy had once stitched me up by making such a call at the Excelsior Hotel in Glasgow – and had forgotten all about it, but that night in Gothenburg as I was leaving the pitch there was a guy shouting at me. He said he was from the Italian magazine *Giornale Sportivo* and that they wanted to invite me across to be their guest for a week at a big event they were hosting. The gist of it was that Lorraine and I were treated to a week's holiday in Rimini in a beautiful five-star hotel on the beach front and taken along to an open air show that was being beamed to fifty-two countries. It was an awards ceremony as well –

the first prize went to the Italian player Massimo Bonini from Juventus, the Belgian striker Erwin Vandenbergh was runner-up and I was third. It was a star-studded occasion, I remember Franco Baresi being there, and the whole week was amazing. They took us to San Marino to do a photo-shoot for Fiat cars, the guy who owned the magazine offered the loan of his Ferrari – which I declined – and we had two members of staff looking after us throughout. Of everything that happened during that year of 1983, getting that wee trip to Italy is probably the thing that I remember most."

But, getting back to the goal itself . . .

"At the time I scored it, it was just another goal. I knew it was a really important one, but the enormity of what I'd done didn't sink in immediately. Even the celebrations afterwards back at the Fars Hatt were, for me at least, pretty low-key. It wasn't until we flew back into Aberdeen and I saw people standing on the roof of the airport that I began to understand its significance. And then there was the drive all the way in from Bucksburn, over Anderson Drive and down Queen's Road and there were people lined up all the way along the route. When we hit Holburn Junction and the bus turned, it was just incredible. You couldn't actually see Union Street, it was totally covered by people all the way down. There must have been two hundred thousand of them; they were hanging out of windows, standing on balconies. It was just unbelievable. And that was the point when I thought to myself, 'Hold on, I scored the winning goal last night and look what it's meant to all these folk.' When we eventually got down to the Castlegate and turned the corner there, King Street was exactly the same. Pittodrie Street was mobbed and when we got into the stadium it was jam-packed, there were even people sitting on the red ash track all round the pitch."

The following season John stayed fit, and featured in fifty-seven games for the Dons. In fact, apart from the '84-85 campaign where he did incur injury problems, he did not dip below thirty-five matches in the remainder of his time at Aberdeen. By the end of his Dons career Hewitt had played 361 games, 107 of those as substitute, and netted ninety goals, leaving him just outside the top ten in the all-time list of scorers.

In addition to the medal collected in Gothenburg he won the Super Cup Final later that year, Premier Division championship medals in '83-84 and '84-85 and a League Cup winner's medal in '85-86. He played in three successful Scottish Cup Final teams for Aberdeen, 1982, '83 and again in 1986 when he at last scored (twice) in a domestic Final, helping Alex Ferguson to collect what was to be his farewell trophy with the club.

"Eric had been having his dispute with the manager, he'd been tapped up to go abroad, so he was left out and it was myself and Frank McDougall that started the match. I'd been playing well in the run-up to the Final, and I was feeling really confident about my own game. Hearts had been having a fantastic season, they'd been in the running for the double, but Celtic pipped them for the league and we always knew that if we got them on a big pitch like Hampden's we'd beat them. We had better players, we could hold the ball better and create better opportunities, and as it turned out we were comfortable winners."

Aberdeen had been majestic in the domestic knock-out competitions that season. They won six matches without conceding a single goal to lift the League Cup, and although it had not been such plain sailing in the Scottish – it took extra-time in the replay to see off Dundee in the quarter-finals – Hibernian had been thrashed 3-0 in the semi and Hearts were about to suffer a similar beating as their campaign crashed and burned in seven desperate days.

With just five minutes on the clock John drifted in towards the middle of the park, slipped past Craig Levein and drilled a low left-footed shot into the bottom corner from nineteen yards. Less than three minutes into the second half he struck again. Peter Weir teased Walter Kidd down the left wing, darted in to the penalty area and cut back a low cross, McDougall dummied, and Hewitt scooped the ball inside the post from seven yards. Billy Stark's diving header simply compounded Hearts' misery.

"Gothenburg was brilliant, but not the sort of thing you ever dared dream about. With Aberdeen regularly reaching Scottish and League Cup Finals I did dream about scoring at Hampden, and always wanted the chance to prove I could do it. That day I did."

Within five months Alex Ferguson had left Pittodrie and Aberdeen FC would never quite be the same again.

"That was when the decline set in. Ian Porterfield took over and for a while we still did ok, his record was actually pretty good, but as a manager he was hopeless. There was no discipline, he wanted to play me out of position and I really wasn't enjoying it."

John's final start for the Dons was on April 1st, 1989, a 1-0 win over Dundee United in which Charlie Nicholas scored the only goal. He had decided it was time to move on, and when Billy McNeill offered him the chance to join Celtic in a £250,000 switch, John signed on.

"To be honest with you I would never, ever have left Aberdeen had it not been for Porterfield, and even though Alex Smith had taken over, I'd given big Billy my word and couldn't go back on it. In hindsight I wish I'd never done it because the Celtic move was just a disaster. I was out of football for a whole year with the knee injury and I never really got a look in when I returned from that. The problems began in a game with St Mirren, I fell awkwardly after challenging Campbell Money, and I could feel right away I'd done my cartilage. The club left me for nine weeks then put me back into training, and while I could run as fast as anyone in straight lines, I couldn't turn, and if I tried to even just pass the ball with my instep I was in agony. Anyway, I was just back in training, hadn't played in a couple of months, and Billy comes to me on the Friday and tells me I'm playing the next day against Aberdeen. I tried to explain I wasn't fit, but he insisted I played, so I did after getting a cortisone jab, and Celtic won 1-0. I actually played the next couple as well, but after the last one against Dundee I woke up at three o'clock in the morning in sheer agony. I was staying at the Hospitality Inn, so I got reception to call me a taxi and it was so painful I was in tears by the time I reached the hospital. I got all sorts of scans, but they couldn't find anything, and it wasn't until they opened me up they discovered the medial ligament had snapped away from the bone completely."

The ligament was stapled back on and Hewitt began his rehabilitation. It was months before he regained full fitness, but even when he did, and after eight goals in three reserve matches in a week, he never got called back into the first team squad.

"Billy left and Liam Brady came in, but he never spoke to me, never even gave me the time of day, and I knew my Celtic career was over."

John had a brief loan spell with Middlesbrough, but injury prevented him from making a first team appearance there, and when he did get fit again his next port of call, in 1992, was St Mirren, then about to be relegated to the First Division.

"It was a hard time for them, they were just about going into administration, but I actually enjoyed it there working with Jimmy Bone. There was myself, Campbell Money and Kenny McDowall as the three senior players and the rest were all kids, and we did ok, nearly getting them back up into the Premier Division."

Raith Rovers romped to the title that year, but Saints just missed out on the second promotion place, finishing two points behind Kilmarnock.

"It was ironic because Tommy Burns and Billy Stark were at Killie then and they'd asked me to join them in the summer of '92, but because I'd settled in well at St Mirren I decided just to stay at Love Street."

John's career then took a bizarre and totally unexpected twist.

"A month before I was freed by Celtic Mark Reid was bought by St Mirren and given a £100,000 signing-on fee. By the time I got there just a few weeks later the money had all gone and although Jimmy Bone wanted to keep me that next summer, he had no cash. I knew the boys who were running Deveronvale at the time and they were offering me £10,000 to go and play for one season in the Highland League, while Jimmy couldn't pay me a penny."

With his family settled in the Glasgow area Hewitt was reluctant to move back north, but felt he had no choice. Money talks!

"I'd warned the guys that if I found it wasn't for me I wouldn't be hanging around. I lasted just three or four games and knew I'd made the wrong decision, that I should still be playing at a higher level, so I called Jimmy and explained the situation and said that if he still wanted me I'd go back down the road."

He stayed with St Mirren for three more seasons, playing almost one hundred matches, but it was a very different club from that which had competed well in the Premier Division in the late 1970s and early '80s, and they never even looked like challenging for promotion.

John's next port of call was Dundalk in the Irish League, where he was appointed player-manager.

"That was just a shambles. I'd been offered three jobs; Sligo, Finn Harps and Dundalk, who were first to get in touch and because they were the biggest and with the Irish clubs there's always the chance of getting into Europe, I thought I'd give it a go. I went across, and the ground was a bit of a shock, it was more like a junior set-up; there was broken fencing, an old shed in one corner, but the Chairman was as nice as ninepence and we agreed what I'd be able to spend to bring players in. He basically sold me the job, but it certainly never worked out the way he'd suggested!"

Not realising that at the time, John moved his family from Scotland to begin their new life across the Irish Sea.

"Worst thing I ever did. I should have waited a few months to see how things were panning out first. I was at a board meeting just six weeks into the job and the Chairman said, 'If we don't get any money in by Christmas we'll be bust again' which came as a complete shock to me."

The job had begun well enough, John managing to persuade Roy Aitken to take Aberdeen across for a pre-season friendly which the Irish side won 1-0, Hewitt ironically scoring the only goal. They lost to Hearts and then took on a Liverpool team boasting the likes of

McManaman, Fowler and Barnes and were only beaten by a single goal. Despite that, John realised his squad was not up to scratch. Of the sixteen players on the books he says eleven were not good enough, and the club was not operating as a professional outfit should.

"When I took my first training session only seven boys turned up! I tried to change things; through a contact I agreed a deal with O'Neills, the big sports manufacturers in Dublin, to supply kit for the next three years. I got training kit too, up until then the guys were turning up for training wearing Liverpool or Celtic shirts, and I got them boots. I even installed a second-hand washing machine and tumble drier under the stand, before that we were sending the kit out to dry-cleaners and it was costing a fortune. The local council had a YTS-type scheme, so I managed to get four or five kids along to paint the main stand, freshen the place up, make it look a bit more respectable."

In addition to the problems he was facing at the football club, John's family were finding it difficult to settle, not helped by a flaring-up of sectarian unrest.

"They told me it was the worst trouble they'd had in twenty-three years, and Lorraine was near suicidal. After about nine and a half months she said she'd had enough, she needed to get out of there, so I sent her back to Aberdeen with Jemma and Niki. I was on the phone regularly to Fergie and he kept telling me I was wasting my time, that I should keep working hard at the job there while at the same time trying to find something at home. Believe it or not, there was a point when, to save more money, I was going to be leaving my rented accommodation and moving in with my bank manager, and that was when I thought 'nah, enough's enough' and I resigned. That was a real experience!"

Escaping his Irish nightmare, John got a call from his old pal Neale Cooper, then in charge of Ross County. The Dingwall club, in just their second season in the Scottish Football League, were gunning for promotion from the Third Division, and Cooper wanted a bit of experience for the run-in. John played in the final seven games, County unbeaten during that spell, and scored his last goal in senior football, at Hampden Park in a 2-1 win over Queen's Park, but there was to be no dream ending as the Highlanders lost out to Forfar on goal difference.

"I had a good time up there, and it was a shame the club never went up. From there I was off to Cove with big Dougie."

Another former Dons team-mate, Doug Rougvie, had been appointed manager of Cove Rangers, the Highland League club based in the southern outskirts of Aberdeen; John was to be his assistant.

"We had a good run there, were well placed to win the league for the first time, but we knew the squad was short, that we needed more players. Dougie went to the Chairman Allan McRae to plead his case, but Allan said there was no money, that the previous managers had spent it all! He was always going on about having ambition, but he wasn't prepared to show any at that time. We were committed to the club, we gave him a list of five names we wanted to sign and asked him to show the same commitment, we guaranteed him that if we got them we would win the league, but it never happened. We were down to the bare bones, Dougie and I were even having to play, and then we lost a cup-tie at home and the following day he called me to say that was it, he was quitting."

Huntly went on to take the title that season and Cove would have to wait until 2001 before clinching their first Highland League Championship.

Cove was very much a part-time post, at least in terms of wages, and by then John had found full-time employment outside the game thanks to his close friend Terry Allan.

"Terry started me off with Tulloch Recruitment where I began to learn the business for six weeks. He then bought ABC, renamed the company Team Recruitment, and I worked with them for ten years. In 2006 I moved to Talisman Energy and I've been there ever since, based in Peterhead, as a logistics co-ordinator."

211

It is a very different life from that Hewitt knew as a professional footballer, one it can take a little time to adjust to.

"When you leave football you think your world's ending. Like many players I didn't really plan for life after the game, football was my life, and I had a very successful career, and when that time comes it leaves a massive void. When I came back from Ireland I had a big decision to make; do I look for a job in the game or do I have to look elsewhere, and that's where Terry came in. I'll never forget, I was standing at the traffic lights at Union Terrace Gardens when he drew up in this lovely white Mercedes convertible. I couldn't believe it was his, and he laughed, gave me his card, we arranged to meet up for lunch and the rest is history."

John is still a regular at Pittodrie, either through his membership of the Former Player's Association or through his friend Terry, Team Recruitment having been major sponsors of the football club in recent years.

"Nothing would give me greater pleasure than seeing the current team winning something. Having been out there for so many years, I know what the boys are going through, know just how desperate they'll be to bring success back to the club."

Even if they do, there seems little chance they, or indeed anyone else from Aberdeen in the future, will be able to emulate John's finest achievement. He remains the last Scottish footballer to score the winning goal in a major European Final; it may be quite some time before that accolade is taken from him.

Apart from that historic goal, mention John Hewitt to any Aberdeen fan of a certain age and the response you will get is, 'Super Sub'. Does that still bother him three decades on?

"Yes," he says slowly and pointedly, "very much indeed."

He was smiling as he spoke, but there is no question the tag still rankles.

"I keep telling people to look at the history of Aberdeen Football Club, to check the statistics, and they'll see that I started far more matches for Aberdeen than I ever did coming on as a substitute, but it seemed to be that it was the important games I came on and quite often scored, and that's how I got the 'Super Sub' label."

Despite the injury problems he suffered, John is in the top ten of all-time appearances for the Dons alongside his team-mates from that glorious era, Willie Miller, Alex McLeish and Jim Leighton. Had he not taken that fateful and reluctant decision to leave for Celtic, he might well have made the top five.

"Ach, I don't really mind it, it's history now, but every so often I'll hear somebody say, 'There's Johnny Hewitt, Super Sub' and it just winds me up a bit. The bottom line is, I played for the team I loved, still love, scored goals and had a wonderful time. That's not bad, is it?"

CHAPTER THIRTEEN

ALEX FERGUSON

My one big regret in writing this book was my inability to secure an interview with the man who masterminded Aberdeen's success story between 1979 and 1986, Sir Alex Ferguson. Unlike most of the other main characters, I had no relationship at all with Sir Alex, having gone into broadcasting at Northsound Radio six months after he had left the north-east, and the few interviews I had done with him over the years were unlikely to have stuck in his mind.

I could have asked some of my friends in the game to put in a word for me, but did not want to leave them in a potentially embarrassing position, so instead took the direct route, establishing that Karen Shotbolt, Football Media Manager at Old Trafford was the person to contact. Karen was very helpful and polite, but having checked with the great man, quite firm in her response. Had this been a project directly commissioned by Aberdeen FC he would have found time to do the interview, but because it was something I was doing on my own he did not want to get involved. It was made clear to me that I should not take this personally; he turns everyone down in such circumstances!

Fortunately there was no shortage of archive material to draw from, and of course I did have access to those who were closest to him during the Pittodrie years – his assistant, Archie Knox, and all the players, and between them they provided me with more than enough information and memories from which to construct this profile of the man and his methods.

Ferguson's story has been told many times and anyone with more than a passing interest in the game will know it all too well; from his childhood in Govan to the shipyards as a staunch socialist and union man; his largely undistinguished and yet still fairly prolific playing career as a bustling goal-scorer; the first step on the managerial ladder at lowly East Stirlingshire and his revitalisation of St Mirren; the unimagined success with Aberdeen and the unparalleled victory march since with Manchester United.

There was little I could add to that picture, instead I wanted to carry out a more in-depth analysis of his time at Pittodrie and to do that I had to take a step inside his inner sanctum.

As mentioned in Chapter Ten, John McMaster was the first of his new players to meet Ferguson, and it is fair to say his early impressions were not entirely favourable.

"He looked so young, he was skinny and had those spindly legs, and to be honest we weren't sure how to take him at first. He was clever, he'd relate stories about the players he'd had at St Mirren, comparing me to Tony Fitzpatrick; Frank McGarvey with McGhee and Joe Harper; and right through the team, and that fired us up, made us more determined to prove we were better than they ever were."

That might have been John's take on those early days, but I discovered it certainly was not a view shared by a number of his team-mates, among them Gordon Strachan.

"I learned from that, I decided that when I was taking over a new club I'd never mention what I'd done before or how good my old players were because it can get up people's noses. It took Alex a while to realise that – we had good players and they didn't like it."

Alex McLeish was just a teenager in those early days of Ferguson's reign, but he too became aware of some dressing-room unrest.

"The older players could give you a better impression because I was just a kid when the boss came in. I remember hearing the gossip though and Stuart Kennedy in particular wasn't happy with being compared to St Mirren players . . . they eventually made it clear to him and he backed down a wee bit, which was good management in itself."

Like most of his team-mates, John Hewitt found the new manager a unique proposition, and initially at least, not necessarily an easy one to handle.

"Discipline was the first thing, he instilled that into the club. When he first came we'd never experienced anyone like him and he was just a raving lunatic. We had to work hard, he always used to tell us we had to train as we played, it was always competitive and it was all about trying to improve you as a player."

The one player more than any other Ferguson had to set up a close working relationship with was club captain Willie Miller, and after a few early disagreements, the pair began to hit it off to the point where there was a strong bond and a solid and mutual respect.

"I think so. I think most managers were initially dubious of me because of my training style, I trained well in football terms, but I didn't like running. I know Billy McNeill told Teddy Scott he wasn't sure about me, but once Alex got to know me we were fine. One of his great strengths is knowing which players he can trust and if he decides he can't trust them, he gets rid of them. He knew he could trust me and we did form a formidable partnership."

Down the years one of the big talking points about that squad and the success it achieved has been the insatiable desire to succeed that was evident throughout those glory years and whether it was there anyway or needed instilled by Ferguson. In doing the various interviews I did, I discovered the players could not agree on that. As far as Doug Rougvie was concerned, it was the manager's doing.

"That was Fergie that gave us that. I'd been there a few years, so had Willie and Clarky (Bobby Clark), so he had that bit of experience and he had the kids, good kids, coming through, so he was lucky I suppose. But he definitely brought something, a winning mentality, a determination that hadn't been there before."

Alex McLeish however remains convinced that while the manager did some fine-tuning, the components were in the main already in place.

"He did have a core of players, the winning mentality was already there, the players definitely had the hunger, but he hand-picked a couple of the right types as well, the likes of Mark McGhee and Peter Weir, so he deserves credit for that."

Eric Black was one of the youngsters given his chance during that period and he found Ferguson both demanding and inspirational.

"He was never satisfied. You climbed one peak and he was immediately working out how we were going to climb the next one . . . he had an insatiable attitude to succeed, to meet the next challenge, and I can see now just how strong he was."

McLeish remembers it as being a hugely demanding time, every day was a challenge if you were going to live up to the manager's expectations.

"When we started getting seriously good as a team the boss demanded more and he had to test us to see if we wanted more and the ones who didn't were culled. We grew with him in terms of our desire."

The manager was ruthless and nothing or no-one was going to stop him from achieving his goals. Neale Cooper says Ferguson thrived on positivity, his own and that which he encouraged from others.

"There was never any negativity . . . he put belief into the players . . . no matter who we played, no fear factor . . . anything he could do to motivate you he would do . . . whether it was Bayern Munich or Morton, he had the same attitude."

Alex Ferguson had very quickly become the dominant figure inside Pittodrie, every employee would see him, and be addressed by him, almost on a daily basis, something that impressed goalkeeper Jim Leighton.

"He knew the name of everybody who worked at the club, he knew all the wives' names, all your kids. My dad would go to every game and he always made time to speak to my dad . . . he just had a great way about him, a way of making everyone feel special, and he saw that as his job I suppose to get us all pulling in the same direction. There were no factions, no cliques. He would go into the ticket office and fire them up there . . . he made no distinction between the footballing staff and non-footballing staff, everyone was important."

One of the manager's first priorities had been to set about establishing the ground rules, ensuring everyone knew what was expected of them. His force of character was overwhelming, his ability to get everyone on his side almost unmatched, and as fringe player Walker McCall remembers, he left no stone unturned when it came to psychology and man-management.

"We would go down to Celtic Park and as we got off the bus there would be Billy McNeill, Bobby Murdoch or Jimmy Johnstone, members of the great Lisbon Lions team, waiting to greet us, and you would look at these guys and be in awe and you were one down before the game even started. Fergie changed all that; he told us to march off the bus staring straight in front, heads held high as if we owned the place. A minor detail, but all part of his plan to take the fear out of going to Glasgow and taking on the Old Firm."

Archie Knox believes that was one of the cornerstones to what followed, that Ferguson quickly identified what his team needed to do if they were to start to break down the barriers and become a force in the game.

"He drummed into them that Glasgow was the place, you had to go there to Parkhead and Ibrox and win on a regular basis, and it was expected of them. Dundee United were coming along at the same time as Aberdeen but they never managed that, not in the manner Aberdeen did."

Ferguson was determined to topple the Glasgow giants, that he correctly believed was the only way to get the Dons winning trophies, and his unquenchable desire was an inspiration to the young Alex McLeish.

218

"Right away he set the bar high. He came in and was talking about winning things, where our mentality had been that we'd done well if we got to the semi or the Cup Final. That was never good enough for Fergie and he kept setting targets. Initially he wanted us to be a 'one trophy a year team' and after we'd done that, a 'two trophy a year team', he was always driving us on."

Alex Ferguson clearly grew as a manager during his time at Pittodrie and Gordon Strachan believes there must have been times when he found it difficult.

"He was just a boy when he arrived, mid-thirties, and he had a lot to learn himself. We were open to what he wanted to do . . . but we were also scared of him, petrified."

That was a feeling Ferguson engendered in most, if not all, those players and Neil Simpson was no exception. But it was by no means the only tool the manager used.

"It was fear, but it was respect as well. He got you into the way of thinking, 'we're Aberdeen, we're the best team, we're the best players'. I'd be walking along the corridor and he'd see me and say, 'how's my best midfielder today?' and it was years later I discovered he'd also been saying that to Neale Cooper and Gordon Strachan and all the others. At the time that gave me such a lift and I was puffing my chest out feeling great."

By the time Peter Weir arrived at Pittodrie, Fergie was already master of all he surveyed, his reputation growing, and the winger had a few concerns about being reunited with his old boss from Love Street.

"I'd been warned he's ruthless and to beware of his temper . . . very early I realised standards were higher at Aberdeen than at St Mirren, the way they went about things."

But Weir very quickly bought into the programme, and it dawned on him he was now part of something potentially very special indeed.

"We just went Wednesday, Saturday, Wednesday . . . big game after big game . . . there was no fear. Fergie and Archie Knox had us well prepared every time . . . we'd have an hour long meeting, we knew everything about the opposition and we knew what we had to do . . . the knowledge those two had helped us enormously, they were ahead of their time, definitely, and Archie and Fergie's training was first class."

The relationship between the pair – and Teddy Scott – was a key component of the success that followed, and the seeds were sown almost immediately Knox arrived from Forfar Athletic.

"Right from day one we hit it off. He was happy for me to take the training, in fact he still joined in back in those days, causing havoc in the five-a-sides! Remember they'd won the league the season before I joined, so the winning mentality was already there. He'd done a lot of work in that respect, and he had some good experienced players on board. His mentality was already well established within the club . . . if you didn't want to be a winner, or couldn't live up to the strain of being a winner or his expectations, then you would fall by the wayside. They had to climb on board and face up to all the pressure he would put them under to make them better players."

Jim Leighton recognises how important the management team was, and how they blended so well.

"They dovetailed great because they were both keen students of the game and wanted football played the right way. Fergie might come in at half-time and blast one of us for two minutes and then he'd move on and Archie would come over and sort the problem out . . . sometimes anyway, quite often it was a real bad cop, bad cop set-up! They worked so hard though, put in so many hours in training and they made it fun, enjoyable, and that played such a big part in what we achieved. Archie would do most of it with Fergie watching on, overseeing everyone, but he was never slow coming in if he wanted something sorted out. I'll bet to this day he's still first in each morning and last to leave every night."

Fergie's fiery temperament has become famous, or perhaps infamous, with tales of players and journalists being terrorised if he deemed them to have crossed whichever line he had drawn on any given day. Not one of his Dons squad missed out on what became known as 'the hairdryer', in fact Peter Weir experienced it on a number of occasions.

"I had my run-ins with him, but in general, nobody messed with him. He knew who to pick on and who to have a go at . . . and when he did have a go at me, I knew what he was doing – he'd bought me, paid all that money for me and if you weren't playing well he'd let you know big-style . . . he'd run at you, shout at you . . . and how you handled that was a big thing. I saw some good players at Aberdeen that couldn't handle it and ended up playing for lesser teams. Aye, I stood up to him . . . it was hard to take, sitting there with fifteen team-mates round about you . . . I remember one game at Ibrox and I'd had a shocker of a first half and I wasn't looking forward to what was coming at half-time, but when I got to the dressing room he was already in the corner having a go at Dougie Rougvie and he left me alone . . . other times I've come in thinking I've done well, I've made a goal, scored a goal and he's verbally assaulted me . . . you never knew what was coming . . . that was his way . . . don't let anyone kid you, he had that fear factor with everyone in the dressing room.

"There was one game against St Mirren, we were still in the hotel beforehand and for some reason he really gave it to me . . . I decided I wasn't taking that, told him to shove his team where the sun don't shine, grabbed my bag, went to reception and ordered a taxi . . . I was planning to go to my mother's in Barrhead then get a train back to Aberdeen . . . Stuart Kennedy came running out and grabbed me, told me not to listen to him, told me they needed me that day . . . he calmed me down – it took forty minutes – and Fergie never said another word about it. He overshot the mark that day – it was a full ten minutes of stuff I couldn't repeat . . . even the other players were shocked because they were all talking about it in the bus on the way back up the road."

One of the accusations levelled at Alex Ferguson was that he over-used the talented youngsters he brought through, that he played them in too many high-profile and demanding matches too early in their careers. The facts seem to back that up, with Cooper, Simpson, Hewitt and particularly Black all suffering horrendous injury problems within a few years. It is a point not lost on those involved, something they all reflected on with me three decades later, but Neale Cooper says it was never on their minds at the time.

"I loved playing football. I'm struggling now with my knee and my foot, Johnny Hewitt's struggling, Eric Black's struggling with his back. We played a lot when we shouldn't have, but we were so keen to play. He played us too much, definitely, he knows he did and that's why I think he's so nice to us these days! Beckham, Ryan Giggs – he rested them when they were coming through because he'd learned from what he did with us . . . but there's no doubt, we wanted to play in those games."

Archie Knox admits that too much was perhaps expected of those kids, 'Fergie's Fledglings', but believes it would be wrong to be too critical of decisions taken over thirty years ago.

"I think they all fulfilled their potential . . . but the amount of big games these lads played in before they were really fully developed maybe had a bearing on their careers as they went on. Then they were playing in Europe, Cup Finals and in a really tough, competitive league . . . maybe we did play them too much, but they always wanted to play, never wanted to miss a game."

Cooper believes the bond Ferguson forged with his players, particularly the younger ones, remains as strong now as it was back then.

"It was as if we were his sons, his boys. I was down visiting Carrington [United's training complex] one time and Ryan Giggs came up and asked if I was the boy who impersonated the manager and he had me doing the 'pwoud, vewy pwoud . . .' line and the guys loved it. Fergie once pulled me up about it after one of his friends had seen me doing him at a dinner. He called to complain, pretending to be angry, but eventually started laughing. He was hard, of course he was, but he was very caring about the boys."

That has not been the case with all that team as Ferguson's relationships with a number of the players, among them Eric Black, Gordon Strachan, Jim Leighton and Mark McGhee, soured for a variety of reasons, some obvious, others less so. Despite their fall-outs, the guys still recognise the part Fergie played in their development and all learned things along the way they were able to put to good use in later life. McGhee still does not know why, having been close to Sir Alex for years, he was dropped like a stone, but bears no grudges.

"I've heard all sorts of suggestions as to why he cut me off. I don't know for sure, but I believe that having helped me get the Wolves job, he felt that I should have done better there than I did. I've got no problem with what happened, he couldn't have been more helpful to me in those early years, and to this day I wouldn't have a bad word said against him."

One of the points Gordon Strachan picked up on was an understanding of how he should treat his players and how hard he should drive them on as a coach and manager.

"Training, I learned you had to push yourself, to work hard all the time. It's character building. He'd have us running, we'd stop, throw-up, get kicked in the backside and told to go again. He never let up."

While for Jim Leighton it was about managing the different personalities and characters in the dressing room, and a psychological approach.

"Fergie did instil so many good traits and beliefs in us all and he made every one of us a better player. You always felt ten feet tall going out onto the pitch. He made you believe you were a better player than you really were . . . and he's still doing it. I think he grew up and had an invaluable apprenticeship through those European runs, it must have been a great experience for him as a young manager to be going up against the likes of Bayern and Hamburg, trying to out-fox some of the best managers from all across the continent, and coming out on top."

For striker Walker McCall it was Ferguson's attention to detail and his ability to outthink and outsmart opposition managers that really shone through during his time at Pittodrie.

"We were playing Rangers at Ibrox and the papers had been full of stories that Davie Cooper, Ally McCoist and John McClelland would miss the game through injury. Fergie was talking us through what he thought the Rangers line-up would be when Jock Wallace walked by and tried to keep up the pretence. Fergie just laughed and told him that his mother-in-law lived in the high-rise flats over-looking the Albion training ground and that he had been there the day before spying on them, watching them train. Cooper, McCoist and McClelland all played as Fergie had predicted."

Leighton also believes preparation played a major part in all the success achieved by Alex Ferguson and his team; no stone was left unturned in the manager's pursuit of his ultimate goal.

"We were always so well prepared. Everyone knew their own jobs and everybody else's jobs. We could be drawing 0-0 with five minutes to go and he'd make a substitution and the player coming on would score the winning goal, in so many games throughout his career that's happened with him. You'd argue there's a lot of luck involved in that, but there's a lot of skill too . . . he's got the Midas touch."

The Midas touch, is that really what it is? Does that explain the unparalleled triumphs he brought first to Pittodrie and later to Old Trafford. Or is it simply down to hard work; is it possible there is no magic ingredient, nothing he brings to the table that no-one else could possibly recreate? The views of his Aberdeen captain Willie Miller:

"There's no X factor, not really. Could another manager have done what he did at Pittodrie? It's difficult to say, but given everything he had to offer, I really don't know that anyone else could have had similar success. We had the nucleus of a good team, but he was the one who pulled it all together, gave us that belief . . . so, on balance, you've got to say no . . . no other manager could have done it."

Alex McLeish is one who has kept in close contact with his old boss down the years, studying him and his methods. Like his old defensive partner, McLeish remains in awe of what Ferguson was able to do, and agrees there was no secret to how it was carried out.

"It's only now that I've got older that I realise what a great thing Sir Alex Ferguson, Archie and Teddy, and that team did. The manager takes huge credit for gelling us, for giving us the final push, getting over the hurdle that Aberdeen couldn't get over before."

For Alex Ferguson it was never about winning popularity contests, it was all about winning trophies, a trait Eric Black became all too aware of.

"There were times when I didn't like him and wasn't convinced about what he was saying to me . . . but looking back now, I see how driven he was, still is. To have that, to be so consistently on top of everything, putting pressure on everyone . . . it's all right doing it for a week or so, but to still be doing it thirty years later is remarkable, absolutely remarkable."

Since leaving Pittodrie in December 1986 Alex Ferguson has created a dynasty at Old Trafford, having completely rebuilt and transformed Manchester United. His first few years were not easy down there, and legend has it he was on the verge of getting the sack in January 1990 when Mark Robins' goal earned a 1-0 FA Cup Third Round win away to Nottingham Forest to spare him. Ferguson has since denied that, agreeing the goal was important, but refuting suggestions he would have definitely been axed without it. Whatever the truth, the Alex Ferguson in those early years was very different to the present-day version, as Alex McLeish notes.

"I always wondered how he would do moving down to the big-time in England . . . to go on and do everything he's done is just beyond anything you could have comprehended. To build that club into what it is now . . . that's down to him. The whole city of Manchester, never mind just Manchester United, is thriving and he's made a huge contribution towards that. Nowadays of course, he

225

would never have been given the chance, not after that start he had, and he knows that, he admits that."

While he went on to eventual greatness with United, carving out a place for himself in the history books as a legendary figure both sides of the border, the fortunes of the club he left behind headed on a downward trajectory. For John Hewitt, the man who handed Ferguson the most prized reward of his Pittodrie career, it was a sad and disappointing few years.

"It was really the start of the decline. You can't replace someone like him, you just can't. He is the best manager Britain has ever produced . . . you could probably say he's the best manager in the world. His record is absolutely phenomenal . . . once in a lifetime you come across someone like him and we were very fortunate to be able to play for him, to be managed by him. There'll never be another Fergie!"

CHAPTER FOURTEEN

MARK MCGHEE

SV HAMBURG 0-0 ABERDEEN
Tuesday November 22nd, 1983
ABERDEEN 2-0 SV HAMBURG
Tuesday December 20th, 1983

Ten days after Gothenburg and a week after closing out their Premier Division campaign with that 5-0 thrashing of Hibernian, Aberdeen lifted their second trophy of the season. It was a flat performance by the Dons in the 1-0 victory over Rangers, Eric Black notching the extra-time winner to secure a second successive Scottish Cup triumph. By that stage of his team's development it was not just about winning for Alex Ferguson, it was about winning with a bit of style, and his dissatisfaction was there for everyone to see and hear as he lambasted the players in a post-match interview. Only his defensive triumvirate of Leighton, Miller and McLeish was spared.

For young Neale Cooper it was a bizarre and frightening experience.

"We were all sat in the Hampden changing room, totally silent apart from him shouting at us. He was saying the three boys had won the Cup Final on their own and that the rest of us were rubbish and an embarrassment. I was shell-shocked. I was physically shattered anyway after such a long season; we've just come in having lifted the trophy and he's going round individually slaughtering us, telling us we should never wear an Aberdeen jersey again."

Neale even had to check with best friend John Hewitt that Aberdeen had actually come out on top.

"I whispered to Johnny, 'We did win the Cup, didn't we?' and he just shook his head and said, 'Aye.' It was unbelievable, he was acting like a loony."

Gordon Strachan had been just about to get the celebrations underway when he got prior warning of what was about to unfold.

"I was about to open a bottle of champagne and Archie said, 'You'd better not open that, he's out there going berserk' and I couldn't believe it. It wasn't right. Most of us had played up to seventy games that season and when we got in after the game we were absolutely drained, we were literally shattered, we had nothing left."

The outburst, naturally, put something of a dampener on the after-match celebrations. Neale Cooper recalls a sombre journey away from the national stadium.

"Our families were all waiting on us, delighted with the result, but we all trooped onto the bus in silence and were taken from Glasgow to the Old Course Hotel in St Andrews for the party. No-one said a word all the way there and Fergie just sat down at the front with a face like thunder. All the supporters' buses were going by and the fans were cheering and laughing and we're just sitting there unable to respond."

The players all went to their rooms to get changed, and it was only once everyone had reassembled in the dining room that the manager's mood finally lightened.

"He stood up at the top table and apologised, admitting he had been out of order. He said it was down to the high standards that we had all set, that he was immensely proud of what we had achieved, and that he was sorry for saying what he had. At that moment it was 'yahoo!' and the party hats went on."

And so that remarkable season of 1982-83 was put to bed, imprinted indelibly on the history of Aberdeen FC and of Scottish football in general.

But there was still some unfinished business.

Back in the 1980s the winners of the Cup Winners Cup played against the holders of the European Cup in a two-legged Super Cup Final. Aberdeen's opponents later that year would be their old foes SV Hamburg. The Germans had eliminated Ferguson's side from the UEFA Cup a couple of seasons previously, but two years down the line his men were more street-wise and battle-hardened; they had learned what it took to win ties against top-class continental opposition, and they were determined to become the first Scottish club ever to win two European trophies.

The first leg was in Germany on November 22nd, 1983, by which time the Dons had already qualified for the quarter-finals of that season's Cup Winners Cup with wins over Akranes and Beveren. The club's exploits had also been recognised by France Football magazine and Adidas who had named the Dons as European Team of the Year. Now the players had to go out and prove it.

There was a crowd of 15,000 at the Volksparkstadion that night and the home fans were to endure a frustrating night as Aberdeen put in a thoroughly professional, if mainly defensive-minded, performance. Hewitt, McGhee and Weir were asked to work hard to prevent Hamburg building from the back, forcing Ernst Happel's side into a more direct style, and that played into the Dons' hands, the height of Cooper and Rougvie being deployed in the full-back areas either side of Miller and McLeish to counter the aerial threat of Dieter Schatzschneider. On the occasions that the Germans breached the visiting rearguard, Jim Leighton dealt comfortably with any threat.

Alex Ferguson reflected afterwards on a job well done.

"We defended as I had hoped and we were aware of Hamburg's strengths. Our midfield had to stay focused as they have real quality in there, but we were ready for them. We still have to win the tie, but this result gives us a marvellous platform to finish the job in front of our own supporters."

In fact, the platform could have been an even better one as Aberdeen came close to snatching what might have been a crucial away goal. Unsurprisingly, it was the club's all-time top scorer in European competition, Mark McGhee, who very nearly gave them the win, cutting in from the left, as he so often did, beating two defenders and firing in a shot which was well saved by Uli Stein.

Mark was one of the key components of that marvellous team. Not only could he hold the ball up to allow midfielders to flood forward, he had mesmerising dribbling skills (although there were times when none of us, least of all him, seemed sure of where he was going next), energy to burn and an unerring ability to find the net.

In his five full seasons with the club McGhee finished top scorer in three of them. Steve Archibald was leading marksman in 1979-80 and Gordon Strachan in 1981-82, his tally of twenty that campaign edging out his close friend by a single strike. In the other years Mark was dominant and during those glorious seasons of '82-83 and '83-84 averaged almost a goal every two games, 51 in 106 matches.

Eleven of those came in Europe; his record-breaking total of fourteen (in just thirty games) in continental competition likely to stand the test of time.

Mark was signed by Ferguson in the spring of 1978, clearly earmarked as the replacement for Dons legend Joe Harper who, by dint of injury and a fractured relationship with the manager, was approaching the end of his glowing Aberdeen career. By then McGhee had already amassed a variety of experiences, but he might have been lost to the game altogether had he followed his boyhood dream.

"I wanted to become a gymnast and at the age of fourteen or fifteen gave up football completely to concentrate on that. The local priest, Father Kirby, was a football enthusiast and he ran the Sacred Heart primary team, but when I moved on to high school the gymnastics became more important to me."

Around that time a friend invited him to play for Cumbernauld Burgh in a match in Dundee, and sensing a good day out, Mark went along for the ride. He scored a hat-trick and fell in love with the game again.

"We weren't a great team, and playing against sides from Glasgow and Stirlingshire we took some heavy beatings. I always remember losing a match 18-1 and my dad asking if I'd scored the one; when I told him I had he said, 'Don't worry, you did your job.' It was a good experience though and it got me back playing again."

It also got him spotted, and led to a two-year stint with Bristol City which he thoroughly enjoyed, even though he never made it into the first team. In 1975, still just seventeen, Mark thought it was time to come home and he was handed the perfect opportunity, a trial with his boyhood heroes Celtic in a testimonial match against East Kilbride Thistle.

Celtic won 5-2, Mark scoring twice, but within days Jock Stein was involved in the serious car crash which almost claimed his life.

"Sean Fallon had taken over and he said they were keen to sign me, but that they would have to wait until Jock recovered as he had to make the decision. I'd also had a trial for Morton in the Renfrewshire Cup against St Mirren, and had done well, so when Hal Stewart offered me the chance to join them I decided to go for it."

The Greenock side, having just been relegated, were then in the First Division and McGhee made a big impact, scoring almost forty goals in less than two seasons playing in a side packed with some legendary characters, among them the maverick Andy Ritchie. His Cappielow exploits led to a move to Newcastle United, and Ritchie inadvertently played a part in sealing the transfer.

On the night before a league game against Hamilton Andy was giving Mark a lift home and stopped off at a local hostelry to meet a few friends. Naturally, given Andy's involvement, one thing led to another and the teenager was well and truly led astray.

"I woke up the next morning with a terrible hangover and feeling awful. I asked my mum to call my work to say that I wouldn't be in (Mark was training to be an architect and playing football part-time), but she refused. So I had to go into the office all day and then off to the game, still really suffering. I scored four goals that night and got the move to Newcastle off the back of it!"

United also signed Mike Larnach from Clydebank at that time – Mark believes they just went down the list of top scorers and bought them – but neither got much of a chance at St James Park.

"When I arrived there, the manager, Bill McGarry, had no idea who I was!"

He did manage almost thirty appearances in a Newcastle shirt, and bagged a few goals, but it was clear he had no long-term future there. It was then that Alex Ferguson made his approach and Mark's career really took off.

"McGarry was fine with me. He said it was up to me whether I went or not, he certainly didn't push me out the door, but Alex had already come in for me when he had been at St Mirren, and he did a great job selling Aberdeen to me. I'd never even been to the city before, but it felt right."

That 'selling job' included a remarkable pledge by the Dons manager.

"He told me that within five years he wanted to be winning in Europe, not just games, but winning tournaments! I'm not sure I believed him, but I loved his confidence, ambition and vision."

Five years later Fergie, and McGhee, had lived that dream.

Mark made his Aberdeen debut in a 1-0 win against his old team, Morton, on April 4th, 1978 and scored his first goal ten days later, his soon to be best friend Gordon Strachan setting him up for the winner against Partick Thistle. The following season was to provide the big breakthrough both for Mark and for the club, as the Dons collected their first trophy under Ferguson, the 1979-80 Scottish Premier Division title. McGhee featured in around half the matches, scoring ten goals, and learning all the time playing alongside Steve Archibald.

"Steve was just a joy to play with, he taught me so much about the art of striking. Not just about scoring goals and getting into position, but working hard and closing down the opposition. He really was a fantastic player."

The following campaign was a relative disappointment, Aberdeen finishing runners-up to Celtic in the league, and suffering cup exits at the hands of Dundee and Morton (Andy Ritchie applying the killer touch!), but it did offer McGhee his first taste of European football, and his first goal, the only one in a 1-0 aggregate success over Austria Memphis. Liverpool humbled the Dons in the next round, but the overall experience opened Mark's eyes to the delights of those big nights against the cream of continental opposition.

I flew down to meet up with Mark in Bristol shortly after his return to management with Rovers. He looked fit and healthy, certainly much better than during the difficult, at times harrowing, end to his previous job at Pittodrie, and over a leisurely lunch at the city's Cote Brasserie, he reflected on those memorable times.

"Those European games I felt probably twenty percent better a player than I did on a Saturday. Willie [Miller] and I spoke about this years later, and there was that extra something special when we went out to play in those ties, for some reason it just charged us up. You know when a team runs out of the tunnel and you take a few paces and jump up and do a pretend header? On those European nights I used to jump a foot higher, it felt physically different. We just loved it . . . and we loved the Duty Free. You've got to remember those were very different times back then, sometimes the Duty Free was incentive enough to get through!"

During those years Mark and his team-mates had plenty opportunity for tax free shopping as they won matches, gathered momentum and carved out reputations for themselves across the continent, culminating of course in that rainy night in Gothenburg. Mark did not score against Real Madrid, but he did, as discussed in previous chapters, set up the winner for John Hewitt. He laughed when I relayed the confusion in Hewitt's mind as the striker wondered when, indeed if, his partner was going to deliver the cross, but told me that was one occasion when he had no option.

"To be honest, because of the conditions and the fact that the pitch was soaking, the ball held up and I just thought I've got to get this in. I was tired and I gave it all my concentration, particularly as it was on my left foot and there was more chance of me scuffing it along the ground to the near post than finding Johnny Hewitt's head. When he scored it was a unique kind of celebration, the players all seemed to celebrate on their own. It's always reminded me of that Monty Python sketch, 'the 100 metres race for people with no sense of direction', that's just what it was like. We were running off all over the place, it was just mental. To be honest, I don't think we knew how to react to something like that."

Mark spoke to me of a crushing fatigue that settled on all the players afterwards, an unreal sensation almost of anti-climax, but that was soon lifted when they met up with their families and the party got underway.

There was however to be a dramatic and explosive interruption to the celebrations when the squad finally made it back to Pittodrie.

"I know this has been written about before, but I've rarely spoken about it because I've always felt I was the one in the wrong, and as such didn't have the right to tell it."

As is so often the case, the demon drink had a big part to play in what unfolded in the tunnel as a packed stadium waited to acclaim their heroes.

"Basically, we were all pissed. We'd been drinking on the plane and then on the open-topped bus fans were throwing up bottles of champagne, and who can refuse champagne? Especially from an Aberdonian! When we got back I was standing at the end of the tunnel composing myself, ready to go out, when I noticed the Cup was lying on its side, so I picked it up and at that moment Fergie came out of nowhere and yanked it out of my hand, saying that Willie was going to be taking it out. I had no intention of taking it out anyway and for some reason I flipped. He was standing with his back to the boot room door so I just grabbed him and ran him through the door and down to the back wall of the room. I was just about to set about him when Archie and the boys dragged me back and while they're grabbing me he's taking a punch or two because he's got nobody holding him back of course!"

234

Oblivious to all this, the more than 20,000 fans crammed inside the stadium were chanting for the team to appear. Meanwhile, the club's top scorer had been taken to the board room.

"You've got to remember that I was a married man with a child at the time, and who came in to calm me down? My mum and the Chairman Dick Donald! I eventually made it out for the second lap of honour."

The following morning realisation began to dawn on the fast-sobering McGhee, and he feared for his future.

"I'm thinking, 'My career's over, what have I done?' and so I decide I have to face the music and go and find him. I went down to Pittodrie and the steel shutters at the main door were open just a little, so I went in and there he was standing on the big AFC motif on the floor. I began to speak and he cut me off and said, 'I was out of order, it's over, it's done', and then he told me we were going down to the harbour to meet the *St Clair* as it was due to dock."

A relieved McGhee duly followed his boss down to greet the returning fans, the pair showing off the trophy and posing for countless photographs, but it was the brief encounter at the stadium that has lived with Mark.

"That was one of the biggest lessons of my managerial career. I learned then not to pre-judge anyone or anything – no player's ever assaulted me, to be fair! – and have always remembered what he did. If he was prepared to forgive me for that, I should always think twice before being too quick to judge my players."

Another lesson Mark has perhaps learned is to think twice about his choice of clothing. Admittedly he had other things on his mind that morning, but the hideous jumper he wore that day will haunt him forever, or at least it should . . .

"I quite liked that jumper," he says, rather too quickly and defensively, before smiling. "I still get asked to sign photos from that day, and the picture still gets used in articles, so I'm never going to forget it!"

And of course it had to make it into this book!

The second leg of the Super Cup Final was played out in front of a capacity 22,500 crowd at Pittodrie on Tuesday, December 20th. There had certainly been a sense of anticipation building in and around the city in the intervening period since the goalless draw in Germany, and while it did not quite feel like the run-up to the Bayern game, or indeed Gothenburg, I do certainly recall getting pretty worked up in advance. We arrived early that night and chose seats in the same area as we had for the win over Munich, halfway up the South Stand and almost adjacent to the Merkland Road 18-yard line. It was to prove a good omen, and the perfect vantage point to witness the two second-half goals which saw the Dons officially crowned kings of Europe.

Aberdeen started the match well, Strachan and McGhee forcing saves from Stein, and remained well in command throughout the first half without securing the advantage their play merited. The only threat at the other end was a long-range Hartwig effort easily dealt with by Jim Leighton.

"They were up for it," Mark remembers, "in fact, in some ways it was probably bigger for Hamburg than it was for us, they were European Champions, there would have been bigger spin-offs for them than for us. I remember talking to the guys once I joined the club and they were deadly serious about that match. The other thing they said was how impressed they had been by the Pittodrie crowd. Manny Kaltz once told me he thought the Aberdeen fans had been special and had a big influence on the outcome that night."

The atmosphere was good, partly, I believe, because many fans who had decided not to go to Gothenburg saw that Hamburg match as their substitute, their chance to really feel a part of the whole experience, and we were all of course lifted by the way the Dons took a grip on the game shortly after the restart.

Two minutes into the second half Peter Weir took off down the left wing and chipped the ball into the box. John Hewitt got there ahead of a defender, but was forced wide before he could shoot, so instead played it across the six-yard box. The ball was partially cleared, but only as far as Neil Simpson, who blocked it before opening up the space he needed to drive a right-footed shot low into the corner of the net. A special moment for all of us, but for Simmy in particular.

"It was a great achievement for the team and fantastic for me to score that goal. Someone said to me that I'm the only Scotsman to have scored for a Scottish club in a European quarter, semi and final all in the same year or season; if that's true, it's something to be really proud of."

Neil scored against Bayern and Waterschei in the Cup Winners Cup run, and completed his treble with that opener against Hamburg, and my initial research suggested he had indeed carved out a niche for himself in Scottish football history, but a little more digging revealed him in actual fact to be part of an exclusive group of two, Alex Scott having netted for Rangers in ties against Borussia Monchengladbach, Wolves and Fiorentina in the 1960-61 Cup Winners Cup. Still, not bad!

One-nil up against the European champions, the Dons were rampant. John Hewitt volleyed just over and Mark twice came close, with an angled drive then a close-range header, frustrated on each occasion by the increasingly overworked Uli Stein. But the clinching goal was only being delayed and it was McGhee who finally settled the tie.

It was the 64th minute of the match and Aberdeen had forced yet another corner. Peter Weir swung it in with his left foot, Eric Black rose but failed to make connection and the ball shot across to Willie Miller, lurking at the back post. His first-time return pass caught the German defence flat-footed and Mark had the easiest of tasks to slip the ball into the net. His celebration was that of a relaxed, self-confident player; a smile and an almost nonchalant raising of his right arm. A couple of team-mates, Dougie Bell and Alex McLeish, patted him on the back, but that was it, there was no repeat of the frantic celebrations sparked by Hewitt's goal in Gothenburg seven months earlier. As Pittodrie erupted the Aberdeen players simply returned to their positions ready for the restart, ready to see the job through, ready to be acclaimed the best team in Europe.

They saw it out comfortably, in fact the winning margin might have been much greater. Simpson had a goal disallowed and Black was twice denied late on as the Dons kept driving forward, continually pressurising the beleaguered Hamburg back-line.

In the end it was 2-0, a score-line which flattered the Germans and saw Willie Miller collect the most unusual 'trophy' of his career.

"It was a shield, and I didn't know what to do with it. How do you lift a shield? To be honest, that took the shine off it a little bit, somehow it didn't feel quite as special because we weren't given a trophy."

Strictly speaking, I suppose what the team won was a plaque, a wooden board adorned with a gold UEFA badge and a small rectangular strip detailing the event. It hardly seems fitting, but I don't remember being in any way concerned on the night. As the exhausted Aberdeen players trooped round on yet another lap of honour we simply drank in the noise, the atmosphere, the uncontained joy. Life as a Dons fan simply could not have been any better.

It was, for all of us, another fantastic memory, another occasion to treasure, but for one of the players we had been cheering it was to be an even more memorable night.

Peter Weir never deviated from his match-day routine. He liked to sleep in the afternoon before heading down to the Ferryhill House Hotel for the team meal. Then it was off to Pittodrie, further meetings with Alex Ferguson and Archie Knox, the warm-up and the game. He had kissed his wife Mary-Anne goodbye, leaving the house, as he always did, before the rest of his family had arrived. He needed to be left alone to concentrate on the ninety minutes ahead.

As he played his part in that landmark victory for his team Peter had no inkling of the drama unfolding a few miles away at Foresterhill Hospital.

"It was only two or three minutes after the final whistle and I see Ian Taggart (then the occasionally fearsome, chain-smoking club secretary) jumping over the dugouts, onto the pitch and heading straight towards me. I thought he was just looking to say well done, and he was, but not in the way I was anticipating. He said, 'Congratulations, you're a father again' and I'm looking at him as if he's daft. When I left home my wife was busy making dinner for my parents arriving and I'm shouting at him, 'What are you talking about?' Turned out Mary had been whipped into hospital about quarter to six, had the baby, then sat and watched the game live on Grampian TV. Word soon spread of course and it was crazy in the dressing room, the boys were all covering me in talcum powder and I'm just sitting there trying to take it all in. I got a shower and went straight up to the hospital and they weren't going to let me in, they said I was too late, so I'm trying to explain who I am and what I'd been doing. Eventually a kind nurse let me in, but only for five minutes, and then she kicked me out again and it was back to the house in Bridge of Don for a double celebration."

Young Stuart was a brother for Colin, the Weirs' second child, and I wondered whether Peter might have been a little upset that no-one had told him of his son's impending arrival. His answer could not have been more definitive.

"No, no, no. Oh, Fergie wouldn't have entertained that! I remember a couple of the boys being told if their wives were pregnant to pack them off to their mother's or mother-in-law's, don't have them in the house bothering you. Mary wasn't due that night, she'd been taken in a couple of weeks early because her waters had burst, but no, I'm glad I didn't know. I know it's different these days, I read of players missing games because their wives are about to give birth, but if I'd said that to Fergie – which I wouldn't have done -- I'd have been hung! You just went by Alex Ferguson's rules, I'm not even sure he would have known my wife was pregnant, to be honest with you."

The following night's *Evening Express* featured a large photograph of Peter, Mary, Stuart and the 'trophy' on the front page, while the *Press & Journal*'s back page headline blazed 'THE EUROPEAN

SUPER DONS', veteran Dons correspondent Alastair MacDonald excitedly writing, 'The Dons are the kings of European football – that's official'.

By the time of that Super Cup Final Mark McGhee was halfway through what would be his final season at Pittodrie, but there was still time for one last magical European night.

In their defence of the Cup Winners Cup Aberdeen had secured a quarter-final meeting with the legendary Hungarians Ujpest Dosza. The Dons went into the first leg in Budapest on the back of a twenty-eight match unbeaten run stretching back over five months which had taken them into the last eight of the Scottish Cup and six points clear, with two games in hand, at the top of the Scottish Premier Division. Confidence could hardly have been higher, and the team played well that night at the Megyeri Stadium, but there was one problem; they simply could not put the ball in the net. Gordon Strachan rounded goalkeeper Szendrei but shot against the post and McGhee then had an even more glaring miss. Szendrei dropped a cross at his feet and from less than a yard out the striker shot weakly, the ball rebounding off the keeper's prone body to safety.

"Fergie didn't just give me the 'hairdryer' after that one, it was a pyrotechnic blast. That miss had been in the last couple of minutes and I knew what was coming. He came right up to me, face to face, and slaughtered me, screaming, 'That was the worst fucking miss I've ever seen in my fucking life!' He was absolutely furious. Back at the hotel he sent us all to our rooms and told us we had to stay there, but wee Gordon [Strachan] – I don't know what had got into him – decided we would go down for a few beers and I tagged along. Really, I just wanted to see what would happen, but when we got to the bar there was no sign of the manager, it was just the press, so we sat until the early hours drinking beer, the wee man the whole time hoping Fergie would show up and there would be a confrontation. He never did, probably just as well. Anyway, we told the journalists about his reaction to the miss and I remember telling them, only joking, 'Never mind, I'll get a hat-trick in the second leg' and of course I did."

Which was just as well, as despite the Dons dominating that encounter in the Hungarian capital it was Ujpest who won it 2-0 thanks to a couple of second-half goals.

A fortnight later Pittodrie was bristling, the fear of elimination from a tournament we had come to love mixed with the hope and anticipation of what might just be a sensational night ahead. It was the first time in four years the Dons had lost the first leg of a European tie; the question was, could they possibly pull back such a deficit? In truth, they very nearly didn't.

As in most of those big games at home Aberdeen went at their visitors from the off, playing at high-intensity, swarming forward time after time, Strachan and Dougie Bell probing and teasing the Hungarian back line. But the Ujpest defence repelled their attacks and with half an hour gone, and the game still goalless, frustration was beginning to set in. And then came the breakthrough.

Alex McLeish acrobatically kept in an overhit John Hewitt free-kick, he and Willie Miller exchanged passes, then teed up Gordon Strachan at the edge of the box. The midfielder delivered an inch-perfect cross, finding Mark with the freedom he craved in front of the Beach End. A nod of his head and the Dons had halved the visitors' advantage. They almost threw it away immediately, Miller fouling Steidl in the box, a clear penalty, but not given by the Belgian referee. Dougie Bell had a long-range effort saved and John Hewitt was also denied before the half-time whistle. McGhee then scrambled a shot against the back post as the Hungarians defended desperately. 1-0 at the break, Aberdeen still behind on aggregate.

Roared on by the 22,800 crowd Aberdeen pressed incessantly for the leveller, but their efforts looked like being in vain; Eric Black having missed with a header and Strachan having crashed a shot off the crossbar with a well struck free-kick. Finally, with just two minutes remaining on the clock, substitute Willie Falconer drove in a low cross which eluded the Ujpest players and McGhee calmly side-footed the ball home. All hell let loose, the noise pouring from the stands was deafening, and although Aberdeen couldn't force a winner in the seconds remaining of regulation time, there was only going to be one winner in the extra half-hour. The goal which settled the tie came shortly after the restart, Stewart McKimmie and Black linked up, Strachan sent another inch-perfect delivery into the box for his mate McGhee, who arrived unmarked at the back post to complete his treble, his low shot flying off the keeper's foot and up into the roof of the net. In doing so he became just the second Don to score a European hat-trick, matching the feat of Francis Munro in the club's first ever European tie, a 10-0 win over KR Reykjavik in September 1967.

"Funnily enough, my main recollection from that game is their keeper nutting Alex McLeish and getting himself sent off."

Jozsef Szendrei had indeed been red-carded for head-butting the Aberdeen central defender, an act of folly after an aerial challenge by McLeish, and one which firmly erased any lingering hopes the Hungarians had of salvaging the match.

That magnificent night was to be McGhee's final fling for the club in Europe, the Cup Winners Cup adventure ending in the semi-finals as Porto won both legs 1-0. His hat-trick saw him reach that record-breaking Aberdeen total, and left him with plenty of memories.

"That really was a fantastic occasion for all of us, and a special one for me . . ." He smiled, before adding, "I'd always wondered if I was the club's top European scorer, and I never knew my stats until now. Fourteen in thirty, eh? Not bad."

Throughout his playing career Mark was generally fairly transient, a year or two here, a year or two there, his spell at Pittodrie being his longest with any one club. He admits that was partly down to the success the team enjoyed, partly because there were not any offers made known to him. It certainly was not down to the financial rewards on offer at Pittodrie.

"The money was rubbish. Our wives would literally be sitting in the stands watching the games and knowing if we won the Cup we'd be going on holiday, if we didn't we wouldn't, simple as that."

In relation to the average fan, the salaries paid to the players were of course quite decent, but when you consider what that team achieved, the glory and the finance they helped bring to the club, then you can understand why, once they began to make a name for themselves, some of the top stars were quick to leave and cash in. Mark was among the first to move on, in the summer of 1984.

"In my final year at Pittodrie I was paid £33,000. I know that because the transfer fee Hamburg had to pay was based on multiples and Aberdeen got £330,000. When I went to Germany I signed a sponsorship contract with Adidas which paid me more than that, quite apart from what I was getting from the club. The day after I signed I went to the company's facility near Nuremberg and they took me down to the factory to get me some gear. I was thinking, 'Great, I'll get a couple of shirts and a few bits and pieces', but I ended up leaving with two huge bags full of tracksuits, suits, tennis racquets, you name it! Back at the hotel I was introduced to Adi Dassler, one of the founders of the company, and a guy who turned out to be the Chairman of Volkswagen and he asked if I needed a car. When I told him the club had given me a nice Mercedes he asked if my wife needed one, and when I agreed that she did, he promised to send us one. Three days later a trailer turns up at the house with this beautiful Golf, all leather seats, electric windows even – I'd never seen anything like it! The guy says there you go, a wee present from Volkswagen. So things like that, the forty grand from Adidas, the wages from Hamburg which were a helluva lot more than Aberdeen had been paying me, there was no way we could stay for simple economic reasons."

There had been interest from Italy, and there was more money on offer there, but the Germans sealed the deal thanks to a football legend.

"My agent called and said Gunter Netzer wanted to meet me. He flew over in a private jet and got a taxi to my wee flat in Ferryhill. That was good enough for me!"

He began his Hamburg adventure shortly after that and found it difficult initially, a series of niggling injuries compounded by hernia problems. He did manage to get a few runs in the team and there were some real highlights during his time there.

"I was at training one Friday and had damaged my ankle ligaments, but it was Bayern Munich the next day and I wasn't missing that. I got this ludicrous bandaging all round it, it was more like a stookie, I couldn't move it at all. Fifteen minutes in I chase a long ball down, cut in on to my left foot at the edge of the box and hit a cross-cum-shot which the wind carries over the head of Jean-Marie Pfaff and straight into the top corner! But when I was running back after scoring I get this excruciating pain right up from my heel and I have to go off, couldn't even put my foot down on the ground. We won 1-0, but that was me out for months, I had to have an operation, didn't recover well, and eventually it seemed right to come back home again."

Home indeed to his boyhood heroes Celtic, signed by Davie Hay, and although it again took him longer to settle than he might have hoped, he had a successful time there winning the Premier Division and the Scottish Cup twice each, including the double in the club's centenary season of 1987-88. He left the following year after a highly productive season in which he finished joint-top league scorer with Charlie Nicholas, then playing with the Dons.

"I never got presented with my Golden Boot until the first game of the following season when I had rejoined Newcastle, so that achievement kind of went missing."

Given that he had been in such good form, why had he left Celtic that summer?

"Big Billy [McNeill] had decided the previous year that he wanted to get in younger guys and that I was surplus to requirements, but I was playing so well, I was really fit and bursting for a chance. I missed the first couple of months, but eventually I got on as a sub against Honved in a European tie and scored right away. Andy Walker had got injured so Billy decided to 'give me a chance' and I got a hat-trick when we beat St Mirren 7-1 on the Saturday."

He then got a run in the team, scored another treble a few weeks later in a 8-0 beating of Hamilton and also netted in a win over Rangers, going on to score sixteen league goals.

"I was really flying, but for some reason Billy still wasn't convinced and when Newcastle came in for me I felt there was still a wee bit of unfinished business and so I went back there."

Mark carried on his good form at St James's and formed a lethal partnership with Mick Quinn, but the first season was to end in heartbreak.

"Jim Smith was the manager. I scored twenty-six league and cup goals and Quinny I think got thirty-seven, and we never got promoted, we lost to Sunderland in the play-offs. I had a double hernia that summer, Jim got the sack, Ossie Ardiles came in and I never got back to the fitness I needed even for that division. He bombed out all the senior players and I left."

Mark then had a brief spell in Sweden with IK Borlange – not as is often reported IK Brage – as he attempted to get fit again. He had enquiries from Hearts and St Mirren, both clubs keen to tempt him back to Scotland, but Alex Ferguson counselled him against that and to concentrate instead on securing his first break into coaching. He did not have long to wait as Reading, then in the third tier of English football, offered him a job as player-manager.

John Madjeski had just taken over the club and was in the process of beginning to completely overhaul it, but it was tough times in those early days.

"In the three and a half years I was there I spent a total of £110,000 in transfer fees, but I was lucky in that I made good signings, the likes of Shaka Hislop and Jimmy Quinn."

Reading won promotion in 1993-94 and were well placed midway through the next season when McGhee shocked them by walking out. Reading only just missed out on a second successive elevation while Mark's new club, Leicester City, were relegated from the Premiership.

"Alex [Ferguson] told me not to go there, told me they had no chance of staying up, and I should have taken his advice. Anyway, I had been there a year when Alex told me Wolves wanted me, and I was persuaded against my gut feeling to walk out. I shouldn't have done it, but I did, and Leicester went up under Martin O'Neill."

He kept the Molineux club up then launched a promotion challenge in 1996-97, only just missing out on an automatic place before losing to Crystal Palace in the play-offs. The following year Wolves reached the FA Cup semi-final, losing 1-0 to Arsenal, and six months later, with his side adrift in the promotion race, McGhee was sacked.

"Leaving Wolves really took it out of me, and by the time I felt I was ready to get back into management, no-one was offering me a job."

When one did come along it was at Division Two Millwall in the autumn of 2000 and McGhee led the team to an immediate promotion then finished fourth in what is now the Championship twelve months later, losing in the play-off semi-finals to Birmingham City. Mark loved his time at the New Den – there was only one problem; the Chairman Theo Paphitis.

"Personally we're fine, friends even, but I just couldn't work for Theo any longer. He was the best, he challenged you in a way that meant you had to be on the ball, to think about any decision you made, but he became too intense, and by the end when he called on a Friday night to ask what team I had selected, we'd be having four-hour conversations about it, and it just became too much."

Mark was out of work for a few weeks before Brighton came calling.

"In my first home league game we lost 4-1 to Bristol City, but by the end of that season we beat them 1-0 at the Millennium Stadium in the play-off Final. We got up to the Championship and stayed there the next season despite our top scorer being Adam Virgo with just seven goals. Wee Gordon [Strachan] reckons that if they did a count-back on that season they'd discover that we'd actually been relegated, that somebody must have miscounted."

They stayed up by one point, but not before a worrying ninety minutes on the final afternoon of the season.

"We needed at least a draw against Ipswich, and we got it, 1-1. They were already in the play-offs but by the end they had about seven strikers on the park, including Darren Bent. I'll never forgive Joe Royle for that, he did everything to try and beat us. Honestly, it was obscene how much effort they put in that day!"

Money was pouring out of the club at that time as they faced a third public enquiry in their efforts to finally build a new stadium back in the city. McGhee had to sell his best players and was not allowed to replace them. The almost inevitable relegation followed, as did Mark's sacking despite earlier reassurances from the board of directors.

In the summer of 2007 Mark finally returned to Scotland, taking up the managerial post at Motherwell. He had been investigating the possibility of moving abroad, but got a call from Alex McLeish alerting him to the vacancy at Fir Park and decided, for both family and professional reasons, the job appealed to him.

"From day one everything seemed right. I got on with the directors and could tell I could work with them."

That was borne out by results, Motherwell comfortably finishing the season in third place having played some sparkling football, with Chris Porter, David Clarkson and Ross McCormack all hitting double figures. Inevitably, the success led to interest from elsewhere and Vladimir Romanov was keen to lure him to Tynecastle.

"I'd agreed terms with Hearts. It was a fantastic offer, a sensational offer, and I got on the plane at Gatwick heading for Lithuania and I just had this overwhelming feeling that I was doing the wrong thing for all sorts of reasons, chief among them the fact that my son Archie was to be born that summer and I had promised to be there for Maria. Had I taken the job Romanov would have had me all over the place watching players. Add that to the reservations I already had – I'd been making noises about taking a team into Europe for the first time and I didn't feel right walking away from that – so I got off the plane, phoned John Boyle and said, 'Make me an offer and I'll stay.' He called back five minutes later and we agreed a deal."

I wondered how his fellow passengers had reacted to Mark's sudden decision not to fly . . .

"I was only going for the night so I just had hand luggage . . ." he replied, then after a pause, added, "That's a point you know. Had I had luggage in the hold I might well have just stayed on the plane. Sliding doors . . ."

During that first season Mark had been on the shortlist to become Scotland boss following the sacking of the hapless Berti Vogts. Also in the frame were the late Tommy Burns, Graeme Souness, Billy Davies and the successful candidate George Burley. McGhee was quite sanguine about Burley's appointment, but less happy about how he discovered he had been overlooked.

"I wasn't absolutely certain I wanted the job, and I certainly wasn't about to leave Motherwell mid-season, so I'd made it clear I wouldn't be available until that summer. I didn't get word from Gordon Smith [the then SFA Chief Executive], I was on the trackside before a midweek game and someone came up to me and told me George had been appointed."

That led to an embarrassing appearance by Gordon on the following Saturday's *Sportsound* programme on BBC Radio Scotland during which he claimed not to have had Mark's telephone number, something anyone else in football could have supplied instantly.

He may have missed out on the Scotland manager's post, but he did, during his Aberdeen career, at least have the honour of wearing the national colours on four occasions, scoring twice. One came against Canada on a summer tour in 1983, the other, more significantly, against England in a 1-1 draw at Hampden in the last ever Home International meeting between the countries the following year.

"When I went to Hamburg I got injured and I was called into squads but never played, and even when I came back to Celtic I was still fighting to get fully fit. By that time Maurice Johnston and Brian McClair and other younger strikers had come to the fore. I know why it happened, but I'm still disappointed I never won more caps. Having said that, to score against England was absolutely fantastic."

A quarter of a century later McGhee simply got on with the job in hand at Fir Park, but after that successful first campaign, his second was not quite as easy, Motherwell slipping down into the bottom six. Despite that, he was a man in demand. There were vacancies at Celtic Park and Pittodrie and Mark was well in the frame for both.

"I hung about in Glasgow for most of that summer of 2009 waiting on the Celtic job and I was given some encouragement that I had a decent chance of getting it. Willie [Miller] knew the situation, and eventually on the Friday I was told to expect a call from Dermot Desmond. By ten o'clock that night it hadn't come, so before hearing anything from them I called Willie and told him I was coming."

The following morning Mark got a text from Desmond telling him they had chosen one of the other candidates, Tony Mowbray. By then it was well into the summer and the new season was fast approaching.

"I didn't have time to do the due diligence I normally did before taking on a new job and I suppose I just assumed Aberdeen would be the club I remembered. It wasn't. Regardless of what you might say about me being one of the legends, I found that I had no standing either from the fans or within the club. It didn't work out for me, it didn't work out for the club, no hard feelings."

His reign began with a "totally disastrous" 5-1 thrashing in the Europa League by Sigma Olomouc in front of a disbelieving Pittodrie. That was our record home defeat in European competition, the 8-1 aggregate score-line was also a record. Mark admitted to me from day one he realised it was not going to work for him back in the north-east.

In truth, it never looked like working. The Dons were knocked out of the League Cup by Dundee and by another First Division side, Raith Rovers, in a Pittodrie replay in the Scottish Cup. I was working at the game that night and had never felt lower as a fan; the drive back home was interminable, punctuated only by the stream of texts and calls from friends who support other teams offering 'sympathy'. Aberdeen finished ninth in the SPL table.

The following season began more optimistically with back-to-back wins sending the Dons to the top of the league. It was not to last, and a run of six defeats in eight matches sent the team to Celtic Park just two points clear of bottom place. Saturday, November 6th, 2010 was to be the darkest day in the club's history, bringing as it did our heaviest defeat in 107 years. The final score was Celtic 9, Aberdeen 0.

On a Saturday afternoon I normally present the programme from the studio hosting Open All Mics, but as fate would have it most of the matches were postponed that day due to the referee strike. Plan B entailed me conducting *Sportsound* from the stadium, with the game going out as our main live commentary. I slid deeper and deeper into my seat as the goals flowed and the Celtic fans around me in the main stand offered good-natured banter. By the end I was emotionally shattered, and yet had to grab the microphone and host the rest of the programme as professionally as possible. I did however let my mask slip once. In his post-match interview Mark at one point said, ". . . it was only three points . . ." Picking up after, my angry response was, "It may only have been three points for Mark, but my team, the team I have supported for forty years, died out there this afternoon."

His comment and my reaction were both picked up by the Aberdeen directors. In fact, having been in discussion with Chairman Stewart Milne and others throughout the following day, Mark called me that Sunday night, not to have an argument, just to try to get a grip on how I and others were feeling in the wake of the humiliation. It was to be the last time we spoke until I called him almost a year later to try to set up the interview for this book.

"It is a hard one to get your head around, trying to come up with the right things to say in a situation like that, particularly right after the game. I was trying not to make excuses. I knew it wasn't just three points, I knew it was more than that."

Milne showed incredible patience and support, but by that stage Mark was 'dead man walking' and the axe finally fell three weeks later, McGhee becoming just the latest in a line of Dons bosses sacked after losing to Kilmarnock at Rugby Park.

I wondered whether the news, when it finally came, was something of a relief.

"I didn't want the sack, that's the wrong attitude, but I couldn't see any way out of it. I didn't have the real backing of the staff. Willie and the others didn't do me any harm, I've no complaints about them, but Stewart wasn't the Chairman I needed."

Mark was out of the game for over a year, eventually returning as Bristol Rovers manager a fortnight before we met up. Batteries recharged, he was ready for the challenge again, and looking forward to guiding a club on the up. With plans well underway for a long-awaited move to a new stadium and a general air of optimism around the place, the positivity he loves to feed off was almost palpable, the memories and hurt of his dismal return to the Dons fading into the past. He steered Rovers well clear of relegation from League Two, helped by a ten-match unbeaten home run, and eventually finished the season mid-table and full of optimism for the future.

CHAPTER FIFTEEN

THE SUPPORTING CAST

Alex Ferguson, the eleven who started in Gothenburg and substitute John Hewitt have rightly attracted most publicity and praise down the years. It is inevitable the spotlight has, in the main, shone on those thirteen men. But they have all been quick to point to the contribution of others; the players, the backroom team and the board of directors who all played their parts in this incredible story. It would be doing those individuals an injustice not to recognise their efforts in this book.

Standing alongside Ferguson during the peak years of his Pittodrie success story were two men, Teddy Scott and his assistant manager Archie Knox. Knox would himself go on to enjoy a stellar career as a number two, assisting Walter Smith during Rangers' nine-in-a-row era, but when Ferguson chose him to replace Pat Stanton at Aberdeen, Knox was managing lowly Forfar Athletic.

The part-time Angus side had, under his guidance, been minutes from the biggest shock score-line in Scottish football history, leading Rangers 2-1 in the 1977-78 League Cup semi-final, only to concede a late equaliser and then be overrun in extra-time.

That was the outstanding highlight during his time at Station Park, in the main the job was all about the day-to-day frustrations of running a small-time club, wondering whether players with full-time jobs would turn up for training or indeed on match days.

Knox had started up the Tayside Reserve League, a chance for him to pit his wits against bigger teams in the area like Dundee, Dundee United and, of course, Aberdeen and it was after one such encounter with the Dons that he received a surprise job offer.

"Alex asked to see me in my office and asked me straight out if I'd like to be his assistant. I said yes and he invited me up to Pittodrie the next day to watch the friendly against Twente Enschede. I met the Chairman and it was all agreed, there was no negotiating terms, it was just a case of here's the job, it's yours if you want it."

Archie was working full-time with local builders Webster & Pattullo selling squash courts and swimming pools in addition to his job at Station Park, but within a week he had tied everything up and begun coaching some of the country's finest young talent at Pittodrie. He admits it was daunting to start with.

"I hadn't really known Alex at all before then, it turned out it was my old boss at Dundee United, Jim McLean, who had recommended me, and I was going into a club which had won the title the previous season. It was a big step up."

The relationship blossomed right from the start, Archie organising training and keeping the kids on for afternoon sessions.

"I honestly can't remember ever having a day off with those boys. The older, more experienced players might have had, but apart from Friday afternoons I had those kids in working with them every day. That's the best part of coaching, getting out with the balls and helping those young lads develop and come through. I loved it."

Aside from the technical and mental aspects of the game, both Alex Ferguson and Archie were big on discipline and expected their players to live their lives in a professional manner. Breaches of the code of conduct were rare.

"I did get a call from one of our landladies complaining about some of the boys. She was looking after Eric Black and Bryan Gunn and a few others and said they were running up and down the stairs and wearing out her carpets. Turns out they were playing hide and seek! Here was a group of seventeen- and eighteen-year-olds and that was what they were up to. We used to use those boys as babysitters! You'd never get away with it these days, but Alex and I would ask them 'What are you doing Saturday night?' and they would hate that question. They'd say they were going out and we'd say 'No you're not, you're babysitting, be there at seven' and these were boys that were playing in the first team at the time! I ask my kids now 'Who was your best babysitter?' and they say it was big Bryan Gunn, because he used to take them down to the garage for sweeties."

Archie also became the club's European super spy; he was the one heading off to all corners of the continent and naturally encountered a few memorable moments. One such came when he travelled to Poland to watch Lech Poznan ahead of their Second Round meeting in that '82-83 season.

"I arrived in Warsaw and got picked up for the trip to Lodz where they were playing. The guy spoke no English and the trip took over two hours. Eventually he stopped on a wee side road and jumped out, presumably to take a leak, but he was away for twenty minutes and I was wondering what the hell was going on. I was just about to drive away myself when he reappeared and off we went, without explanation. We got to the hotel and it turned out we were sharing a room! I never slept a wink. About half-two there was a banging on the door and he ended up having a huge argument with someone out in the corridor. It was a nightmare."

The only team Archie did not scout during that Cup Winners Cup run was Dinamo Tirana; even he could not find a way into communist Albania. He did find his way to Spain on May 1st, 1983 for the last day of the Primera Division season where the Dons' Final opponents Real Madrid were due to take on Valencia. Real needed to win to clinch the title, Valencia required a victory to avoid relegation. Incredibly, Archie left Dyce Airport on the morning of the game, so it was always going to be something of a race against time.

"It was organised through Harry Hynds Travel. It was Aberdeen to London and on to Alicante, and then I had a hire car to drive to Valencia. It was a wee 1100 engine and it was struggling. There wasn't another car to be seen; turns out I had taken the toll road, and along the way the car overheated and I had to pull over with steam pouring out of it. I had to wait half an hour for it to cool down before I could set off again. By the time I got to Valencia I was running late and had no idea where the hotel was – I was supposed to meet Real Madrid there and travel to the game on their bus. I stopped a taxi driver and paid him to lead the way and I followed, but by the time we got there the bus had left. They had said they would leave the tickets if I hadn't arrived, but when I asked at reception, nothing. I went up to my room and got changed into the Aberdeen suit and tie. I got a taxi and told the guy 'Don't worry, I'll pay the fines, just get me to the stadium in time' and to be fair he did what he could, breaking speed limits, dodging in and out of the traffic, but we hit gridlock so I paid him, got out and ran the rest of the way.

By the time I got there I was soaking with sweat and it was ten minutes after kick-off. I went round and round the stadium trying to persuade people to let me in, showing them the Aberdeen tie, but no-one was interested. Eventually I just made a run for it past the stewards and up the stairs, but they grabbed me and frogmarched me out! There were some policemen there so I went over to explain and one of them said 'No-one could make up a story like that' so he took me over and distracted the stewards and I nipped up a different set of stairs. The stadium was packed; it had been a total sell-out for six weeks, so all I could do was kneel down in an aisle with my notebook peering through a guy's legs to try to watch the game, it was the only way I could see the pitch. I had just got there when Valencia scored the only goal of the game, they stayed up and Athletic Bilbao won the title. I learned absolutely nothing about Real Madrid, I would have been better off sitting in a bar watching it on the television.

"I finally got back to the hotel and remember seeing their manager Alfredo di Stefano standing at the bar drowning his sorrows with a large whisky. I went up to the room to have a shower and get changed and I'd just got there when there was a knock on the door, and here was the boy from reception with my tickets for the game, and on the envelope it read Mr Billy McNeill, Celtic Football Club. Unbelievable!"

While Alex Ferguson was clearly the boss, Archie had his say and the pair would adjourn to 'Ted's Room' (Teddy Scott's remarkable bolthole filled with all forms of memorabilia, photographs and the daily football diaries he maintained religiously, recording every game played by the club, line-ups, scores and scorers, and every significant, and quite often not so significant, happening within the walls of the stadium) two hours before kick-off to finalise their team selection for the day.

"One day we'd agreed on the side and went into the dressing room to announce it, and I'm thinking 'that's not the team we chose' so I let him finish and when we got back outside I asked him. He said that he'd had a last-minute rethink – he had changed three of the side – and I said that's fine, but Drew Jarvie was in the starting line-up and now he's not even on the bench, and Alex said, 'For Christ's sake I forgot about him' and I had to go tell one of the young lads that there had been a mistake and that he wasn't a substitute and that Jarvie was."

Ferguson's at times fiery nature meant he had to spend SFA-enforced periods watching matches from the stand when his only means of communication with Knox in the dug-out was by bulky, brick-like walkie-talkies. As you might imagine these were generally red-hot given the flow of instructions from manager to assistant. During one game Ferguson leapt to celebrate an Aberdeen goal and in sitting down again brought his walkie-talkie crashing on to the bald head of the Lord Provost Alex Collie who was sat in the row in front. He spent the remainder of the match dabbing blood from the Provost's head with his handkerchief.

"It was bizarre, every time I looked round that was all I could see, Alex wiping the blood from the Provost's head. I could hardly concentrate on the game."

Knox stood side by side with Ferguson for over four years before being offered the chance to go it alone as manager of his boyhood heroes, Dundee, in 1984.

"It was great to get the chance, but I never really enjoyed it the same. I went from a team capable of winning things to a team fighting relegation, and while we had good players like John Brown and Robert Connor I knew they were going to be sold. I never got used to working with guys who weren't quite at the same level as those I'd left behind."

He returned to Pittodrie two and a half years later as co-manager. "That was a strange thing, I never bothered about titles, but because I'd been manager at Dens Alex wanted me to have the same title back with him." But it was to be a short-lived stay. In November 1986 Manchester United came calling and the pair were off to Old Trafford.

"We were training at Seaton Park and I saw Alex's Merc reversing along the track. My mum hadn't been well at the time so I thought he was there with bad news and I ran over. He never even got out of the car, just wound down the window and said, 'We're going to Man United.' He told me that I'd be offered the job at Aberdeen and it was up to me, but I knew right away I was going with him. I knew I would never be able to recreate what we had done."

There was never any discussion regarding a contract, it was all just agreed with the United board on the spot, and Archie went home to his late wife Janice and their children and told them, 'Pack your bags, we're off to Manchester.'

He stayed with Ferguson at Old Trafford for five years and then, with the club settled and about to embark on a two-decades-long domination of the English game, Archie quit to join Walter Smith at Ibrox.

"It was all about stepping up in my career. I hadn't made much money from the game, I had bills to pay, and believe it or not, I was being paid more by Rangers than I ever was at Manchester United. In fact when I left Aberdeen to go to United I got a pay rise of just five grand a year. Can you imagine that?"

After a trophy-laden spell with the Govan side, Archie joined Walter for a return to England with Everton. He was also assistant to Scotland manager Craig Brown and later took charge of the Under-21 national team. Among other appointments added to the CV were stints with Livingston, Bolton Wanderers and Blackburn Rovers. After a year out of the game he joined up with Craig Brown at Motherwell and the oldest managerial pairing in the game did so well they were poached by Aberdeen in December 2010, Archie returning to Pittodrie to find his old club rock-bottom of the SPL. The pair immediately moved the Dons away from relegation trouble and set about trying to return them to at least a level of respectability.

"I still love being out there working with the boys. I'm feeling the cold a bit more than I did thirty years ago right enough, but there's nothing else I'd rather be doing."

The players I have spoken to in researching this book have generally described Archie as the 'good cop' in his managerial partnership with Alex Ferguson, something he refutes. Perhaps he feels that would be bad for his image, but there clearly was a strong bond with that team, and two of them, Eric Black when he was manager at Coventry and Mark McGhee when he was in charge of Millwall, brought him in as assistant boss. When I suggested that showed the high regard his players from back then still held him in, Archie was typically self-deprecating.

"Well, either that or they couldn't get anyone else."

The other member of the management team behind Aberdeen's glory days of the early to mid 1980s was a quite remarkable man, one who preferred to remain very much in the background and quietly get on with the job, but who was nevertheless a key component of the success story.

Teddy Scott was born in Ellon in 1929 and began his football career as a player with Bournemouth while doing his national service. He returned to the north-east after being demobbed and joined junior side Sunnybank who he helped win the Scottish Junior Cup in 1954 (one of only two such successes for Aberdeen sides in the history of the competition, the other being recorded by Banks o' Dee three years later). Teddy caught the eye of Dons manager Davie Halliday, signed

258

for the club on March 3rd 1954, and was part of the squad that won the club's first ever Scottish championship, but not a huge part; he was to play just two competitive matches for the first team. Instead his contribution to the club, which saw him inducted into the Aberdeen FC Hall of Fame, was to come in countless other areas.

His various titles included trainer, kit-man, reserve team coach and physiotherapist, but no label could accurately reflect his tireless work over forty-nine years until his much-delayed retirement in 2003.

Alex Ferguson saw him as an invaluable member of his backroom team and remained in contact long after leaving for Old Trafford. In fact when Teddy was awarded a testimonial match in January 1999 Sir Alex brought along a full-strength Manchester United team to celebrate the occasion, and such was the high esteem everyone held Teddy in, the game drew Pittodrie's first sell-out crowd in years.

Archie Knox is in no doubt just how vital Teddy was to their operation.

"He was remarkable, just remarkable. I've never known anyone to spend the amount of time as Teddy did at this football club. He would arrive at 7am, and for years he was getting the bus in from Ellon in the morning and getting the 10pm bus back home from the top of the road. The club eventually got him a wee Fiesta van, but for years and years he made that trip every single day."

Teddy was almost evangelical about his work with the young-sters and reserve players who needed a game and would arrange matches almost every Sunday, roping Knox in along the way.

"He had me driving the mini-bus about all over the place, to Deveronvale, to Elgin, all over. He liked to make sure the Highland League clubs were looked after; it suited them and it suited Aberdeen to have those games. He took the reserves every week, he washed all the laundry, looked after all the kit. He'd be working on for hours after getting back from matches. He was a phenomenal man, just phenomenal, and never had a bad word to say about anybody."

There is not a single player who encountered Teddy Scott who does not have a tale to tell, and all remember him fondly.

John McMaster was just one of many whom Teddy took under his wing.

"He was my guardian, he looked after me. We had to buy a settee for our first flat, I couldn't afford to pay it all at once, and I needed a guarantor for the finance and he said no problem, signed it just like that. He never had his favourites though, he would have helped anyone. He liked the west coast boys, he loved our mentality, the arrogance we had. He was just an incredible character."

While he worked with all the players, he did pay special attention to the younger ones, among them Eric Black.

"Teddy had a massive influence, he got on well with everybody, but still set standards and put great store in discipline; we were always having to check the dressing rooms were tidy, the washing done and the carpets clean. I was in the first team at that time, but he never let you get above your station, there was a constant reality check."

One story has gone down in legend, and it has a number of variations, but the bones of it are that Aberdeen arrived in the dressing room before the away leg against Sion to discover that Teddy, who had not made the trip, had packed the wrong colour of socks. Alex Ferguson decided that he would sack Scott on returning home and Gordon Strachan piped up, "Oh yes, and which ten people are you going to get to replace him?"

That is a question that could have been asked many, many times over the five decades Teddy Scott loyally served the club and it was no surprise that Ferguson was there leading the tributes at Ellon Parish Church when Teddy died after a long illness at the age of eighty-three in June 2012. A club statement accurately described him as a 'true Aberdeen legend'.

The board of directors at the time was a tight close-knit unit consisting of three men: Chairman Dick Donald, his son Ian and Vice-Chairman Chris Anderson and they set about supporting the manager in his vision.

I only ever knew the Chairman as Mr Donald, I couldn't bring myself to call him Dick, and while he was a slight and unremarkable looking man, he did have something of an aura about him. He certainly attracted respect from all who dealt with him and his contribution to the club was enormous.

Mr Donald signed for the Dons in 1928, but played only infrequently for the first team during two spells interrupted by a year long sabbatical with Dunfermline. Two decades later, having immersed himself in the family business empire, a thriving company which included cinemas, the ice-rink in Spring Garden and His Majesty's Theatre, he was invited to join the Pittodrie board of directors, eventually taking over as Chairman in 1970. He always knew the value of money and was at times parsimonious, but forged an excellent working relationship with Alex Ferguson, prompting the manager to describe him thus, "As a chairman, he was a colossus, and nobody had to tell me that I had little chance of ever working for his like again."

Dick Donald died after a lengthy illness in 1993, having been too ill to attend the official opening of the Richard Donald Stand, the massive edifice constructed in place of the old Beach End. His loss was mourned by all who knew him, his funeral attended by former players and managers with Sir Alex, fittingly, among the pall-bearers.

Ian Donald had joined the Pittodrie board in 1980 following the end of a playing career which had begun at Manchester United and ended at Arbroath. A hotelier, Ian followed his father into the family business, expanding it into other areas of the world of entertainment and leisure, and officially took over as Aberdeen FC chairman in 1994. By then it was a very different club to that which his father had run so prudently and after four years in the post – during which he was the last Dons chairman to oversee a trophy win – made way for local businessman and multi-millionaire Stewart Milne. Ian remained an active board member until 2004 when he was named honorary president.

The third member of the board in season 1982-83 was Chris Anderson OBE, a forward-thinking visionary credited as the brains behind much of the good that happened in and around the club at that time. It was he who was instrumental in turning Pittodrie into an all-seated stadium; he was also one of the driving forces behind the creation in 1975 of the Scottish Premier Division, a new league set-up which contributed to a healthier and more competitive environment and one in which Aberdeen flourished. Like his fellow board members Chris played for the club, and with a little more success than the Donalds, before becoming a director in 1967 and vice-chairman a few years later. In tandem with his football career Chris was a key figure at Robert Gordon's Institute of Technology, taking early retirement as secretary there in 1984. Within months he began to experience physical problems, unusual for the still ultra-fit then fifty-nine-year-old, and he was given the shocking diagnosis that he was suffering from motor neurone disease, for which there was no cure. Within two years he was dead, a tragic loss to his family and friends, a desperate loss too for Aberdeen FC.

In a touching obituary, reprinted in his book *The First 100 Years of the Dons*, the highly-respected journalist Jack Webster, a close friend, wrote: 'In facing up to his greatest battle so courageously, Chris Anderson remained conscious till his very last day. But he was trapped inside an immobile body without means of communication, except for the flap of an eyelid. The man who loved fitness and freedom was finally a prisoner. And, in the fading minutes of Tuesday night, he was mercifully given his release'. Chris Anderson's ambition had been to lead the club he loved into the twenty-first century as its chairman, and had he been spared Aberdeen FC might have entered the millennium in an altogether stronger position.

The board of directors at that time placed trust in their manager and allowed him to manage the club, never interfering unless asked to do so. Archie Knox perfectly sums up their approach.

"Dick Donald would come into the dressing room sometimes just to wish us all the best, occasionally Ian and Chris, but it would just be a quick chat. We had an AGM one year and it lasted two minutes, we never had board meetings . . . we'd all just sit down with a bowl of soup in the canteen and that was it. That's how they ran the club, it was a remarkable operation."

Of the players who kicked-off the Cup Winners Cup Final against Real Madrid, the nine who made most appearances during the 1982-83 season all featured. Willie Miller played in all sixty competitive matches during that campaign, Jim Leighton missed just one, the others fewer than ten. Black, McMaster and Hewitt found themselves sidelined more often because of injury problems.

The highest name on the appearance list not to feature in Gothenburg was Stuart Kennedy whose career was ended by that knee injury during the semi-final second-leg in Belgium. It was a cruel twist of fate for the rock-hard full-back. Stuart's team-mates have described him as being among the most mentally-tough players they have encountered, his determination unmatched and he, as much as anyone, deserved to be out there facing Real Madrid. Alex Ferguson gave him every chance, bending over backwards to allow him to prove his fitness, but in the end even Stuart had to concede he was not ready and it was an act of great compassion, and a clear indication of the esteem in which he held Kennedy, to name the unfit defender among the five substitutes.

The players I spoke to for this book were queuing up to praise their old team-mate. Alex McLeish recalled Kennedy's unshakable self-belief.

"Stuart compared himself to the best right-backs in the world, he was always dismissing wingers and telling them, 'Look you'd better go over to the other side and see if you can get any joy out of the left-back because you're getting nothing out of me.' He just talked opponents off their game."

Gordon Strachan told me, jokingly, he might have to take some responsibility for Stuart's early retiral.

"He was one of the first full-backs I wrote off! I played into my forties but you look at any right-back that played behind me – they barely made it to thirty before having to chuck it . . ." and after a wicked chuckle, ". . . so I thank them all! He was strong-minded and had delusions of grandeur when he got forward – he thought he was Manny Kaltz, but he wasn't – everything he got was through sheer determination and hard work and he was great for me."

John McMaster still feels a deep sadness when he recalls that fateful night in the city of Genk.

"That will always live with me, Stuart's injury. His knee just buckled . . . there was no reason why it should happen. He was a strong wee bugger, tough, sinewy . . . the dressing room afterwards was like a morgue, because we lost, but also because of what had happened to Stuart because we knew it was a bad one."

As is so often the case in football, one person's despair is another's opportunity and Kennedy's injury had a silver lining for McMaster.

"I don't think I'd have played in the final if Stuart had been there. It would have been big Dougie at left-back and Stuarty at right-back . . . I know that, he knows that . . . it was so, so sad . . . that was our biggest regret about that whole time, but he was there and he was the same old Stuart winding us up, pushing us on."

When Stuart's knee was opened up the surgeon discovered his cartilage had split in two and there was further additional damage to his joints. He was told in no uncertain terms his playing career was over. He remained at Pittodrie until 1986, helping with the reserves and doing some scouting, but by then he knew it was time to move on.

"I was a proud athlete, I didn't want to hang around, limping about the place, so I headed home to Grangemouth and bought a pub, The Woodside Inn, in Falkirk. I really enjoyed that, it was a great pub with great customers, and that became my life."

Stuart ran the pub until 2003 when he decided it was time to look for something new. Just five days after selling it he was sitting at a T-junction when a double-decker bus crashed into the side of his car, pushing him forcibly off the road and through a hedge, causing a catalogue of serious injuries. His leg was in plaster for fourteen weeks and he had to endure a lengthy rehabilitation phase. Unsurprisingly, he calls it "the worst time of my life". During that time he and his wife Anne bought the Grangeburn Guest House in Grangemouth, returning the property to the family. Anne had been brought up in the house and her mother had run the business for years before selling it sometime previously. Stuart helps in the running of it, but says, "Anne's the boss", which might come as a surprise to his old team-mates who remember what a forceful, argumentative and dominating figure he was in the dressing-room.

Stuart maintains an interest in football, doing a bit of scouting to keep his hand in, and still loves getting together with that Gothenburg squad. He recalls with pride the fact that Alex Ferguson wrote in his autobiography that Kennedy had given him 'monumental service' and had allowed him to be part of that famous win over Real Madrid. "That wasn't his style, normally it was a case of 'once you're used, you're used' and I really respected that he gave me the opportunity. Mind you, when he told me afterwards he couldn't put me on at 2-1, I told him he was wrong, that I'd have gone on and scored a couple of goals to settle the match! To be fair, the substitution he made that night wasn't a bad one, was it?"

Kennedy started forty-two matches that season and at least had the comfort of getting a medal in Sweden, but his team-mate Dougie Bell, injured in the Scottish Cup semi-final win over Celtic, was not so lucky. Alex Ferguson could not afford to have two unusable substitutes on the bench and it was Dougie who missed out. Bell had been signed by Ferguson on a free transfer from St Mirren in 1979 and became a key squad player, often being deployed in the bigger domestic games and European ties. The 5-1 thrashing of Waterschei was perhaps the best match of his Dons career, Dougie was unplayable that night, but there were countless other occasions when his direct running and mesmerising skills swung games Aberdeen's way. He was sold to Rangers for £160,000 in 1985 and went on to play for a dozen more clubs on both sides of the border before calling a halt to his career in the late nineties, following that with various management and coaching positions in junior football and with First Division Clyde.

The bench in Gothenburg was completed by goalkeeper Bryan Gunn and midfielders Ian Angus and Andy Watson.

Gunn spent half a dozen years at Pittodrie but, because of the astonishing consistency shown by Jim Leighton, played only eighteen games. His career, during which he won six Scotland caps, really took off when he moved to Norwich City. In more than a decade at Carrow Road he featured in over 400 games, the highlight being a UEFA Cup win over Bayern Munich (a decade after the Dons' famous victory over the same side) which helped him be inducted into the club's Hall of Fame. Bryan had a brief spell with Hibernian, but returned to Norwich, and among his various jobs with City was a period as manager which ended ingloriously with a 7-1 home defeat to Colchester United. Away from the game Bryan and his wife Susan suffered personal tragedy in 1992 when their two-year-old daughter Francesca died from leukaemia, prompting the pair to help set up a cancer charity which eventually raised in excess of £1,000,000 to help fund research and to provide resources for local hospitals.

Ian Angus had a similar length of time with the Dons, but was perhaps overshadowed by fellow youngsters Cooper, Simpson, Hewitt and Black. He never established himself in the way they did, but still featured in 120 matches. Moves to Dundee and Motherwell, where he won a Scottish Cup winner's medal in 1991, followed, and he then enjoyed a two-year spell with Clyde. 'Og', as he was known to his Pittodrie team-mates, finished his career with a brief spell at Stirling Albion and an even briefer one with Albion Rovers before slipping out of the game entirely.

Andy Watson made his Aberdeen debut against Ayr United, the same day as Steve Archibald, as a substitute for Dom Sullivan on a freezing cold afternoon in January 1978. The game ended 1-1 and I felt a certain pride watching him enter the fray as he, like me, had attended Skene Square Primary School. Andy barely featured over the next two years, but made a huge contribution in the title-winning season of 1979-80. A virtual ever-present in the final three months of the campaign, he scored four goals, with one, a late equaliser against struggling Hibernian, being particularly important on a night when our championship challenge seemed set to evaporate. Watson left that summer of 1983 to sign for Leeds United and had later spells with Hearts and Hibernian. He became assistant to Alex McLeish when his former team-mate took over as manager of Motherwell and the pair were side by side for the next seventeen years until Alex decided to employ Peter Grant as his number two when taking over at Aston Villa in 2011.

There were just two other players who started matches during that momentous season.

Right-back Brian Mitchell played twice, in the League Cup win over Dumbarton in September and then in the 5-0 thrashing of Kilmarnock in the penultimate league match. Brian spent seven years at Pittodrie but found regular first-team football difficult to pin down as he played understudy first to Stuart Kennedy, then to Stewart McKimmie. He did however feature during the successive title wins in 1983-84 and '84-85 and collected a League Cup winner's medal playing at left-back in the 3-0 beating of Hibernian in October 1985. It is a period Brian looks back on with great fondness, "It was a fantastic experience just to be involved. I was just a squad player I guess, but I learned so much about football and about life in general; the good values, work ethic, man-management. Fergie was great with me, always interested in what was happening in my life. He was autocratic, and you wouldn't get off with some of what he did these days. It could be unpleasant at times, but I certainly learned all about discipline both on and off the pitch." He went on to enjoy a six-year stint with Bradford City and had season-long stays with Bristol City and Hull City before retiring in the mid-'90s. Brian went to university and earned a Management Degree and a post-grad qualification in Management Studies while also spending time coaching college students in the USA. He later had a three-year stint as SFA Development Officer in Aberdeenshire and worked as a Sports Development Officer with the local council before taking on his current job as Active Schools Manager with Sportscotland in 2004. He still attends Aberdeen home games compiling reports and statistics for the Press Association.

Ian Porteous turned eighteen during that campaign and made a single appearance, in that beating of Kilmarnock the week before Gothenburg. He would spend most of the decade at Pittodrie, but was another who never really became a first-team regular. He started just twenty-two games for the Dons, but still managed to score ten goals, the best of which was a screamer from twenty-five yards in a 3-0 humbling of Rangers on the day Jock Wallace returned to take over his old club. "The main problem was the quality I was up against for a place, competing with the likes of Strachan, McGhee, Weir, Black and Hewitt. It was difficult, but a real honour to be involved with such a talented group of players. I should have left perhaps a year earlier, but the club and city were so special to me it was a real wrench doing so." After leaving Aberdeen Ian spent a season in Denmark with Herfolge, returning to Scotland for a productive five-year spell with Kilmarnock. His career in Scotland wound down at Elgin City and at Arbroath, and then in 1996, thanks to Dons legend Bobby Clark – who was at that time New Zealand national coach – Porteous emigrated to sign for Wellington United. He retired from playing a year later, taking the step into coaching, and has since worked for various clubs in the Wellington area, most recently with Waterside Karori. Ian says he still employs methods drilled into him as a youngster at Pittodrie. "Sir Alex was a hard task master, and along with Archie Knox had an amazing will to win. The main impression they left on me, and one that lives with me to this day, is never accept second best."

Four other players made fleeting appearances.

Walker McCall was in his second spell with the club, returning after stints with Ayr United, St Johnstone and in America. His most productive time came in 1980-81 when he netted ten times in just fifteen starts, but by 1982-83 his Dons career was on the wane and he was only twice called upon from the bench. McCall left to join Dundee, retiring in 1986. Former Dons team-mate Joe Harper was at the time with Abbey Life and introduced Walker to the insurance industry, where he worked for a few years. He later ran a laundry business before joining the Weatherford oil company in the mid 1990s; he still works there as an Asset & Inventory Controller. More into his golf than his football these days (he was once a 4 handicapper and still plays to single figures), Walker is an occasional visitor to Pittodrie and keeps in touch with his old colleagues through the AFC Former Players Association. He recalls Ferguson and Knox as, "the best management team I ever worked under" and was, like every other player, subjected to the odd dressing-room savaging. One in particular stands out. "It was the game against Hamburg and I was on the bench. He was about to switch one of the midfielders, but changed his mind, and I was thrown on without even getting a chance to warm-up. Sure enough, almost immediately I get a chance six yards out and I blasted it over the bar, in fact it was nearly over the Beach End roof! (The Dons won that 1981 UEFA Cup first-leg tie 3-2, the Germans scoring late on and eventually winning 5-4 on aggregate.) When I got back inside after the game he absolutely slaughtered me, tore me to shreds."

Left-back Derek Hamilton made his Dons debut against Morton in April 1979 and went on to start thirty-two matches in his five-year Pittodrie career. His involvement in 1982-83 was limited to three substitute appearances and he departed that summer for a highly successful six-year stay with St Mirren, during which he collected a Scottish Cup winner's medal in 1987. His senior career ended with Stranraer and Morton before he dropped down into the Ayrshire Juniors.

Steve Cowan was brought to Aberdeen from St Mirren by Alex Ferguson and made his name as a seventeen-year-old scoring the winner against his old team in the 1980 Drybrough Cup Final at Hampden. He came on as a substitute five times during the campaign, scoring twice, but was another largely overshadowed by the Gothenburg Greats: "I loved my time at Pittodrie and learned so much, every day was an education working with Fergie." He went on to star for both Hibernian and Motherwell and is fondly remembered by supporters of both clubs. In the early nineties he had a successful spell in Irish football with Portadown, winning League and Cup honours and scoring goals aplenty.

During his Motherwell days Steve had begun planning for the future, learning the ropes with Edenvale Financial Services, and after retiring in 1994 he took a full-time job with the company, later moving into recruitment. He coached Salvesen Boys Club in Edinburgh and also had four years at the Hearts Academy, training some of the kids who have recently made the first team at Tynecastle. "That was a great experience, there were some really talented boys there, and it gives me such a sense of satisfaction to see them moving on and taking the next steps in their careers." Steve also successfully entered the world of broadcasting, joining me as a summariser and analyst on *Sportsound*.

Striker Willie Falconer left the bench twice during the campaign, in the 1-0 defeat to Waterschei in April, then four days later in a 1-0 league win over Celtic. His best season at Aberdeen was his last one, 1987-88, when he netted eleven goals in forty starts, including one at Hampden when the Dons lost the League Cup Final in a penalty shoot-out to Rangers after drawing 3-3. He went on to enjoy a long and successful career. After six years down south with Watford, Middlesbrough and Sheffield United, Lou Macari signed Willie for Celtic in a £350,000 deal. Later stints with Motherwell, Dundee and St Johnstone followed until he called time on his career in 2003 after one final season with Clyde. He had a spell coaching with Motherwell's under-19s before moving into the football agency business.

In all, a total of twenty-three players featured during that 1982-83 campaign.

Their contributions varied of course, from the fleeting appearances made by some of those mentioned above to the staggering effort put in by captain Willie Miller, who did not miss a single one of the 5,400 minutes of competitive football played by the Dons.

But the story of that squad, that season, has inevitably and justifiably to focus on the players who faced up to, and beat, the mighty Real Madrid that rainy night in the south-west of Sweden, the dozen men who brought the club its greatest ever triumph, becoming along the way Aberdeen legends.

CHAPTER SIXTEEN

THE GOTHENBURG GREATS

Leighton, Rougvie, McMaster, Cooper, McLeish, Miller, Strachan, Simpson, McGhee, Black, Weir and Hewitt. The twelve who graced the turf inside the Ullevi Stadium on that most memorable of nights, May 11th, 1983.

As I have just outlined others played their part in the story, in some cases a major part in the story, but the men listed above were those who most directly influenced the outcome against Real in Gothenburg.

That group of players was together for three full seasons at Pittodrie but incredibly the starting line-up in the Cup Winners Cup Final was chosen only on one other occasion by Alex Ferguson, ten days later in the Scottish Cup Final victory over Rangers.

That staggered me as I would have sworn they must have been fielded numerous times, but having checked and re-checked, I can only come up with that single additional competitive match. The absence of Stuart Kennedy in Sweden had a bearing on that, as did lengthy injury spells suffered by John McMaster in 1982-83 and Eric Black the following season. There were a number of games in which ten of the eleven played, a few where Hewitt started and Black replaced him, and others where Dougie Bell, Andy Watson and/or Ian Angus stood in for members of the Gothenburg XI. The fact remains, the most famous team-sheet in the history of Aberdeen Football Club and it was only ever selected twice.

The statistics surrounding the Gothenburg Greats are mind-boggling.

Between them the twelve who took on the Spanish superstars picked up 101 winner's medals. Given the size of club they were playing for, that is a truly astonishing statistic, even more so when you consider ninety-seven of them were amassed in a seven-year spell under Alex Ferguson. The exceptions were two League Cup wins for Willie Miller in 1975-76 and 1989-90 and Alex McLeish with a Cup double in that latter campaign.

Eric Black started just 150 games for Aberdeen and collected eight trophies. That represents a winner's medal fewer than every nineteen matches. Neale Cooper started 195 games and got his hands on nine pieces of silverware; his average is almost as impressive.

Between them the twelve played in 4,469 matches for the Dons starting with Willie Miller's substitute appearance against Morton at Cappielow on April 28th, 1973 and ending with Jim Leighton's all too brief last-ever Scottish Cup Final on Saturday, May 27th, 2000. Again, that is remarkable; a span of over twenty-seven years between the first and last appearances of a Gothenburg Great in an Aberdeen shirt.

Their names have been etched indelibly in the history of my football club, their deeds discussed and eulogised over to this day. Their pictures hang in the corridors and on the walls around Pittodrie Stadium, the fruits of their labours fill the club's trophy cabinet.

Almost all who have tried to take their place in the subsequent decades have found the task too demanding, some have buckled under the pressure, others have complained that the ghosts of Gothenburg have haunted them to the point of inevitable failure. A few, a small few, have embraced the triumphs of the 1980s, realising they are something to be cherished and treasured, and not a stick with which to beat successive incumbents in the dressing room and manager's office.

In the long history of Aberdeen FC – over a century and counting now – that was simply a snapshot in time, a coming together of the right manager with the right back-up and a collection of young men eager to do his bidding, desperate to match his unquenchable desire to be a winner. Second place was of no interest to them; winning was all that counted, and winning with a certain style. They played a fast and aggressive attacking game, precise passing mixed with hard-tackling; goals flowing at one end of the pitch, steely determined defenders keeping them out at the other.

For a few glorious years it was heaven and it will never, ever be repeated, not just in that north-east corner of Scotland, but anywhere the world over. Given the way the game has developed in the intervening decades there is no chance a club the size of Aberdeen with its limited resources will dominate at home and abroad in the way Fergie's team did.

Supporters of other clubs will have their own views but for me that team, the Gothenburg Greats, was the most remarkable ever produced in this country and I will, until the day I die, feel privileged to have grown up watching them develop and then perform the most heroic of feats at the game's top level.

Writing this book has been, in equal measure, hugely frustrating and remarkably rewarding, but now that it is laid out in front of me I feel a sense of fulfilment. The joy was in tracking down these guys, interviewing them, listening to their at times emotionally-charged words, reliving the most dramatic and exhilarating moments I have ever experienced inside a football stadium and laughing, plenty laughing! It all came together to make it a remarkable year, bringing to life once again my happiest days as a Dons supporter.

They were no longer those youthful energetic men careering across the pitch. Waists and bellies have thickened, hips have been replaced and hair has either been lost or gone grey. Joints have stiffened and memories have dimmed.

But get them talking about that time, about that team, and the eyes sparkle and the smiles broaden and they are hurled back into that dressing room, pulling on those famous red strips, readying themselves for battle. The manager's words reverberate around the room. Archie Knox gees-up any who need a last-minute boost, Teddy busies around making sure they all have their tie-ups, and their studs and boots are fine. And then the referee calls on them. One last word from Fergie, there's a rumble, a growl of determination, and the dressing room door is flung open and out they go, up that tunnel, out on to the Pittodrie turf and the cheers of the adoring Aberdeen fans . . .

THANKS AND ACKNOWLEDGEMENTS

As ever, in an undertaking of this size, there are countless individuals who need to be thanked. First and foremost my undying gratitude goes to the players and coaching staff from that period, all of whom graciously gave of their time and shared some wonderful memories and stories – most of which I was able to include in the book! Various other people supplied quotes or helped with information and/or contact details, or in a variety of other ways. Among them, and in no particular order: George Adams, Graham Rhind, Graham Shand, Jon McLeish, Kevin Stirling, Jim Traynor, Eric McCowat, Duncan Davidson and Chick Young. To anyone whose name I might have missed out, I apologise.

Thanks also to the staff at Aberdeen City Library, where I spent many enjoyable hours looking through old copies of the *Evening Express* and *Press & Journal* and reminiscing. And to all at Black & White Publishing and to my agent, Kevin Pocklington, for much needed support and guidance.

The following publications were of great help for research purposes . . .

Aberdeen FC: A Complete Record by Jim Rickaby
Managing My Life by Alex Ferguson
The Aberdeen Football Collection by Clive Leatherdale
The First 100 Years of the Dons by Jack Webster
The Don: The Willie Miller Story by Willie Miller with Rob Robertson
The Miller's Tale by Willie Miller with Alastair Macdonald
Sent Off at Gunpoint by Willie Johnston and Tom Bullimore

And I also drew on an article about Teddy Scott by Michael Grant, printed in the *Sunday Herald*, April 13th, 2003.

The most valuable resource of all was the www.afcheritage.org website, which never let me down on all the countless occasions I turned to it for help or back-up.